Information
Assurance

Information Assurance

Managing Organizational IT Security Risks

Joseph G. Boyce
Dan W. Jennings

An Imprint of Elsevier Science

Amsterdam   Boston   London   New York   Oxford   Paris
San Diego   San Francisco   Singapore   Sydney   Tokyo

Butterworth–Heinemann is an imprint of Elsevier Science
Copyright © 2002 by Elsevier Science (USA)

Library of Congress Cataloging-in-Publication Data

Boyce, Joseph George, 1951–
  Information assurance: managing organizational IT security risks /
    Joseph George Boyce, Dan Wesley Jennings.
    p.   cm.
  Includes bibliographical references and index.
  ISBN 0-7506-7327-3 (pbk. : alk. paper)
  1. Computer security. 2. Data protection. I. Jennings,
    Dan Wesley, 1954- II. Title.
QA76.9.A25 B69 2002
005.8 — dc21   2001056663

British Library Cataloguing-in-Publication Data
A catalogue record for this book is available from the British Library.

The publisher offers special discounts on bulk orders of this book.
For information, please contact:
Manager of Special Sales
Elsevier Science
225 Wildwood Avenue
Woburn, MA 01801-2041
Tel: 781-904-2500
Fax: 781-904-2620

For information on all Butterworth–Heinemann publications available,
contact our World Wide Web home page at: http://www.bh.com

10 9 8 7 6 5 4 3 2 1

Printed in the United States of America

To my parents, my brother, my wife Odette,
my two wonderful children, Kimberly and Alan,
and my friends, Bishop John Neumann and Dr. Biddle.

Joseph George Boyce

To my wife and best friend, Denise, who reminds me
about what is important, and to all my security staff, past
and present, from whom I continue to learn and grow.

Dan Wesley Jennings

Among the natural rights of the colonists are these: First a right to life, secondly to liberty, thirdly to property; together with the right to defend them in the best manner they can.

—Samuel Adams

The personal right to acquire property, which is a natural right, gives to property, when acquired, a right to protection, as a social right.

—James Madison

Contents

APPENDICES   201

Foreword

We are in the midst of evolutions and revolutions throughout the world. These evolutions and revolutions do not come about without conflicts. These conflicts are often between those who want to maintain the status quo and those who want not evolution, but revolution. Add to that the world of business, which now more than ever, because of information and information systems, spans the globe (in a nanosecond), and the global marketplace, where competition is fiercer than ever. Combine that with the political power of nation-states, where economic power equates to global power and influence. In this new playing field and battlefield, where information is used to gain and maintain power, you have a global breeding ground for global threats to information and the information systems that store, process, display, and transmit that information around the world.

Information systems are more vulnerable than ever, and more and more miscreants around the world are attacking information systems for pleasure or political purposes, or to gain business advantages.

We are indeed living in exciting times full of hopes, fears, and challenges. There are few more challenging professions in the world than those involved in the protection of information and information systems. Yes, the world is changing, and it seems to be changing faster and faster with each passing year. In recent times, the world has seen:

- The end of the Cold War
- A "new world order," where the new competition is for global marketshare and pursuit of advantage against competitors throughout the world
- The raising profile of global hackers, terrorists, and espionage
- Espionage shifting from the theft of nation-state secrets to theft of corporate information and the use of the Internet to conduct Netspionage (network-enabled espionage) by techno-spies, netspionage agents, and information brokers
- Increasing challenges caused by both new and old threats using new and old methods
- The growth of E-business as part of corporate business
- The demise of military superpowers and an increase in regional alignments such as the European Union and NATO; the geographic spread of Islamic Fundamentalism; and conflicts in the former Soviet Union
- In the more modern nation-states, a shift from manual labor to "brain power"

Quite frankly, the world has always had problems, conflicts, crime, internal wars, international wars, and technological improvements, all causing changes in societies throughout the world. So, why should we expect otherwise from humanity, when our technology belies the fact that as evolutions in humanity have taken place, we are still barely out of the caves when it comes to crimes, wars, and other conflicts? We will continue to be challenged from all parts of the world by those who are dissatisfied with how things are done and what they have, and who want to take from others without compensating the owners. They want it no matter if it takes illegal means to get it. What security professionals must keep in mind is that information and information systems are the Achilles' heel of any business or government agency.

Today, we have the old phenomenon of information warfare brought to new heights by these global miscreants who use high technology — the microprocessor-driven products — as weapons. This has drastically and dramatically changed how we view the importance of information defenses to support businesses and governments. Because of information systems, the use of other high technologies and our dependence on them, and automated information, the world is in the midst of global information warfare. These wars are being fought on all fronts by nation-states, businesses, and various hackers, terrorists, and other groups. They are all bent on achieving their goals by attacking the vulnerabilities of our information systems. They are using information warfare tactics to steal, destroy, disrupt, exploit, and corrupt the information and information systems we are employed to protect.

Today, those of us involved in information and information system protection are learning new, sophisticated tactics, philosophies, and processes to protect these valuable corporate or government assets. Phrases such as "information superiority," "defensive information warfare," "information operations," and "information assurance" are just a few of the newer terms being used to identify processes that can better defend our valuable information and information systems so that our nation-states and businesses can gain a competitive advantage while still protecting these valuable assets.

Information Assurance (IA) is one of the newly refined processes of information protection that has evolved from computer security and information system security. Is it InfoSec by another name, a subset, or just the other way around? There is some argument about that. However, after reading this book you will be in a better position to decide that for yourself. According to the United States government, IA is described as follows:

> Information Assurance (IA) is information operations (IO) that *protect and defend information and information systems by ensuring their availability, integrity, authentication, confidentiality and nonrepudiation. This includes providing for restoration of information systems by incorporating protection, detection, and reaction capabilities* (U.S. DoD 3600-1).

For the purposes of this definition, the following meanings also apply:

- IA Authentication: Security measure designed to establish the validity of a transmission, message, or originator, or a means of verifying an individual's authorization to receive specific categories of information (National Telecommunications Information Systems Security Instructions (NSTISSI) 4009)

- IA Availability: Timely, reliable access to data and information services for authorized users (NSTISSI 4009)
- IA Confidentiality: Assurance that information is not disclosed to unauthorized persons, processes, or devices (NSTISSI 4009)
- IA Integrity: Protection against unauthorized modification or destruction of information (NSTISSI 4009)
- IA Nonrepudiation: Assurance the sender of data is provided with proof of delivery and the recipient is provided with proof of the sender's identity, so neither can later deny having processed the data (NSTISSI 4009)

IA is one of the "new, basic concepts" on which today's information-based and information-dependent nation-states and global corporations are developing their information protection strategies. They may also develop new concepts, and some of the above may be integrated into them and/or renamed. Regardless, when one tries to understand the information and information system protection strategies, policies, plans, and processes, one must clearly understand the concept of today's IA concepts and processes.

The authors of this book, Joseph G. Boyce and Dan W. Jennings, add to the body of knowledge that we all need to know in order to successfully defend and protect today's valuable resources — information and information systems. *Information Assurance: Managing Organizational IT Security Risks* provides the reader with an introduction into the world of Information Assurance. Read it, learn from it, and apply what you have learned so that you can better defend your information and information systems from the miscreants of the world.

Dr. Gerald L. Kovacich
ShockwaveWriters.Com
Whidbey Island, Washington

Preface

Private (profit-motivated) and public (non-profit-motivated) organizations operate throughout the world within the bounds of their geopolitical environments to provide products and services to fulfill the needs of individuals, groups, and other organizations. Inherent in any organization that emerges to fulfill such needs are three known fundamental tendencies or basic drives. These involve the tendencies to perpetuate its own existence (survival), to integrate the functions of its parts (coexistence), and to grow and develop (growth). Private and public organizations are distinct legal entities within a democratic society. Therefore, such fundamental tendencies or basic drives could equate to rights that every organization must have and be free to exercise within the bounds of law. Nations have developed judicial, police, and military infrastructures to counter perceived threats to the rights of their citizens to survive, to coexist with other citizens, and to prosper. The unique situation that confronts private and public organizations is that their geopolitical operating environments can extend beyond the bounds of a single nation (i.e., multinational operations). However, such organizations have to protect their rights. The protection of these rights gives the organization, and those that interact with it, an opportunity to prosper to the fullest extent. The social, political, and economic orders at the local, national, and international levels are at stake if such rights are not protected.

Also, private and public organizations are responsible for protecting information that they possess and legally own and information that they possess but do not legally own. This involves information related to such parties as employees, customers, suppliers, and organizations that form partnerships or joint efforts with other organizations. At the very least, the organization's reputation, and therefore its credibility, could be at stake if such information is not sufficiently protected.

Information is unquestionably critical to an organization because it could serve as its output as well as a resource to produce the output. The protection of an organization's information is imperative to ensure its survival, coexistence, and growth, just as an organization's cash flow determines its financial posture and its productive capabilities determine its operational posture. There are conditions that could threaten the Information Assurance (IA) posture of an organization and, therefore, the protection of its information.

IA provides a means for protecting and defending organizational information and information systems. Fundamentally, because information is so integral to the management and operation of any organization, the protection of this information equates to the protection of its right to survive, coexist, and grow.

We wrote this book to provide organizations with a practical systemic approach for developing a comprehensive IA program based on a Defense in Depth strategy. The Defense in Depth strategy can be applied to organizations of all sizes, industries, and nationalities, whatever the extent of technological use and dependency and the technological products in use (for example, Microsoft, Dell, UNIX, Java, Cisco routers). The layers of defense presented in the book are universal. Organizations will vary in their commitment of resources to each of the layers as a matter of strategy for achieving their desired IA posture. People who would benefit from the information in this book include, in no order of priority:

- Organizational Information Systems Security (INFOSEC) managers
- Organizational Information Technology (IT) managers
- Organizational Chief Information Officers (CIOs)
- INFOSEC testers and evaluators
- IT auditors and inspectors
- Business owners
- Organizational senior and general managers
- Undergraduate- and graduate-level IT and INFOSEC students
- Undergraduate- and graduate-level organizational management students
- Organizational contracting people who are responsible for negotiating and formalizing the outsourcing of IT or INFOSEC functions
- Organizations that provide the outsourcing of IT and INFOSEC functions

This book is the result of our years of work experience, training, and education as INFOSEC professionals within the United States Department of Defense (DoD). We each provide our own perspective on the IA issues and problems confronting an organization. The DoD offers unique opportunities beyond other work environments to gain extensive knowledge and experiences in IA. We have been fortunate to gain experience by participating in the following areas:

1. Designing, testing, and evaluating of the IA posture of highly classified and complex applications during the security certification and accreditation process
2. Developing, updating, and enforcing IA policies at the organization-wide and individual organizational unit levels
3. Testing and evaluating the IA posture at the individual organizational unit level during the security certification and accreditation process
4. Assessing the vulnerabilities of information systems and organizational units
5. Managing the IA posture of individual organizational units

Also, the DoD has made significant contributions to IT. The first computers resulted from the needs of war. The Internet owes its existence to the DoD. The DoD has produced INFOSEC standards and guides. These INFOSEC standards and guides have been referenced by countless books, articles, and studies. No other organization could provide its INFOSEC professionals with exposure to such a broad range of hardware, operating systems, applications, system architectures, information classifications, information architectures, and communication technologies. In recent years, private organizations have been adopting INFOSEC principles, concepts, and methodologies that have been in use in the DoD for many years.

Our work experiences, training, and education permitted us to develop two perspectives concerning the writing of this book: the "macro" and "micro" perspectives. We believe that the combination of these two perspectives has enabled us to present a book that comprehensively addresses the development of an IA program for a broad array of organizations. An organization must address IA from a higher level ("macro"), organization-wide managerial perspective. That is, the components of the IA program must be defined for the organizational entity as a whole, and as a means to measure the posture of the organization from an IA perspective. The IA posture (Chapter 5) provides a means of representing the current state of an organization's security relative to the confidentiality, integrity, and availability of the information that is so critical for its survival, coexistence, and growth. This posture provides the organization with a basic means to measure the extent of its IA uncertainties (i.e., risks) and its IA certainties relative to the achievement of its defined IA needs (Chapter 4). Also, from a "micro" perspective, there are issues relevant to the implementation of the IA program within the organization. The book provides samples of relevant documents, implementation checklists, and references to Internet Web sites for obtaining more detailed information.

This book is distinct from other books involving INFOSEC subjects in the following ways:

1. The book provides a discussion of the principles and concepts relating to the securing of information.
2. The book provides a practical experience-based process for developing an IA program based on a Defense in Depth strategy within an organization from both organization-wide managerial (macro) and program implementation (micro) perspectives. This process is a model that can apply to organizations of all sizes, industries, nationalities, whatever the extent of technological use and dependency and technological products in use. Underlying significant IT devices such as personal computers, workstations, servers, firewalls, and routers are fundamental concepts that have not changed since the inception of the computer. The greatest changes that have occurred over time involve the increasing speed and volume with which computers can process, store, and communicate information and the increasing integration of computers into organizational processes.
3. The book attempts to counter the continuing perception of IA and organizational operations as two distinct, mutually exclusive functions that require indirect trade-offs within an organization; that is, the misconception that as organizations commit more of their attention and resources to IA, the organizations face reductions in their performance and output. Also, the book presents IA from a basic managerial perspective. IA is an organizational function in the manner of production, marketing, finance, and so on. Therefore, the managerial process common to all the organiza-

tion's operations can be used to manage IA within an organization. These common business processes define, measure, predict, produce, control, report, and accept the organization's financial and operational postures. The reality that faces modern organizations is that the application of technology is at a point where "the system is the business." Therefore, overall organizational posture and the IA posture have become inseparable as organizational dependency on technology and timely, reliable information has expanded to a great level.

4. The book provides valuable references to additional sources of information on a variety of subjects as well as recommended tools and methodologies to use to execute the process.

The organization of the book follows the process of developing an IA program within an organization. This organization involves 16 chapters divided into three sections.

Section I: The Organizational IA Program: The Practical and Conceptual Foundation

Chapter 1 ("IA and the Organization: The Challenges") discusses some major IA issues that organizations have historically faced as well as new challenges that have emerged and need to be addressed. Chapter 2 ("Basic Security Concepts, Principles, and Strategy") provides the concepts and principles that serve as the foundation for building IA within an organization and introduces the Defense in Depth strategy.

Section II: Defining the Organization's Current IA Posture

Chapter 3 ("Determining the Organization's IA Baseline") describes the means for defining the physical and virtual boundaries within which the organization processes, stores, and communicates its information. Chapter 4 ("Determining IT Security Priorities") introduces the concept of *Critical Objects* as a means for defining the IA needs that must be accomplished by an organization to ensure its survival, coexistence, and growth. Chapter 5 ("The Organization's IA Posture") describes an approach for defining and measuring the IA posture of an organization.

Section III: Establishing and Managing an IA Defense in Depth Strategy within an Organization

Chapter 6 ("Layer 1: IA Policies") describes the purpose of IA policies, how they relate to organizational objectives, their format and structure, and their development and approval. Chapter 7 ("Layer 2: IA Management") discusses the objectives of IA management, how it relates to the organization's other management functions, its size and positioning within an organization, and tools and methodologies to support it.

Chapter 8 ("Layer 3: IA Architecture") defines an IA architecture, its components, and the process for its development and change. Chapter 9 ("Layer 4:

Operational Security Administration") describes a process for establishing and managing accounts to permit personnel access to organizational information and services.

Chapter 10 ("Layer 5: Configuration Management") defines configuration management, its criticality to the organization, how to establish it, its political and technical dimensions, and an approach for performing it. Chapter 11 ("Layer 6: Life-Cycle Security") describes the process for building security into the design of automated information systems (AISs) and networks and testing the security prior to the incorporation of the AIS or network into the IA baseline. Chapter 12 ("Layer 7: Contingency Planning") provides a means for defining contingency planning requirements for an organization and a process and tools for meeting these requirements.

Chapter 13 ("Layer 8: IA Education, Training, and Awareness") discusses the importance of IA education, training, and awareness and a means of providing it within an organization. Chapter 14 ("Layer 9: IA Policy Compliance Oversight") describes the need for IA policy compliance oversight and a process and tools for its performance.

Chapter 15 ("Layer 10: IA Incident Response") defines the need for an incident response capability within an organization and a means to develop and implement such a capability. Chapter 16 ("Layer 11: IA Reporting") discusses the purpose of establishing a reporting structure, the information that should be reported and its format, and a process for establishing a reporting structure.

Some of the chapters cite applicable appendices to provide readers with practical tools, methodologies, references, and approaches for successfully accomplishing the objectives of the chapters.

We hope that this book helps to protect the rights of organizations and the individuals who both support and depend on the organizations to meet their needs.

Acknowledgments

We express our gratitude to the staff of Butterworth–Heinemann, especially Mark A. Listewnik, Laurel A. DeWolf, Jennifer Packard, Maura Kelly, and Kevin Sullivan, as well as a former employee, Rita Lombard, for their time, effort, and support in making this book a reality. Without their support and guidance this book truly could not have been written.

Disclaimer

The views expressed in this book are those of the authors and do not reflect the official policy or position of the Department of Defense (DoD) or the U.S. government.

I: THE ORGANIZATIONAL IA PROGRAM: THE PRACTICAL AND CONCEPTUAL FOUNDATION

1. IA and the Organization: The Challenges

CHAPTER OBJECTIVES

- Provide an understanding of the meaning of IA and its significance relative to the operation of private and public organizations
- Provide a definition of the fundamental rights of private and public organizations as well as the role that information and IT plays relative to these rights
- Provide a description of some significant examples of challenges that have emerged to threaten the fundamental rights of private and public organizations

THE MEANING AND SIGNIFICANCE OF IA

IA is the process for protecting and defending information by ensuring its confidentiality, integrity, and availability. At its most fundamental level, IA involves protecting the rights of people and organizations. There are two perspectives to consider. First, IA can provide organizations with the ability to protect their own rights as entities to survive, coexist, and grow, since information is so integral to their management and operations. Second, IA can provide organizations with the ability to protect the rights of other parties that support and interact with them. These parties include employees, the existing and potential consumers of their products and services, suppliers, and other organizations that are allies as a result of partnerships and joint ventures. This chapter will further describe the fundamental rights of organizations and the contributions of information and IT to achieving those rights, and it will explore the emergence of threats that challenge that achievement.

THE RIGHTS OF ORGANIZATIONS

As the needs of people evolve throughout the world, private and public organizations are established and operated to provide products and services to fulfill these needs within the bounds of their defined geopolitical environments.

There are three fundamental tendencies or basic drives inherent in these organizations. These involve the tendencies to perpetuate existence (survival), to integrate the functions of organizational parts (coexistence), and to grow and develop (growth). The fundamental tendencies or basic drives equate to rights that every organization must have and must be free to accomplish within the bounds of law. Such rights give organizations and those that interact with them the opportunity to prosper to the fullest extent.

The three tendencies manifest themselves as three interrelated, interconnected, and interdependent organizational components or "subsystems." The three are interrelated in that each fundamental tendency or basic drive has an independent effect on the behavior of the organization as a whole. They are interconnected in that the effect of the organization as a whole is the synthesized effect created by the interaction of all three. They are interdependent in that the actual effect created by the organization as a whole depends on the interaction of all three. Therefore, it is critical that an organization maintain a balanced state between these three tendencies if it is to fulfill the needs of its customers within its geopolitical operational environment.

The organization's tendency or drive to perpetuate its own existence (survival) results in its "technical" component or subsystem. The term "technical" is used to refer to the organization's component or subsystem that is responsible for producing the products and services that meet the needs of its customers. Indeed, Automated Information Systems (AISs) and networks can be considered to be a part of this "technical" component since they can both directly provide information and services to customers and support the production of products and services such as automobiles and electrical appliances.

The organization's tendency or drive to integrate its parts or functions results in its "political" component or subsystem. This component serves as a catalyst for action and enables the organization to move from one point in time and space to another. The organization's ability to integrate its parts or functions is dependent on the extent to which its political component aligns itself with the direction prescribed by the technical component.

The organization's "cultural" component or subsystem results from its tendency or drive to grow and develop. The cultural component serves as the conceptual foundation by which direction and movement remain congruent with the environmental "need." The organization's ability to grow and develop is dependent on the extent to which its cultural component aligns organizational values with those of the geopolitical environment within which the organization operates.

In summary, the "success" of an organization can be construed as the extent to which its rights can be protected to ensure that it can:

1. Technically produce a product or service that the environment values and is willing to "pay" for. This will ensure the organization's survival.
2. Provide an internal political order that will permit work to be divided up and integrated such that each member feels he/she is valued and is making a meaningful contribution. This will promote coexistence by creating a common vision around which each member can manage him- or herself.

3. Provide a culture in which members share a common set of beliefs of the direction, movement, form, and substance needed to fulfill the needs of customers. This will ensure that the organization grows and develops at a pace commensurate with the needs it has emerged to fulfill (Cook and Smith, 1986).

THE CONTRIBUTION OF INFORMATION AND INFORMATION TECHNOLOGY (IT) TO ACHIEVING THE RIGHTS OF ORGANIZATIONS

Information and IT significantly contribute to achieving the rights of organizations. Their contribution to the technical component of an organization will be briefly discussed since it involves the organization's tendency to perpetuate its existence. This tendency is dependent on the extent to which the technical component can produce an output that the consumers within its geopolitical operational environment accept and are willing to acquire.

Organizational Output

Organizations must make decisions daily that move them closer to consumers. However, there are uncertainties and, therefore, risks associated with this requirement. First, it may be difficult to precisely define the needs of consumers within the environment and these needs may rapidly change. New product and service preferences are the result of an aging population, changing family structure, and flexible lifestyles. Organizations need to adapt to these factors.

Second, consumers have unique needs. An organization must know its consumers on a personal basis to really meet their individual needs. It is not enough to know consumers by market segment, climatic zone, demography, or income level. Organizations must know their consumers and be able to recognize and acknowledge them each time a contact is made. For example, a mature "loyalty" program can provide mutual benefits to consumers and organizations.

Third, organizations need to sufficiently manage the availability of their products and services as well as controlling their costs and associated profit margins. For example, retail businesses need to manage the inventory levels at their stores and control the markdowns and profit margins of their products. Inventory to which consumers do not react becomes "unproductive." This results in greater interest expense and a barrier to reinvesting in merchandise that is selling. The unproductive inventory will require markdowns to liquidate, with a negative impact on profit margins.

The third point is dependent on the level of success achieved with the first two factors. If an organization has sufficiently collected, analyzed, stored, and communicated to the appropriate decision makers the information necessary to understand their consumers and are able to adapt to their changing needs, then favorable organizational performance will result (Steerman, 1999).

The fundamental objective for an organization is to reach some level of understanding of predictable consumer behavior in order to achieve a stable and predictable level of organization performance. In the private sector, nothing seems to cause more turmoil in the stock market than when major corporations announce quarterly earnings that are lower than expected (predicted).

Business Intelligence

Organizations have been collecting, analyzing, storing, and communicating to appropriate decision makers information about consumer needs through the use of IT. This information about consumer needs has been incorporated into business intelligence areas. Business intelligence has been useful to (a) analyze past performance, (b) gain insight into current trends and facilitate the integration of this information into the business plan, and (c) develop assortments that truly work to reflect the needs of the consumer and of the organization's performance objectives (Steerman, 1999).

Internet

The Internet has been a significant factor in collecting business intelligence for organizations as well as a means of providing direct sales of products and services to consumers. Businesses have learned to stay competitive and survive by exploiting the Web as a source of business intelligence information.

THE EMERGENCE OF NEW CHALLENGES

Organizations have been confronted for quite some time with situations that have challenged the capabilities of IT to support their rights of survival, coexistence, and growth. However, new challenges have emerged in recent years because of the continuous capabilities of IT, as well as its widespread understanding and availability and the interconnectivities between organizations.

Organizational Vulnerability to Chain Reactions of Environmental Events

The internal operations of organizations that operate in today's world are becoming increasingly vulnerable to the impact of external events because of the vast interconnectivities that IT creates. The world's financial, stock, and news markets offer the best example. These markets are essentially "world-wired" to an extent never before reached. Investors at home or at the office can view any number of worldwide financial anchors in real time and track the progress of their holdings via any one of thousands of free market Web sites.

Large investors can send billions of dollars zooming around the globe, sucking capital out of struggling economies with a few taps on the keyboard. Small investors can move their money faster and more cheaply as well. Technology has made us better informed about the marketplace. The intent of more and better

information is to make people act more rationally. In financial markets it sometimes seems to have just the opposite effect. It's not just that an information del-
uge is shortening our attention span. It's also that the enormous amount of new
financial media have made it possible for us to know much more about what
everybody else in the market thinks. However, we are also more vulnerable to
the madness of the crowd. This creates more difficulty in terms of an organization's ability to provide reasonable predictions of market events and, thus, organizational performance.

For example, in 1998, Long-Term Capital Management (LTCM), the giant
Connecticut-based hedge fund, was financially rescued by a consortium of Wall
Street's biggest firms. Computer technology and the information allowed the
firm to make huge, complex bets on minor short-term discrepancies in the prices
of financial assets in a host of different economies. The intent was to eliminate
risk. The end result was the opposite. LTCM placed its trust in computer models and the information they used. This permitted them to make larger and larger
bets worth hundreds of times the firm's original capital. However, the bets failed
and the firm's heavy borrowing magnified its capacity to wreak more havoc in
other markets. Several other big hedge funds were also severely affected. Their
frantic efforts to "unwind" their complex positions knocked stock and currency
markets in seemingly unrelated economies for a loop (Chandler, 1998).

The Significant Rise and Criticality of Unstructured Information

As previously emphasized, information continues to drive organizational decisions. What has changed dramatically is the kinds of decisions that organizations
make and the type of information that influences these decisions.

There are two basic types of information. Structured information results from
the legacy of information systems processing. In the beginning, there was nothing but data — structured data — which represented a collection of distilled facts
that made up a record. Data storage was expensive, so organizations concentrated on the distilling of information into critical data elements. The intent was
to also reduce those same elements into an even more discrete form to save storage space, such as the reduction of dates from four-byte fields to two-byte fields.
The end result of information distillation was structured data that was stored in
a predefined record format. This information was only as good as the ability of
the designer to anticipate precisely which data elements must be stored in the
record. The reliance on a predefined record format that includes some information, but leaves other information out, is the key limitation of structured information sources.

Textual documents, audio, video, voice, images, and graphical objects are
examples of unstructured information. The information is called "unstructured"
because its exact content and organization are unpredictable. Therefore, by definition, unstructured information is any information type where the content
doesn't fit a predefined, descriptive model or arrangement.

As the economy shifts from an industrial model to a knowledge-driven one,
more information is necessary to support the decision-making process. Also, the
dynamic nature of the environments in which organizations operate is such that

less and less of this information fits the structured information model. The ratio of unstructured to structured information in most organizations is easily 9 to 1. It is the unstructured information that has emerged to drive much of the decision making in the key organizational processes. The volume and sources of this information are increasing and not decreasing. There will probably always be a need to create record management applications (databases) to track and manage specific facts about key organizational transactions. These, in turn, will drive other organizational transactions. However, the reality is that this thinking cannot extend to all organizational information needs. It forces organizations to distill information to fit some predefined context or application of that information. This relies on the outdated assumption that it is possible to predict in advance the context (who, when, where, why, and how) in which any piece of organizational information will be useful — today, or at any time in the future.

The industrial economy involved a high degree of predictability. Organizations operated in fairly static environments where change was slow and they had time to recognize it and react. A narrow set of products and services were output to meet consumer needs. Where markets and processes were highly predictable, it was appropriate to rely on predictable processes, supported by structured information sources. However, a new economy has emerged. Instead of producing tangible goods, organizations produce ideas. Ideas are driven by information and because organizations are constantly reshaping what they think, the predictability that defined the old economy is essentially lost.

In this environment, the entire information-processing model is inverted from one of data capture to one of dynamic information assimilation. The organizational process does not depend on predictable (structured) information as input, and for the most part doesn't create any structured information as output, either. The organizational process itself is unpredictable because what is involved is the human thinking process.

In a knowledge environment, the success of an organization depends on the ability of its knowledge workers to sift through all the available unstructured information sources and make decisions fast enough to fulfill the needs of the organization's consumers. There are many sources of unstructured information. Some examples include corporate document bases, the Internet, intranets, extranets, information subscription services, and dialog with customers, suppliers, and competitors. However, organizations will continue to rely on structured information as well. Recordkeeping systems and other databases will store predictable organizational information. The success of an organization will continue to depend on providing confidentiality, integrity, availability, authentication, and nonrepudiation services for both structured and unstructured information (Tucker, 1999).

Expansion of the Use and Criticality of Organizations' Intranets

Organizations that operate within diverse geopolitical environments have found it difficult to ensure that their employees are able to effectively communicate with one another. Mail, phone calls, faxes, and even e-mail have been found to be insufficient. Intranets have been seen as the best means to provide employees with continuous communications and access to key organizational and consumer information. Intranets have become critical information-sharing and collaboration tools.

Intranets are internal networks within one organization. They are a managed assembly of Transmission Control Protocol (TCP)/Internet Protocol (IP) local-area networks (LANs) where each LAN connects to the intranet through a router. Routers are special purpose computers whose job is to move packets between the intranet and the LAN, often asserting certain controls and restrictions. The Internet is a public wide-area network (WAN) that extends around the world and connects millions of computer users. It is a collection of independent WANs and LANs in the hundreds of thousands, or perhaps millions. An extranet involves a network that bridges the public Internet and the private organizational intranet.

Organizations have been expanding the role of their intranets in an effort to better understand and meet the needs of their consumers (survival) as well as to ensure that the knowledge and actions of employees are better coordinated and integrated (coexistence). For example, Wells Fargo & Co. of San Francisco has been making its intranet available to more employees throughout its 6000 branches and offices. The intranet is being used to replace the daily faxes sent to branches to update them on banking processes and procedures or to warn them of fraudulent activities in their regions. Wells Fargo has been enhancing the content on their internal sites, transforming them into true corporate portals. Initially, they used the intranet mainly to make human resources information available to employees. Since then, sites have been created to manage specific projects, procurement, and purchasing. Wells Fargo has also organized the more than 1000 sites through a portal-like central site, called Teamworks, which also includes company news, history, and stock updates.

Organizations are also moving toward more advanced uses of intranets. These uses include providing a central place for accessing internal and external information and accessing core enterprise systems. For example, Lockheed Martin Corporation is interested in consolidating more than 1000 separate intranet sites into a corporate portal environment. The intent is to eventually evolve to providing a common enterprise portal for intranet and Internet systems and, thus, simplify access to all capabilities. The enterprise information portals will replace the separate worlds of intranets and extranets with the new interface that will become as ubiquitous as the Windows desktop is now. This evolution will even further expand the dependencies of organizations on IT and its need to be protected and defended (Hicks, 1999).

Increasing Public Concern for the Privacy of Information

The public's concern for the privacy of their personal information has been increasing in recent years. IT allows government, business, and other interested parties access to a wide range of information about individuals. Personal information such as income, marriage status, credit history, medical records, political party, employment history, military history, and school history is collected and stored in various databases.

Such information can be given freely or collected without a person's consent. Personal information is usually given freely when people apply for credit, a mortgage, heath insurance, or hospital admittance, or when they decide to rent a video or register the warranty on a new purchase. Additional information is also collected without consent. This information is obtained through monitoring of cordless or cellular telephones or collected by credit bureaus and medical information bureaus (Page, 1994).

The privacy of personal medical information has been of special concern to the public. The proliferation of electronic records has allowed medical information to be used in ways that would have been unimaginable several years ago. This has provoked widespread public anxiety about the security of information that once remained a secret between patients and their personal doctors. Americans have long assumed that their medical records are their own business. A solid body of court cases and state laws underlines the tradition of doctor–patient confidentiality and the principle that patients' medical records cannot be disclosed publicly without their permission. Medical privacy is a tradition under assault since the broad technological, scientific, and economic forces are overpowering the old rules. For example, companies that manage pharmacy benefits routinely inspect what patients take and call their doctors to recommend alternatives. The public should be receiving reasonable assurances that when their personal information is collected, the health care system will properly secure it and disclose it only for important health purposes (Allen, 1998).

On October 29, 1999, President Clinton disclosed the first federal protections to safeguard the confidentiality of Americans' medical records. The protections are intended to restrict the conditions under which doctors, hospitals, and health plans can divulge patients' medical information without their consent. Under broad new rules the administration worked on for years, the federal government would ensure patients' rights to examine their own medical records, determine who else has looked at them, and pursue criminal action against anyone who misuses their medical history (Goldstein, 1999).

The Continuing Spread of Corporate Espionage

The use of corporate spooks and saboteurs has continued to grow in today's global, high-tech economy, where the most prized assets can be stored on a disk and surveillance equipment can fit on a shirt button. Congress passed the Economic Espionage Act of 1996 to slow down this growth. This act carries a long prison term for intellectual-property theft. The Federal Bureau of Investigation (FBI) nearly tripled its investigations into corporate espionage in 1998. In 1997, by a conservative estimate, at least $25 billion in intellectual property was stolen from U.S. corporations.

These cases involve foreign spies left over from the Cold War working for new capitalist bosses, as well as U.S. firms turning to Dumpster divers or computer hackers to stay ahead of the competition and disgruntled employees walking off with classified material. In this era of downsizing and diminished corporate loyalty, close to two-thirds of all U.S. intellectual-property losses can be traced to insiders (Eisenberg, 1999).

SUMMARY

Information and IT significantly contribute to achieving the rights of organizations to survive, coexist, and grow. An organization could consist of an entity of any size (small, medium, large), sector (private, public), type (sole proprietorship, partnership, corporation, governmental entity), geopolitical environment (local, state, regional, national, multinational), and output of products and services (automobiles, food, entertainment, books, technical consultation, legal advice, dental services, medical care, medical drugs, and so forth). The rights of organizations are threatened by traditional threats as well as by the emergence of new challenges. IA provides a means to protect and defend the rights of organizations from such threats. This book describes a sequential process for developing an IA program based on a "Defense in Depth" strategy. The process begins with a definition of basic security concepts, principles, and the Defense in Depth strategy that serve as a foundation for IA (Chapter 2 — Basic Security Concepts, Principles, and Strategy). Subsequently, there will be a discussion of the means for defining the totality of the organization's physical and logical boundaries within which it processes, stores, and communicates information (Chapter 3 — Determining the Organization's IA Baseline), for defining the Critical Objects that require protection (Chapter 4 — Determining IT Security Priorities) and for measuring the current state of the organization's risks relative to the accomplishment of the protection of these Critical Objects (Chapter 5 — The Organization's IA Posture). Finally, there will be a description of the complementary layers of technical (hardware and software) and nontechnical (e.g., IA policies, IA management, configuration management, and so forth) defense that provide a means of protecting the organization's Critical Objects and achieving a state of risk that is acceptable to the organization's management (Chapters 6–16).

REFERENCES

Allen, A., "Those Prying Eyes — Why Doctor–Patient Confidentiality Isn't What It Used to Be." *The Washington Post Magazine* (February 8, 1998): 11–15, 27–32.

Chandler, C., "World-Wired Markets: Vast, Fast, Secure. You Sure?" *The Washington Post* (October 25, 1998): C1–C2.

Cook, V. G., Jr., and Fred Smith, *Influencing and Managing Change.* Monterey, CA: U.S. Naval Postgraduate School, 1986.

Eisenberg, D., "Eyeing the Competition." *Time* (March 22, 1999): 58–60.

Goldstein, A., "President to Detail Patient Privacy Rules — Policy Restricts Who Can Access Online Records." *The Washington Post* (October 29, 1999): A1, A9.

Hicks, M., "Corporate Intranets Enter Portal Space." *PCWeek* (November 15, 1999): 104, 106.

Page, T. L., "The Impact of Computers on Privacy." *IS Audit & Control Journal* (Volume III, 1994): 33–38.

Steerman, H., "The Power of Detail." *Teradatareview* (Fall 1999): 48.

Tucker, M., "Dark Matter of Decision Making." *Intelligent Enterprise* (September 14, 1999): 20–26.

2. Basic Security Concepts, Principles, and Strategy

CHAPTER OBJECTIVES

- Identify the primary security services encompassed through IA
- Understand traditional security concepts and principles that provide the foundation for information security decisions
- Present three fundamentally different strategies for developing and implementing a program for protecting an organization's IA baseline and Critical Objects
- Provide an understanding as to the strategy that would maximize the protection of the IA baseline and Critical Objects

BASIC SECURITY CONCEPTS AND PRINCIPLES

Introduction

A total IA program extends beyond mere regulations. It is based on the concept that security begins as a state of mind. The program must be designed to develop an appreciation of the need to protect information vital to the interests of the organization and to foster the development of a level of awareness that will make security more than routine compliance with regulations.

The application of security to any organization, facility, or IT system must be based on certain accepted concepts and principles. These are foundational to the development of the organization's IA policies and critical to dispensing consistent technical security guidance or deliberating sound security judgement calls. Everyone within the organization must understand applicable security policies. However, good security awareness is more than simply ensuring that everyone knows and obeys the rules; it involves knowing the reasoning behind the rules.

Security practices and procedures sometimes cause personal inconvenience. Security is often perceived as regulatory, restrictive, and bureaucratic because often it is all those things. Simply knowing and obeying the rules is not always sufficient. It is natural to want to know why we must comply. An explanation of "because I said so" is not a good response; users want and deserve valid reasons for security policies. One of the best ways to explain the purpose of a given security policy is to help others understand its underlying security principles. A working knowledge of basic security concepts and principles will help equip us to meet this challenge.

The goal of any IA program should be to instill within people a knowledge and awareness that goes far beyond rote compliance. Knowing the basic security principles on which good security practices are built will foster an appreciation for the need for IA. Knowing security tenets will also enable us to make sound security judgments in the absence of specific written guidance.

Basic Security Principles

The application of security to any organization, facility, or information technology system must be based on certain accepted principles. In 1992, a group of international experts developed a list of security principles for the Organization for Economic Co-operation and Development (OECD) as "a foundation from which governments and the private sector, acting singly and in concert, could construct a framework for securing IT systems" (NIST, 1996, p. 4).

In 1996, the National Institute of Standards and Technology (NIST) modified the OECD principles to better suit the needs of federal government systems. This chapter is a compilation of principles from OECD and NIST as well as several other basic security concepts and principles from other sources that underlie sound IA practices. Many of the principles are simply introduced in this chapter and developed more thoroughly in subsequent chapters of this book.

IA Supports the Mission of the Organization

Perhaps the most critical and strategic business resource for any organization is its information (Naisbitt, 1982, p. 15). The purpose of IA is to protect an organization's valuable information, as well as the facilities, systems, and networks that process, store, and transmit that information. Protecting information can be as important as protecting other organizational resources, such as money and personnel.

Information is an expensive, sensitive, and perishable resource that represents a substantial investment, but how we protect the information depends on the form it takes and the attribute(s) it possesses. Although the concept of information is intangible, information can assume various forms:

- Thoughts and speech
- Hardcopy (originals, copies, transparencies, faxes)
- Softcopy (stored on removable and nonremovable media)
- Personal knowledge
- Technical skills
- Corporate knowledge
- Formal and informal meetings
- Telephone conversations
- Video teleconferences

When it is all boiled down, information can be represented in mental thought and speech, written documentation, and electronic communications/computer formats. Information also comes in three states, analogous to the three states of water—liquid (water); solid (ice); or gas (steam). Similarly, at any given moment, information is being transmitted, processed, or stored. This happens irrespective of the medium in which it resides (McCumber, 1994).

Threats to these states of information basically fall into three categories: compromise by unauthorized disclosure; corruption through unauthorized modification; and unavailability through a denial of service. Regardless of its format, information that is worth protecting will possess one or more critical attributes that will dictate what kind of safeguards are required to adequately provide protection against these threats.

Security Requires Auditability and Accountability

Security controls must produce reliable, indisputable evidence that they are working correctly. The evidence can take the form of audit trails, system logs, alarms or other overt or covert notification. With this feedback, management can determine whether the control is functioning properly, making adjustments as required (Wood, 1990, p. 18).

Where auditability refers to the ability to verify the activity of a control; accountability refers to holding individuals answerable, responsible, or liable for specific activities. The system must ensure that individuals or processes with authorized access to the information, and individuals accessing the system, are held accountable for their actions. Individual accountability safeguards (e.g., identification/authentication and audit mechanisms) must be enforced for all information systems to fulfill these security requirements (Wood, 1990, p. 19).

Identification tells the system which user is accessing the system; *authentication* confirms to the system that the user is who he says he is. Think of your Automated Teller Machine (ATM) card as a kind of identification and authentication (I&A) mechanism. Information coded on your card lets the system know which account to access while your PIN number verifies that it is really you doing the accessing.

In the same way, a user account name identifies the user to the system, for access and accountability purposes. For this reason, the identifier must normally be unique. Group, shared, or anonymous accounts should not be permitted when accountability for access must be controlled by weak authentication (i.e., static passwords). Additionally, the naming convention for user IDs must distinguish each individual user in order to provide the level of attribution necessary to enforce accountability. Without individual accountability, audits are going to be of little value since system use (or misuse) can be only attributed to an individual through circumstantial evidence.

Effective accountability must be irrefutable. Authentication, required prior to system access, theoretically proves to the system that you are the person who belongs to that unique user identification. Unfortunately, the authentication process is far from perfect since there are three basic ways to prove who you say you are, and all have their shortcomings:

> (a) *Information you possess.* Passwords are still the most familiar and widely used form of authentication. A password known only to the

owner of the user ID verifies to the system that he or she is actually the account owner. However, passwords are considered weak authentication because they are often shared among friends; easily broken by guessing or public domain cracking programs; or stolen from watching the user type in the password or from finding it written down. "In a survey conducted at a 1996 hackers conference, 72 percent of the hacker respondents said that passwords were the 'easiest and most common hack' used" (*SC Magazine*, 2000, p. 21). In more recent years, password cracking tools, and the dictionaries they use, have become more sophisticated; given sufficient time to run against a password file, potentially all passwords can be broken.

(b) *Objects you possess.* The use of objects such as digital signatures, electronic keys, tokens, and smart cards is considered strong authentication because of the low probability of breaking the encryption used to protect these objects. As with passwords, it is assumed that the possessor is the owner; yet the possibility of loss, theft, sharing, duplication, or spoofing exists. There may also be a heavy administrative overhead associated with the distribution and periodic replacement of the objects, not to mention the expense. Yet, Public Key Infrastructure (PKI) technology is being incorporated into applications and objects to secure electronic mail, Web browsers, virtual private networks (VPNs), single sign-on, and e-commerce transactions. The goal of enabling technology is to provide "an integrated security solution to solve the problems of authentication, single sign-on, and confidentiality across multiple resources" (Abramowitz et al., 2001, p. 1).

(c) *Features you possess.* The field of biometrics — measurable physiological and/or behavioral characteristics — is a fascinating growth area that offers the strongest and most irrefutable authentication. Behavioral characteristics include verification of voice, keystrokes, or signatures. Physiological characteristics include recognition of palm, fingerprint, finger image, finger or hand geometry, iris or retina, vascular patterns, ear shape, and even body odor.

Biometrics also presents three challenges:

1. High number of false negatives — although it won't allow a non-owner access, it may reject the true owner based on a false reading.
2. User acceptance — some methods of authentication such as retina scanning are considered uncomfortable by many users. Less intrusive methods such as iris scanning, facial feature, or thumbprint recognition are proving more acceptable.
3. Physical limitations — a retina scan won't work with users who are blind or have cataracts; finger or hand recognition would not be practical in an environment that required protective gloves; voice recognition may be affected by throat problems.

To ensure that individuals are held accountable for their actions, auditing and monitoring of the information system must be accomplished in a way that, consistent with applicable laws and regulations, assesses the adequacy of security features and generates an audit trail of security-relevant events for all users.

Security Requires Access Control

Access controls limit access to information or information assets. By using access control services, we can prevent a user from seeing or using unauthorized information. We can also prevent the unauthorized modification or disclosure of that information. Access controls may be technical or nontechnical in nature.

There are two basic approaches to applying access controls within systems and networks: one is to permit anything that is not explicitly denied; the second is to deny anything that is not explicitly permitted. In other words, either open up all access to everyone, denying access only by exception, or else turn off all access to everyone by default, opening up access only by exception. The former is called the "Default Permit" stance; the latter approach is known as the principle of minimalism, or the "Default Deny" stance.

> The *default deny stance* makes good sense from a security point of view because it is a fail-safe stance. It recognizes that what you don't know *can* hurt you. It is the obvious choice for most security people, but it is not at all obvious to users. With the default deny stance, you prohibit everything by default; then, to determine what you are going to allow, you:
>
> - Examine the services you want.
> - Consider the security implications of these services and how you can safely provide them.
> - Allow only the services you understand, can provide safely, and recognize as a legitimate operational requirement.
>
> Services are enabled on a case-by-case basis. You can start analyzing the security of a specific service, and balance its security implications against the needs of your users. Based on that analysis and the availability of various remedies to improve the security of the service, you can settle on an appropriate compromise (Chapman and Zwicky, 1995, p. 50).

Other access control principles include:

> *Separation of functions*: The principle of separating roles or functions provides a form of security checks and balances by ensuring that no one individual owns all the processes; controls all the security features; or possesses unrestricted access to all the information. The concept is that, by compartmentalizing the functions or roles within the system, the risk is reduced that one person will totally compromise the confidentiality, integrity, or availability of the information or the system.
>
> *Independence of control and subject*: "The person charged with designing, implementing, and/or operating a control should not be the same person who is to be controlled thereby" (Wood, 1990, p. 17). In any system, it is good practice to ensure independence between the person charged with designing a security control and the person(s) who are to be controlled by it. Likewise, those responsible for enforcing security controls

must be empowered and autonomous to perform unbiased reviews and objective evaluations. The individual responsible for overseeing the security management of information systems, for example, should not report directly to the audit department or the systems operations department in order to eliminate any real or perceived conflict of interest.

Least privilege: Considered by many "the most fundamental principle of security (any kind of security, not just computer and network security)," the least privilege principle requires that each individual be granted the most restrictive set of privileges or accesses needed for the performance of authorized tasks (Chapman and Zwicky, 1995, p. 45). Users are given just the access or privileges they need to do their jobs, but no more than required. For example, normal users are granted only the subset of privileges necessary to perform normal user functions. A system administrator may require a much larger subset of all privileges, or in some cases, the full set of privileges available. Enforcement of least privilege is often easier said than done, particularly when it comes to operating systems that are not designed to enforce separation of functions.

Control: Control is the nontechnical principle that all access to the system must be regulated. No one should gain access to an organization's information system(s) without the explicit knowledge and authorization of a control officer (e.g., Information Systems Security Officer).

Discretionary Access Controls (DAC): DAC are a technical means of restricting access to objects (e.g., files, directories, data entities) based on the identity and need-to-know of users or processes and/or the groups to which the object belongs. For example, access can be regulated or mediated by comparing file types to predefined rules or access lists. The controls are discretionary in the sense that a subject with certain access permission is capable of directly or indirectly passing that permission on to another user or process. DAC roughly equate to Identity-Based Access Control (IBAC) within international standards.

Mandatory Access Controls (MAC): Unlike DAC, MAC prevent this ability to pass on permissions. Instead, they require formal authorization (i.e., clearance, formal access, need-to-know verification) and restrict access to objects based on the sensitivity of the objects (e.g., via object labeling), focusing on data confidentiality. In these cases, access is regulated/mediated by comparing file contents (e.g., based on data labels) to a predefined rule set for each classification level. Within international standards, MAC roughly equate to Rule-Based Access Control (RBAC).

Security Requires Confidentiality

Confidentiality services provide the protection of information, both stored and communicated, from unauthorized disclosure. In this respect, they are a subset of access control since the objective is to technically or nontechnically control the information, ensuring that those who need to see the information can read it and precluding its disclosure to those who are not authorized. This information may be in the form of system- or network-generated data, as well as traditional information.

All information is not equal: organizations typically possess multiple levels of information sensitivity. Some information has no confidentiality requirement; it is deemed public domain and represents an organization's contribution to the universe of information available to everyone. Other information is more tightly controlled and only shared among organizational allies. Still other information is deemed so sensitive that it only may be made accessible to a small subset of individuals within the organization.

Organizations — both private and public — know the value of protecting the confidentiality of information. Private industries are investing heavily in the protection of information from nondisclosure and forcing employees to sign agreements restricting their postemployment competitiveness (Armour, 2000, p. 1). Businesses understand that leaked proprietary information can mean the loss of competitive edge. Public organizations have long depended on the confidentiality of their information as a means of protecting the sources and methods for obtaining that information and for maintaining information superiority over their enemies.

Normally, the nontechnical protection of the confidentiality of information is based on a combination of some kind of classification scheme plus enforcement of the need-to-know principle. Classifications distinguish the information that must be protected from information that is expendable. They also represent the level of protection that must be applied to the information based on established guidance. Of course, these established classification terms are only effective if "everyone who receives the information understands its value and sensitivity and then follows the prescribed protection procedures" (Schweitzer, 1996, p. 36). Access to some classifications may require a security clearance — a formal certification authorizing access up to and including a certain classification level of information.

Need-to-Know

Having an authorization or clearance to see a particular classification level of information, however, is not sufficient reason to see all information at that level. An authorized holder of sensitive or classified information — often the owner of the information — must determine if a prospective recipient legitimately requires access to specific classified information. In other words, does the individual have a need to know the information in order to perform his or her official duties? The individual should possess the combination of clearance, formal access, and need-to-know before being authorized access to the information. No one should be entitled to sensitive or classified information solely by virtue of office, position, rank, or security clearance. Senior management or the data owner must decide who is authorized to make a need-to-know determination.

Data Separation

Some measures prevent the disclosure of information by employing access control mechanisms, thereby keeping an adversary from reaching the information, or by preventing the information from reaching a place where unauthorized disclosure could occur. Data separation mechanisms include physically separating the data (e.g., isolating SECRET information by not allowing any physical connectivity to another classification enclave) or use of a filtering router that screens data by matching character strings or security labels.

Compartmentalization

The principle of compartmentalizing is based on the concept that restricting and isolating access to information will reduce the risk of a total compromise of the confidentiality of the information. Knowledge is power; give too many people too much information and you have increased the possibility that someone will use that information illicitly. If individuals only have pieces of information based on their need-to-know, theoretically, you can reduce the number of individuals who would have enough pieces to enable them to construct the whole picture. Of course, restricting the open exchange of information can also impede the free flow of ideas and creativity.

Classification

Data classification assigns commonly known labels to information in order to identify the appropriate level of protection, handling, and control of the information, based on the originator data owner's determination of its value, timeliness, usefulness, and sensitivity.

> Although the basic aim of data classification is to identify and isolate data which is critical to the orderly and continued functioning of the organization, the process also serves to clarify the extent to which individual data segments need to be protected so that integrity and availability can be ensured (Karabin, 1985, p. 1).

Table 2-1 is a matrix of a model for classifying and controlling classified information.

Encryption

Encryption is the reversible process of transforming plain-text information into an enciphered text by using an encryption algorithm. The algorithm is a mathematical formula that uses a key — a kind of password string known only to the sender and receiver — applied to the text, which renders the text unintelligible until it can be decrypted by reversing the process. Encryption is heavily used today to protect the transmission and storage of information, but it does not provide a complete security solution. The encryption key and unencrypted data must also be protected from theft or hijacking. Also, the encryption software must be properly implemented to ensure data security.

Once the data is properly encrypted via a key, the person(s) on the receiving end must be able to obtain the key in order to decipher the message. Managing the key is the tricky part. The key must be securely generated, securely transferred, securely stored, securely updated, secured used/controlled, securely recovered, and, when no longer needed, securely destroyed. Multiply these requirements by each required key for each and every employee needing to access the information, and you can begin to understand the complexity of key management and its support infrastructure.

Table 2-1 Matrix of a Model for Classifying and Controlling Classified Information

Sample Corporation	U.S. Government Equivalent	Description	Attributes
"Public Use"	"Unclassified"	Information approved for public disclosure	Used for all nonsensitive information
"Internal Use Only"	"For Official Use Only"	Personal, medical, technical, or business information restricted to use within the organization and for purposes related to the organization	Used for general correspondence which is too sensitive to be released to the general public but does not meet the criteria for higher classification
"Confidential"	"Confidential"	Information of higher personal, technical, or business sensitivity and where disclosure must be restricted to those employees who need to know this information to perform their duties	Provides a competitive edge; unauthorized disclosure would be against best interest of organization or individual; shows operational direction over short term; important to the technical or financial success of a product
"Confidential-Restricted"	"Secret"	Information of even higher personal, technical, or business sensitivity where damage to the organization would result because of the serious impact of disclosure outside the organization; information is restricted to a predetermined need-to-know basis	Provides a significant competitive edge; disclosure would damage organization; relates to or describes a very significant portion of the organization's business; shows operational direction over extended period; extremely important to the technical or financial success of a product
"Registered-Confidential"	"Top Secret"	Information restricted to employees on a predetermined need-to-know basis and where strict accountability and maintenance of a history of access is required	Provides very significant competitive edge; outside disclosure would cause severe damage to the organization; relates to or describes a major and very significant portion of the organization's business; shows strategies and major direction over an extended period of time; is vital to the technical or financial success of a product

The integration of digital signatures and certificates, and the other services required for e-commerce, is called the *public key infrastructure (PKI)*. These services provide integrity, access control, confidentiality, authentication, and nonrepudiation for electronic transactions. The PKI includes the following elements:

- Digital certificates
- Certificate authority (CA)
- Registration authorities
- Policies and procedures
- Creative revocation
- Nonrepudiation support
- Time-stamping
- Lightweight Directory Access Protocol (LDAP)
- Security-enabled applications
- "Cross-certification" (Krutz and Vines, p. 165)

Cryptography and its related topics (e.g., virtual private network (VPN) tunneling, Kerberos, Internet Protocol Security (IPSEC), Single Sign-On (SSO), wireless security, etc.) are vast and complex subjects that exceed the scope of this book. Rather than rehash the information already documented by subject matter experts on specialized encryption topics, we recommend that you consult one of the many excellent books already available.

Nonrepudiation

Encryption — in the form of digital signatures, for example — can be used to provide proof of delivery to the sender of data and ensure to the recipient of the data that the sender is who he or she claims to be. In this way, neither the sender nor recipient can later deny having processed the data. This service is dependent on the ability of digital signatures to authenticate a user's identity and on integrity services to ensure that no subsequent changes were made to the signature.

Security Requires Integrity

Integrity is that quality of information that identifies how closely the data represents reality. How closely does your resume reflect "you?" Does the credit report accurately reflect the individual's historical record of financial transactions? The definition of integrity must include the broad scope of accuracy, relevancy, and completeness (McCumber, 1994).

Sometimes information requires protection based not on who may see it, but rather on who could tamper with the information. Transactions can be intercepted and altered, accidentally or maliciously, while en route. Integrity security services protect against unauthorized modification of stored or communicated information to ensure that the data is timely, accurate, complete, and consistent. It can also mean ensuring that the system functions so as to provide data integrity, to include the detection and notification of unauthorized modifications to information and accounting for all authorized changes.

Data integrity services work by performing a calculation on the data being transmitted which results in a value. That value is then bound to the original data and retained throughout the transmission. To ensure that the integrity of the information is still intact, a recalculation is performed. If the new value matches the previous value, it is assumed that no unauthorized modifications occurred during transmission.

We say *assumed* that no unauthorized modifications occurred because these values can be easily spoofed, allowing changes to be made and a new check value generated. A digital signature or some means of encryption may alleviate this problem by preventing tampering with the check value. Protection of information integrity normally is only as good as the design of the application or the effectiveness of the procedures being used.

Security Requires Asset Availability

Availability is the information attribute that requires protection when authorized access to the information and information services must be timely and reliable. Availability is normally thought of in terms of protecting tangible assets (e.g., facilities, systems, and networks) and ensuring that essential assets are properly functioning, but most of the protection applied to these assets comes in the form of intangible processes and procedures. Typically these processes and procedures aid in the quick and complete recovery of essential systems and business operations when availability is lost. The most common practices for protection of information availability include:

- Applying access controls, integrity, and confidentiality
- Closing known security holes in operating systems and network configurations
- Backup procedures
- Data recovery procedures
- Preventive maintenance plan
- Continuity of operations plan
- Emergency action plan

Failure to protect the availability of information and its assets can result in a denial of service. Such denials are often thought of in terms of malicious attacks, but most denial of service incidents occur because of failure on the part of employees to develop or follow good internal procedures. Thus, these unintentional denials of service are usually avoidable.

Security Is an Integral Element of Sound Management

Security is not an end in itself, but it is a critical function that supports the mission of the organization. As such, security is an integral element of sound business management that requires management support at the highest level. In fact, a security manager is only as effective as the support that he or she receives from senior management; it is key to the success of any organization's security program.

Due Diligence

An organization in general, and senior management in particular, is also charged with a kind of civic responsibility when it comes to security. Organizations cannot conduct electronic commerce in a cyber vacuum. There is a social obligation on the part of every organization doing business in a public Internet environment to protect itself against known threats and to ensure its computing environment does not become a threat to others. This responsible action, in turn, contributes to the overall protection of the enterprise.

> Due diligence is required to check your network and examine the vulnerabilities detected, even if you think they are minor. It's those vulnerabilities you may think are too insignificant to require your time to repair, that are the ones adversaries will exploit to gain unauthorized access to your network (Naumann, 2001, p. 1).

Management must understand that failure to provide adequate support and resources necessary to protect against known threats could leave the organization open not only to malicious attack, but also to civil liability as a result of such negligence.

Such due care on the part of management includes:

- "Means to prevent the organization's computer resources from being used as a source of attack on another organization's computer system" (Krutz and Vines, p. 314)
- Capability to recover (e.g., backups, contingency plans, continuity plans, disaster recovery plans, incident handling)
- Ability to detect and eradicate malicious code
- Oversight over local and remote access control
- Elimination of unapproved modem connectivity
- Sufficient organizational security policies, procedures, and guidelines
- Personnel screening procedures to reduce the threat from insiders

Senior corporate executives are increasingly being held liable for failure of "due care" in disasters. They can also face civil suits from shareholders and clients for compensatory damages. The definition of "due care" is being updated to include computer functionality outages, as more and more people around the world depend upon data information to do their jobs (Krutz and Vines, p. 276).

Security Should Be Cost-Effective

The costs and benefits of security should be carefully weighed in both monetary and nonmonetary terms. Security levels, costs, measures, practices, and procedures should be appropriate and proportionate to the value and degree of reliance on the asset and to the severity, probability, and extent of potential harm. Potential harm must always be viewed in a worst-case scenario; underestimating the extent of damage that could result from the loss of information or its assets may result in the inability to justify adequate security controls or resources to protect it. We will devote much attention later in this book to the subject of valuing information.

Security Requires Risk Management

The safeguarding of information and resources (against sabotage, tampering, denial of service, espionage, fraud, misappropriation, misuse, or release to unauthorized persons) is accomplished through the continuous use of safeguards. These security safeguards include administrative, procedural, physical, environmental, personnel, communications, emanation, operations, and information system security. A mix of safeguards is used to achieve the necessary level of security or protection using risk management principles: analyzing the risks and cost benefits; selecting and implementing the appropriate mix of safeguards; and assessing the results, making appropriate adjustments as necessary.

Risk is the expected loss of accountability, access control, confidentiality, integrity, or availability from an attack or incident. This risk should be identified and analyzed to assess the impact to the organization in the event of a loss. A management decision would then determine whether the risk was acceptable or whether measures are required to mitigate the risk to an acceptable level. Risk management also includes the measures required to maintain a level of acceptable risk. Understanding and applying risk management principles is so important and integral to what the security manager does that we will devote an entire chapter to this subject later in this book. (See Chapter 5 — "The Organization's IA Posture.")

Security Requires a Comprehensive and Integrated Approach

Measures, practices, and procedures for the security of an organization's assets should take account of and address all relevant security considerations, security disciplines, and security interdependencies. Information systems security cannot exist in a vacuum. It is dependent on the multidisciplinary nature of security. Risk management, for example, is all about knowing how, when, and where to apply security measures to achieve the necessary level of protection for information and its requisite resources in order to control and reduce risk to an acceptable level. These measures may incorporate personnel security, physical security, communications security, and operational security, but the mixture of measures must be balanced and proportionate to the associated risks. Good IA management today requires this kind of thorough and holistic approach to security.

Security Requires Life-Cycle Management

Life-cycle management is the "cradle to grave" concept that information systems acquisition, integration, configuration, testing, implementation, operation, and disposal are controlled and managed. An entire chapter is dedicated to this concept later in this book. (See Chapter 11 — "Layer 6: Life-Cycle Security.")

Change Management

Change management is the principle that changes must be anticipated and controlled to ensure that authorization, testing, and approval occur before a modification to the operational baseline is implemented. A comprehensive change management process must be implemented and operating to ensure that configuration management of the operational security baseline is maintained. Changes to the IA baseline must not adversely affect critical processes or void existing terms of accreditation. Security controls must be configurable to accommodate the organization's security policy. As those policies change due to risk management decisions, the controls must be flexible enough to change, too. (See Chapter 10 — "Layer 5: Configuration Management.")

License Management

Software copyright laws and licensing agreements must be honored. License management must be accomplished in order to track software license requirements; avoid denial of service from license expirations; and minimize operations and maintenance (O&M) costs by procuring the appropriate number of licenses for the organization.

Security Responsibilities and Accountability Should Be Made Explicit

The obligations, expected behavior, and the degree to which an individual is held responsible for his or her actions should be clearly stated. The security officer is responsible for interpreting, applying, and enforcing higher-level security directives, regulations, and policies within the organization. When these policies need further refinement or in the absence of higher-level guidance, the organization will need to develop local policy to fill the void to ensure that individual expectations are clearly delineated.

Once defined, these obligations and expectations must be supported and enforced by senior management and conveyed to all individuals throughout the organization. This effort is primarily achieved through a robust security training and awareness program.

Security Requires Training and Awareness

Everyone within the organization should know and understand his or her security role and responsibilities. A security training and awareness program must be developed and implemented that instructs users in their responsibility to uphold the organization's information system and security policies, procedures, and practices. Initial training must occur *before* the user is granted access to any information system. After that, a program of ongoing and proactive security awareness and refresher training will remind users of their security responsibilities and reinforce good security principles. Awareness methods (e.g., posters, videos, e-mail reminders) are also used to keep attention focused on security issues and remind personnel of their individual and corporate security responsibilities.

Appropriate system and security training must also consider the level of access. A system administrator requires more detailed training in the system's operation and security features than a person with normal user privileges. With the level of access often at the root or superuser level, privileged users (e.g., system administrators, security administrators, Webmasters) must be your most trusted system users because of their unrestrained system access. As such, this group also represents the organization's biggest insider threat. Some organizations today are requiring a form of licensing or certification for privileged users, to ensure a certain minimum level of understanding and competency. In some cases, an initial or random screening interview or polygraph examination also is used as a means to verify compliance with organizational policy and to act as a deterrent from considering any deliberate deviation from policy.

An effective training plan for procedures, guidelines, and checklists is essential to providing both consistency and continuity of operations. Training is also key to information availability since most denial of service events result from unintentional human error or omission. Personnel must be trained and equipped with all the skills necessary to perform their specific duties, to include good security procedures. As personnel remain aware of proper operational and security procedures, the number and severity of security incidents should drop proportionally. (See Chapter 13 — "Layer 8: IA Education, Training, and Awareness.")

Security Requires Continual Reassessment

An organization and its information, facilities, and systems/networks, as well as the environment in which these operate, are dynamic. Information systems and the requirements for security vary over time. The use of security safeguards must be constantly reevaluated for applicability and effectiveness. Likewise, the effectiveness of the organization's Information Assurance program as a whole must be continually assessed and reevaluated, and the program must be adjusted as necessary. Such corrective action will help keep the IA Program relevant and focused.

Security Must Respect Ethical and Democratic Rights

The use of an information system and its security should respect the legitimate rights and interests of others and "should be compatible with the legitimate use and flow of data and information in a democratic society" (OECD, 1992). Privacy issues fall into two basic forms: information about ourselves that we have revealed for public use and personal information about ourselves to which we want to control access. The principles of ethics and democracy present a double-edged sword. While we must protect the personal and private information of the system user, we must also ensure that the organization's information and systems are used only for authorized and legitimate purposes. For example, all U.S. Department of Defense computer systems are required to electronically display a warning banner for users to read and heed prior to logging in and accessing the system. The banner clearly states that the information system is subject to monitoring and auditing (to include e-mail); users have no expectation of privacy while using the system; and anyone caught using the system for unofficial or unauthorized purposes is subject to administrative action or criminal prosecution. Although security officials cannot legally target an individual's system use, the consent-to-monitoring notice gives the organization legal recourse to investigate and prosecute misuse, if discovered.

> An ethic is an objectively defined standard of right and wrong. . . . An ethic is different from a law in several important ways. First, laws apply to everyone: one may disagree with the intent or the meaning of a law, but that is not an excuse for disobeying the law. Second, there is a regular process through the courts for determining which law supersedes which if two laws conflict. Third, the laws and the courts identify certain actions as right and others as wrong. From a legal standpoint, anything that is not illegal is right. Finally, laws can be enforced, and there are ways to rectify wrongs done by unlawful behavior.
>
> By contrast, ethics are personal: two people may have different frameworks for making moral judgements. What one person thinks is perfectly justifiable, another would never consider doing. Second, ethical positions can and often do come into conflict. . . . Yet, there is no arbiter of ethical positions: when two ethical goals collide, each person must choose which goal is dominant. Third, two people may assess ethical values differently; there is no universal standard of right and wrong in ethical judgements. Nor can one person simply look to what another has done as guidance for choosing the right thing to do. Finally, there is no enforcement for ethical choices (Pfleeger, 1997, pp. 517–518).

Other Basic Security Principles

Choke point: The principle that funneling activity through a narrow channel improves the ability to control and monitor the activity (e.g., toll booth, cash register checkout). A choke point is only effective if all activity is required to use it, without the possibility of circumvention (Chapman and Zwicky, 1995, p. 48).

Consistency: The principle that the system behaves in the same manner each time; there is no unplanned or undesirable variation in the system's behavior.

Control of the periphery: The principle that it is easier to deny entry to intruders than to eject them after they have gained entry. The emphasis here is on protecting boundaries and detecting intrusions upon penetration of that boundary.

Defense in Depth: Operates on the principle that multiple, overlapping layers of controls provide better protection than any single control used by itself. Anyone attempting access to critical assets would first need to defeat multiple layers of security controls. In order to ensure the needed redundancy for effective Defense in Depth, the controls must function independently of each other. (See Basic Security Strategy section below.)

Deny upon failure: The principle that a failed control will default to denial of access or service. In other words, the system or mechanism that is being controlled will cease to function or will, at minimum, deny further access, if the control fails. This is also referred to as a *fail-safe* control (Chapman and Zwicky, 1995, p. 49). Audits, for example, should be configured with the default setting to crash upon audit failure. If functioning audit controls are a security requirement for operational use of the system, when the audits stop working, the system should halt.

Diversity of defense: The principle that additional security is derived from having more than one type or brand of the same control. For example, "using security systems from different vendors may reduce the chances of a common bug or configuration error that compromises them all" (Chapman and Zwicky, 1995, p. 53). The benefits of this principle must be weighed against the trade-offs in additional acquisition, operation, and maintenance costs.

Interdependency: The concept that security services do not act alone, but depend on other services to achieve IA. Alternatively, when one service fails, other security services are impacted, and assurance may not be achieved. For example, integrity and confidentiality are interdependent, and accountability and availability each depend on both confidentiality and integrity.

Override: The system must be designed to permit proper authorities to stop, or otherwise interfere with, the operation of a control only in special circumstances. Any overriding of the control, however, should provide for the reinitialization of the control to normal operational mode. For example, overriding of access controls should be set to expire upon completion of the override period. "If special access-control-related privileges have been granted to a systems programmer so that he or she may fix a problem, these privileges can be defined to expire in a few days. In this way, the probability that these 'god-like' privileges will be used for unauthorized activity is reduced" (Wood, 1990, p. 15).

Reliability: The principle that the system behaves as expected.

Simplicity: As a general principle, less complex usually indicates easier to understand. The more simple a control is, the easier it is to test and verify that the control is working as designed. A simple control is always preferable, but if the choice is between a more complex technical control and mitigating the risk through manual procedures, the technical control should be seriously considered. Procedures are often a weak method of policy compliance because enforcement is often difficult or impossible. Additionally, a security control should always be simpler (i.e., less complicated and/or involving fewer steps) to implement than available options to override or bypass the control. For example, if your organization implements software that enforces a security policy but allows users to override by exception, it should be more intuitive and convenient for the user to implement the security control than to disregard it.

Timeliness: Everyone involved in the prevention of and response to breaches of information security must act in a timely manner. Ideally security must be done proactively, anticipating and preventing security incidents from occurring. The reality is that much of a security manager's job is spent reacting to security problems. As a result, the detection of and reaction to security incidents must be accomplished in a timely manner. Written procedures must be in place to avoid delays in proper handling and reporting of security violations. Contingency planning must be implemented and exercised to avoid unnecessary denial of service.

Universal application/participation: The principle that all personnel and systems within a controlled environments are, voluntarily or involuntarily, subject to the same security policies and controls, without bypassing or opting out (Chapman and Zwicky, 1995, p. 52; Wood, 1990, p. 17).

Weakest link: The principle that a chain is only as strong as its weakest link. The security of a network is only as effective as the least protected or weakest point in the network's defenses (Chapman and Zwicky, 1995, p. 48).

BASIC SECURITY STRATEGY

Approaches to Applying Security Principles

An organization has three fundamental strategies for developing and implementing a program to protect its IA baseline and the Critical Objects that are necessary for its survival, coexistence, and growth. Each of the strategies will be separately described.

Security by Obscurity Strategy

The basis of the first fundamental strategy is stealth. That is, if no one knows that an organization's IA baseline and Critical Objects exist, they would not be subject to threats. The intent is that sufficient security can be achieved by hiding an organization's automated capabilities and the access to these capabilities or at least not advertising their existence. IA does involve the use of stealth to a certain extent. However, the current and growing extent to which organizations have been using their automated capabilities to interact with customers and potential customers does make the strategy option not very practical and realistic.

The Perimeter Defense Strategy

This strategy is more of a concentrated effort of defense and is predominantly technical in nature. Also, this strategy basically focuses on threats from those that are outside the bounds of authorized users to the organization's IA baseline and Critical Objects. The organization's IA capabilities are primarily located within a "zone" or "border" of defense between the "insiders" and the "outsiders." This strategy has been compared to the "Maginot Line" that existed as a defensive perimeter or border between the allied nations and Germany during World War I. An example of this concentrated strategy involves a firewall device that is connected to both the Internet (i.e., outside) side of an organizational border and what is considered to be the organization's own trusted internal network. A public access server is connected to the cables above the firewall and a Web proxy server is connected to the cable below the firewall. The term "demilitarized zone (DMZ)" has been used to describe the defensive perimeter that includes these three devices. The intent of this perimeter is to control the flow of information between the organization's internal trusted network and the untrusted external Internet. Not much of the organization's IA capabilities is allocated to secure the internal systems. The assumption is that perimeter defenses are sufficient to prevent, detect, and correct any intruders so that the internal systems will be secure.

The Perimeter Defense Strategy has two critical weaknesses. First, this strategy does very little or nothing to protect an organization's internal systems from an attack by an authorized inside user such as an employee or contractor. As discussed in Chapter 1 ("IA and the Organization: The Challenges"), it is the authorized insiders who pose the greatest threat to the organization's IA baseline and Critical Objects. Second, if the perimeter defenses (e.g., firewalls and routers) fail, then the organization's internal systems are open to attack.

Defense in Depth Strategy

The Defense in Depth strategy takes a much broader approach by defining a number of operationally interoperable and complementary technical and nontechnical IA layers of defense. The critical fact is that the totality of these layers is what provides a cohesive and integrated process for defense in the same way that the seven layers of the Open Systems Interconnection (OSI) Basic Reference Model provide a process for communications. The Defense in Depth strategy recognizes that, because of the highly interactive nature of the various systems and networks, any single system cannot be adequately secured unless all interconnected systems are adequately secured. An IA solution for any system must be considered within the context of this shared risk environment. Therefore, layers of protection are needed to accomplish IA needs. Also, there is a complementary aspect to a Defense in Depth strategy. Multiple layers offset weaknesses of other layers.

Also, an enclave is defined as an environment under the control of a single authority with personnel and physical security measures and may contain multiple networks. Enclaves may also be specific to an organization or mission. Different enclaves (e.g., office facilities, warehouse facilities, production facilities, marketing analysts, financial analysts) within the organization require a strong perimeter to guard against malicious outsiders. Essentially, there is a need for technical and nontechnical layers of defense to protect against outsiders, as well as those within the enclave (i.e., the insiders). This approach is even more relevant to organizations considering the significant rise in the threat posed by individuals who are formally authorized to access organizational Critical Objects.

The Defense in Depth strategy does not imply that protection is required at every possible point in the IA baseline. The allocation of the IA capabilities can be focused, based on the unique needs of an organization's threats. Further, adopting a layered approach can allow lower assurance solutions (which are generally more cost effective and more user friendly) to be used in many environments, permitting the applications of higher assurance solutions at critical locations (e.g., network boundaries).

The implementation of a Defense in Depth strategy is complicated by the fact that many organizations employ multiple types of external network connections through the enclave boundary. These include encrypted connections to other enclaves, connections to access data on hostile networks (such as the Internet), connections to remote dial-in users, and, if required, connections to other local networks operating at different classification levels. There is a requirement for different types of solutions for each of these connections that satisfy both operational and IA requirements.

Recommended Strategy: Defense in Depth

Every organization that has defined IA needs must address the fundamental issue of what strategy it will use to accomplish its IA needs. We believe that the ever-increasing organizational dependency on automated capabilities for survival, coexistence, and growth requires the broader and more integrated strategy that is inherent in Defense in Depth. Four reasons will be cited to support this conclusion, although it is recognized that many other justifications could be cited.

First, the use of electronic commerce (e-commerce) provides both an opportunity for the organization and some inherent risks. E-commerce could affect every application and database within the organization. The security of the Web server host within the DMZ is not sufficient to address the risks posed by e-commerce transactions. One such risk is that the Web server could start opening sessions to other servers within the organization, thereby providing paths into organizational enclaves. Also, hackers could gain access to the internal organizational network and traverse all internal segments at will. There is no longer the luxury of defending only a single segment of the organization. The reason is that e-commerce is more than just selling online; it gives the organization's customers and partners access to some of an organization's critical data and applications.

There may be a belief that sufficient defenses exist beyond the firewall within the organizational enclaves. However, the architecture of internal organizational enclaves has been driven by several factors: historical accident (we needed it, we added it), performance (based on user complaints, we moved the servers to their own internal segment), and/or reliability (someone will get fired if there's a problem with this application, so we'll buy two of everything). Traditionally, security has rarely been the driving factor in the design of network architecture. Therefore, the firewall is often the only secure portion of the network. E-commerce is an example of an application that requires the same degree of security behind the firewall as is traditionally applied to the DMZ. This requires an expansion of the depth of the defense to within the organization.

Second, traditionally, the threats to the confidentiality, integrity, availability, authentication, and nonrepudiation of organizational information have been perceived as existing outside the physical and logical boundaries of the organization. However, there is more of a realization that employees inside the organization pose a threat similar to that posed by those outside the organization. Certainly, employees who have been granted higher levels of privilege to create user accounts, establish configuration settings, and develop and modify software code represent a potential source of this threat. The National Security Telecommunications and Information Systems Security Committee (NSTISSC) published a manual in July 1999 entitled "The Insider Threat to U.S. Government Information Systems." This document stated that the greatest potential threat to U.S. government information systems comes from insiders with legitimate access to those systems. The insider threat to the private sector would be similar.

Third, the Open System Interconnection (OSI) Basic Reference Model represents the process of communications based on layers. These layers, from the lowest layer to the highest layer, involve the Physical, Data Link, Network, Transport, Session, Presentation, and Application Layers. Each layer represents a task within the communication process required for the movement of information between information systems that are connected to a network. As Chapter 8 ("Layer 3: IA Architecture") will describe, the International Organization for Standardization (ISO) 7498-2, Part 2, "Security Architecture," identifies five types of Security Services that are aimed at controlling security threats. These Security Services are Authentication, Access Control, Data Confidentiality, Data Integrity, and Nonrepudiation. Security mechanisms that are associated with these Security Services should be allocated within the depths of appropriate layers of the OSI Model. Therefore, a layering approach is inherent in the communication of information within an organization and between organizations.

Fourth, there are many possible types of attacks that could be used to exploit organizational information systems. The following represents examples of these possible types of attacks:

> *Passive intercepts and attacks on the wide-area network (WAN)*: These attacks include network traffic analysis, monitoring of unprotected (plain-text) communications, decrypting weakly encrypted communications, and capturing identification numbers and passwords.

> *WAN-based attacks*: WAN-based attacks include attempts to circumvent or break security features, introduce malicious code, or steal data. These can include attacks mounted against the network backbone; exploitation of data in transit; electronic penetrations into an enclave or local-area network (LAN) through the boundary protection devices (including an enclave's remote access entry point); or attacks on an authorized remote user when he or she attempts to connect to the enclave.

> *Insider attacks*: Insider attacks are performed by a person who is authorized to be within the physical boundaries of the information system security processing system and/or has direct access to the information security processing system.

> *Hardware/software distribution attacks*: This type of attack focuses on modifications of hardware or software at the factory, or modifications or substitutions during distribution. Malicious code can be easily imported into a protected enclave through shrink-wrapped software, users swapping media with machines outside the enclave, or other paths that are implemented to import information from outside a protected network. The hardware/software distribution attack refers to the potential for malicious modifications of hardware or software between the time it is produced by a developer and the time it is installed and used. If a user has a remote access capability, these attacks could occur while the remote user's computer is being configured, if it is left unattended (i.e., without proper physical security), or while software is passed to it either over the network or via physical means (e.g., floppy disks).

Implementing Defense in Depth

In our next chapter, we will provide a means for an organization to define the scope or boundaries of what it needs to protect. Physical and virtual boundaries are described. The virtual boundary includes the necessity of defending the network infrastructure, the enclave boundary, and the computing environment. The remaining chapters of this book provide a means of implementing a Defense in Depth strategy for protecting the physical and virtual boundaries of the organization.

Figure 2-1 is a model that depicts the layers of the Defense in Depth strategy. The core of the strategy is information that the organization requires for its survival, coexistence, and growth and the IA baseline that collects, inputs, processes, stores, outputs, and communicates that information. The organization should define its IA needs concerning its information and IA baseline relative to confidentiality, integrity, and availability. The IA posture provides a means of measuring how successfully the organization is achieving its IA needs.

The IA policies (Layer 1) need to be formulated to define the actions and behavior required to accomplish the defined IA needs of the organization. An IA management structure (Layer 2) will need to be formally established to monitor and control the implementation of the IA policy. Layers 3 to 11 involve the technical and nontechnical implementations of the IA policies. An IA architecture (Layer 3) provides the infrastructure of technical security services and security mechanisms and a basis for their allocation within the organization's IA baseline. Layers 4–11 provide the infrastructure of nontechnical functions. Each of the eight nontechnical functions of these layers (operational security administration, configuration management, life-cycle security, and so forth) provides an infrastructure of integrated support to the IA Architecture. The successful integration

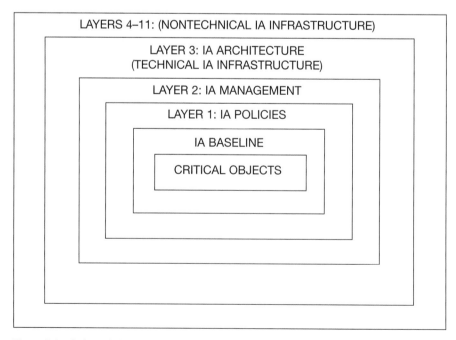

Figure 2-1   Defense in Depth strategy.

of both the technical and nontechnical layers produces the Defense in Depth strategy that maximizes the protection of the organization's IA baseline and Critical Objects. As we will discuss in detail in Chapter 5 ("The Organization's IA Posture"), each layer influences the level of the organization's IA posture. The extent to which these layers collectively operate and complement one another ultimately determines how high or low the level of the IA posture will be for the organization at any point in time.

SUMMARY

Information is one of the organization's most valuable resources. Threats to information security can come in the form of unauthorized disclosure, corruption, or preventing access through a denial of service.

The purpose of security is to protect the organization's valuable resources, particularly the confidentiality, integrity, and availability of its information and the assets that process, store, and transmit that information. Security regulations, policy, and guidance are based on generally accepted security concepts and principles. Understanding those concepts and principles will enable the Information Assurance professional to make educated decisions and issue consistent guidance in the absence of written policy or historical precedent.

Three fundamentally different strategies were presented for developing and implementing a program for protecting an organization's IA baseline and Critical Objects. The strategies described included Security by Obscurity, Perimeter Defense, and Defense in Depth. The Defense in Depth strategy was presented as the strategy that would maximize the protection and achieve the highest IA posture level. The book defines an organizational Defense in Depth strategy in terms of a collective structure of 11 complementary technical and nontechnical layers. Each of the layers will be described in subsequent chapters.

REFERENCES

"A Model for Information Classification and Control." Supplement to *Computer Security Newsletter* (No. 47, January/February 1987).

Abramowitz, Beth, Steve Boczenowski, and Brian McKenney, "Security Enterprise Resources with PKIs." *The Edge*, The MITRE Advanced Technology Newsletter (February 2001; Vol. 5, No. 1).

Armour, Stephanie, "Does Your Company Own What You Know?" *USA Today* (January 20, 2000).

Canavan, J. E., *Fundamentals of Network Security*. Norwood, MA: Artech House, Inc., 2001.

Chapman, Brent, and Elizabeth Zwicky, eds., *Building Internet Firewalls*. Cambridge, MA: O'Reilly & Associates, Inc., 1995.

Garfinkel, Simon, and Gene Spafford, *Practical UNIX and Internet Security*, 2nd ed. Cambridge, MA: O'Reilly & Associates, Inc., 1996.

Information Assurance Technical Framework (IATF), Release 2.0.1 (September 1999).

Karabin, Stephen. "Data Classification for Security and Control." *EDPACS: The EDP [Electronic Data Processing] Audit, Control and Security Newsletter* (December 1985; Vol. XIII, No. 6).

Kovacich, Dr. Gerald L. *Information Systems Security Officer's Guide: Establishing and Managing an Information Protection Program.* Boston: Butterworth–Heinemann, 1998.

Krutz, Ronald L., and Russell Dean Vines. *The CISSP Prep Guide: Mastering the Ten Domains of Computer Security.* New York: Wiley, 2001.

McCumber, John R. "Information Systems Security: A Comprehensive Model," Annex to NSTISSI No. 4011, National Training Standard for Information Systems Security (INFOSEC) Professionals (20 June 1994).

Naisbitt, John, *Megatrends.* New York: Warner Books, 1982.

National Institute of Standards and Technology (NIST) Special Publication 800-14. *Generally Accepted Principles and Practices for Securing Information Technology System.* Washington, DC: U.S. Department of Commerce, 1996.

Naumann, I. E. (Jon), "DNS Attacks: An Example of Due Diligence." *Sans Institute* Article (April 3, 2001).

National Security Telecommunications and Information Systems Security Committee (NSTISSC). *The Insider Threat to U.S. Government Information Systems.* NSTISSAM INFOSEC/1-99 (July 1999).

Organization for Economic Co-operation and Development (OECD). *Guidelines for the Security of Information Systems.* Paris, 1992.

Pfleeger, Charles P., *Security in Computing*, 2nd ed. Upper Saddle River, NJ: Prentice Hall, 1997.

Russell, Deborah, and G. T. Gangemi, Sr., *Computer Security Basics.* Cambridge, MA: O'Reilly & Associates, Inc., 1991.

SC Magazine. "Body Parts" (February 2000).

Schneier, B. *Secrets and Lies—Digital Security in a Networked World.* New York: John Wiley & Sons, Inc., 2000.

Schweitzer, James A., *Protecting Business Information: A Manager's Guide.* Boston: Butterworth–Heinemann, 1996.

Wood, Charles Cresson, "Principles of Secure Information Systems Design." *Computers & Security* (1990; Vol. 9): 13–24.

II: DEFINING THE ORGANIZATION'S CURRENT IA POSTURE

3. Determining the Organization's IA Baseline

CHAPTER OBJECTIVES

- Identify the elements of the DoD's Defense in Depth strategy
- Establish a working model of IA elements
- Discuss physical security requirements
- Outline technical countermeasures used within virtual boundaries

INFORMATION ASSURANCE ELEMENTS

The U.S. Department of Defense (DoD) has adopted a Global Network Information Environment (GNIE) IA strategy called "Defense in Depth" (IATF, 1999, p. 1.1). The approach is based on the ancient principle that multiple layers of protection are better than a single point of failure. Medieval castles incorporated a combination of moat, drawbridge, fortified walls, watchtowers, armed guards, and supplies. Likewise, good computer network defense cannot depend on a single firewall or simple passwords, but rather requires multiple controls and safeguards to provide an acceptable level of defense.

The DoD strategy breaks down IA into three basic elements — people, technology, and operations.

> People are the most crucial aspect of IA. The challenge is to provide the right amount and type of training to all the people and to develop a human resources strategy that brings the right people to bear at the right time and place. . . . [Operations consists of] two main aspects: system management and situation awareness (IATF, 1999, p. 1.2.3).

Operations also include the security procedures required to ensure that system defenses quickly adapt in response to changing threats. The element of technology is where the Defense in Depth layers are applied: within the network at large; at the enclave boundary; and within the computing environment. These layers utilize security countermeasures to provide the confidentiality, integrity, and availability necessary to protect information and its assets from network-based threats. (See Figure 3-1.)

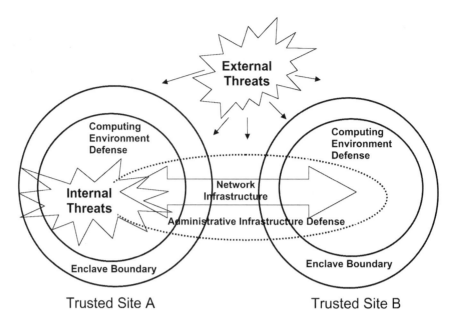

Figure 3-1   Defense in Depth layers.

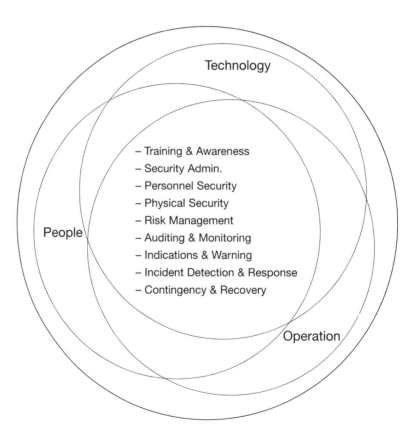

Figure 3-2   Interrelationships of IA elements

While the DoD strategy provides a good Defense in Depth model, it struggles to find the balance between its elements. The tendency is to overemphasize one element over the other, in particular, putting too much stock into the technical layers. Another shortfall is the assignment of certain subelements to each of the major elements. These subelements could apply to all three elements and should not be viewed as exclusive to any single element. (See Figure 3-2.)

By charting out the IA subelements as they equally apply to people, technology, and operations, we can see how all these attributes form a more holistic approach to IA. Personnel security, for example, obviously applies to the People category, but personnel clearances, coupled with the individual's need-to-know, determine levels of access control—itself an application of the technology element. Meanwhile, the operations element of IA must include the personnel security program when assessing the organization's overall IA risk posture (see Chapter 5— "The Organization's IA Posture"). Auditing and monitoring is a function of the operations element, but this function cannot be separated from the people and technology being audited. We see the marriage of all three IA elements as the best way to express the vast range of IA responsibilities and disciplines. Such a model is best supported by a solid foundation of risk management principles and the IA strategic plan, policies, and mission/function statement, all working in concert with the organization's goals and objectives. (See Figure 3-3 and Table 3-1.)

We begin our discussion of IA elements by defining the boundaries of the organization's physical and virtual scope of IA responsibilities. Once this context is established, we will examine in more depth the various other elements of IA in subsequent chapters:

- *Personnel security*: Chapter 9—"Operational Security Administration"
- *Security operations and administration*: Chapter 7—"IA Management"; Chapter 9—"Operational Security Administration"; Chapter 10—"Configuration

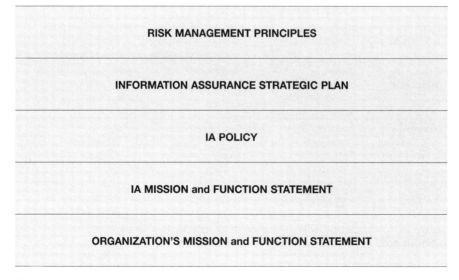

Figure 3-3 IA foundational structure

Table 3-1   Information Assurance Elements

Subelements	People	Technology	Operations
Physical Security	Physical access controls of facilities	Technical access controls of facilities	Auditing and monitoring of physical access controls Traditional risk assessment
Personnel Security	Visitor control Background checks Clearances Indoctrination Least privilege Need-to-know determination Access management	Authentication and accountability measures Access controls Separation of functions Data separation and compartmentalization	Auditing and monitoring of system access controls Data classification Data marking and labeling Traditional risk assessment
Training and Awareness	Security orientation Annual refresher Understanding of role and responsibilities Security Awareness	System training Tech security training Certification and professionalization	Working knowledge of policies and procedures Training program self-assessment
Security Operations/ Administration	General user role Privileged user role Staffing Remote management Outsourcing Coordination Selling IA	Technical security guidance Certification/ accreditation Configuration/ change management Destruction and disposal	Tactical IA plan Testing and evaluation Risk assessment Auditing and monitoring IA metrics Self-inspection checklist Procedural audit (policy review and revision)
Auditing and Monitoring	User expectations and rules of behavior Consent to monitoring Legal limitations Privacy issues Copyright issues Licensing issues	Real-time monitoring Audit collection and retention Technical audits/ penetration testing Tech vulnerability scanning	Audit review and analysis Traditional risk assessment Tech vulnerability assessment
Indications and Warnings	Insider threat mitigation	Intrusion detection Antiviral scanning Firewall monitoring	Enterprise security management Threat assessment
Incident Response	Training Exercised procedures Evidence handling/ chain of custody	Automated response	Procedural response Incident cleanup Reporting
Contingency and Recovery	Depth of coverage Contingency personnel	Backup procedures UPS Disaster recovery plan	Continuity of operations procedures
IA ACTION VERBS	MANAGE; TRAIN; and PREVENT	PROTECT and DEFEND	COMPLY; ASSESS; DETECT; REACT; RESTORE
SECURITY DISCIPLINES	PERSONNEL; PHYSICAL; and OPERATIONS SECURITY	INFO SYSTEMS SECURITY; IPSEC; COMSEC; TECHNICAL SECURITY	INFOSEC; PROCEDURAL/ ADMINISTRATIVE SECURITY

Management"; Chapter 11—"Life-Cycle Security"; Chapter 12—"Contingency Planning"; Chapter 14—"IA Policy Compliance Oversight"
- *Contingency and recovery*: Chapter 12—"Contingency Planning"
- *Training and awareness*: Chapter 13—"IA Education, Training, and Awareness"
- *Auditing and monitoring*: Chapter 14—"IA Policy Compliance Oversight"
- *Indications and warnings*: Chapter 14—"IA Policy Compliance Oversight"
- *Incident response*: Chapter 15—"IA Incident Response"

Physical Boundaries

The terrorist attacks against the United States on September 11, 2001, changed forever the way the world views our need for security. While cyber-threats from viruses and worms had previously reminded us of how vulnerable our information systems are to attack, the events of that fateful day underscored our need for traditional physical and personnel security. The need to physically protect assets from real or perceived threats cannot be overlooked or mitigated by other security disciplines; there is no substitute for good physical security measures.

The extent of an organization's physical security responsibility is normally determined by the organization's physical boundaries. The physical boundaries must encompass the facility and network infrastructure(s) that make up your site. This includes all the facilities that process and store information, as well as all the IT equipment that permits the internal and external communication of information.

If your organization is confined to a single building or office space, then your physical security boundaries are most likely limited to the outer perimeter of that facility or office. If your organization looks more like a compound or campus environment, the physical security may include all the buildings, structures, and offices that process and store information as well as the Protective Distribution System (PDS) that provides the conduit for communication lines between buildings. When physical security responsibilities extend to multiple sites, the physical boundaries of each site must be individually assessed.

Whatever your physical facility layout, the fundamental objective for physical security of the facilities is the same: allow entry to authorized personnel with a legitimate need and deny access to unauthorized individuals. Although this sounds simplistic, a great deal of thought needs to go into developing your physical security protection.

At minimum, two physical barriers should be used, with checks to ensure that each barrier is working properly. Each possible entry point to each facility should be secured, including doors, windows, air vents, and air-conditioning ducts.

Additionally, consider what areas or zones within each facility require more protection. For example, the offices where payroll is done or where IT servers are located require more physical access controls than general office space; general office space may need more physical access controls than an area designated for general public use (i.e., waiting room, reception room). Physical access to servers and workstations should be controlled and identifications verified. For those areas requiring more protection, use a combination of control methods.

There are three basic ways to control physical access:

- People (stationary security guards, receptionists, customer service representatives, and roaming surveillance guards), and/or animals (guard dogs)
- Mechanical devices (locks and keys) used with physical barriers (walls, doors, and fences)
- Electronic devices [automated card readers/badge readers, biometrics, alarm systems, intrusion detection systems, motion detectors, closed circuit television (CCTV) cameras] (Lane, 1990, p. 19).

Of these methods, locks are the least expensive, but keys can be easily duplicated and cipher lock combinations can be guessed. Spin-dial combination locks provide good access control, but are best used for overnight securing; they are impractical in high-traffic areas where regular and frequent access is required.

Using people as an access control mechanism presents a costly and ongoing overhead. Security guards may be an effective means of controlling a small number of people accessing a physical area. That said, it is questionable whether a security guard doing access control can effectively verify (from several feet away) that the thumbprint-size picture of the person on an access control badge is, in fact, the person wearing the badge. A more effective use of a security guard at an entry control point is in conjunction with another control method, such as an electronic device. Having the guard verify that no one bypasses a turnstile entry with personal identification number (PIN) verification provides a better level of secure physical access control. Additionally, the guard could perform bag checks to ensure that no unauthorized device or information goes in or out of the facility.

If a person is to be used as an access control mechanism, ensure that they understand the extent of those responsibilities (Lane, 1990, p. 20). They need to know who is authorized access, who is unauthorized, and whom to call in the event of a problem. Of course, anytime people are used as an access control mechanism, it is assumed that they are physically postured beside or in front of the entry they are protecting.

Certain electronic devices are extremely effective for physical access control, if used properly. However, they can provide an incomplete solution if improperly configured. For example, a card reader system without a turnstile mechanism to enforce single entry will allow multiple users to piggyback on a single user's entry code. Forcing a card reader swipe and/or PIN verification upon entering the protected area without requiring a card swipe upon exiting will provide an incomplete audit trail, if it is necessary to pinpoint who was in the building at a given time.

One of the primary advantages of using electronic access control devices is the ability to control entry locations and times. With a card reader system installed, access to required buildings or offices, as well as expected work hours and days, is entered into a magnetic strip or computer chip on the employee's badge or building access card. The information on the card will prevent entry into a facility outside of authorized access times. Of course, the drawback with this access control, as with most security, is the exception to the rule. The lifting of time restrictions for on-call employees, for example, is a legitimate exception to policy, but it provides an opportunity for undetected illegitimate use.

Another associated consideration for physical access control is an organizational policy for visitor access. Procedures should be implemented to escort any individual not fully authorized to have unescorted access. When considering a visitor access policy, address the organization's position on such issues as:

- Official visits by family members (retirements, award presentations, etc.)
- Unofficial visits by family members (emergency situations when childcare is unavailable)
- Unofficial visits by others (e.g., flower or pizza deliveries)
- Nondisclosure agreements for authorized vendors, contractors, and visitors
- Escort policy for visitors, cleaning staff, and maintenance personnel
- Portable or wireless computing and telecommunication devices and associated media carried in/out of the facilities by visitors (e.g., Personal Digital Assistants or PDAs, laptops, electronic notebooks, cellular phones, modems, devices with enabled infrared ports)
- Audio and video recording equipment (e.g., cameras, video cameras, tape recorders, cassette players with record capability, PDAs and laptops with digital recording capability)
- Procedures for sanitizing work spaces prior to visits from personnel without proper clearances or need-to-know
- Monitor displays (turned away from open doorways and windows to avoid unauthorized disclosure)

All hand-carried items should be subject to inspection before being brought into the organization's facilities. These inspections are useful in identifying unauthorized items; acting as a deterrent for those contemplating a malicious act; and enforcing compliance with applicable security regulations. The legal limitations of the inspectors and the rights of employees during an inspection should be clearly spelled out to everyone. For example, the organization's legal counsel may determine that items carried on a person's body or in clothing worn by the person may not be inspected. However, items carried into or out of the facility, including briefcases, laptop cases, newspapers, notebooks, magazines, and gym bags, may be inspected.

Also consult your legal advisors about the extent to which you may conduct unannounced security inspections within the workspaces. For example:

- Are all spaces subject to periodic security inspections for compliance with applicable security regulations and requirements?
- Are all work areas and equipment subject to inspection for security, health, safety, and other official purposes?
- What items does the inspection include (e.g., computers, computer equipment, removable media, safes, desks, file cabinets, bookcases, and other storage facilities)?
- Who may conduct these authorized inspections?

- What actions are authorized if evidence of regulatory or legal misconduct is suspected or discovered during these inspections (e.g., seizure, inspection, analysis, review, and action by administrative and/or legal authorities)?
- How are employees notified that the terms of their employment and their access to the organization's facilities imply consent to these inspections?
- Are employees required to sign a statement of understanding about the organization's prerogative to conduct such inspections?

Virtual Boundaries

Besides the physical boundary, each networked information system also has a virtual boundary that extends to all intended users who are directly or indirectly connected to the system. With today's network connectivity, it is unusual to have a physical boundary of an organization that is not exceeded by its virtual boundary or enclave. An enclave is

> an environment under the control of a single authority with personnel and physical security measures and may contain multiple networks. Enclaves may also be specific to an organization or mission. Enclaves may be logical, such as an operational area network, as well as being based on physical location and proximity. . . . The point at which the enclave's network service layer connects to another network's service layer is the enclave boundary (IATF, 1999, p. 1.2.6.2).

Examples of enclave boundary environments include:

- A virtual private network (VPN) on a service layer network
- Service layer networks including modem connections
- Local-area networks (LANs) used to tunnel information within a wide-area network (WAN)
- Remote laptop connections to different service networks
- Remote LANs or systems

Organizations often have publicly accessible Web servers; file transfer protocol (ftp) servers; remote facilities with network access; employees authorized to work from home; and traveling employees with roaming connection requirements. These and other situations raise questions to consider in defining the scope of your IT security responsibilities beyond mere physical boundaries. Who is responsible for:

- The security of information accessed by remote network or dial-up connections?
- The control and use of modems from within your facility?
- The activity of deployed or traveling employees with laptop network connectivity?
- The information transferred to and from employees working from home?
- The information accessed on the organization's Internet homepage?
- The information accessible through an anonymous ftp address on your network?
- Portable computing devices that come/go from your facilities?

- Wireless computing devices that operate within your facilities?
- Stand-alone computers within the organization's facilities (i.e., permanent systems with no network connectivity)?
- Systems owned by other organizations that electronically interface with your systems?
- Systems controlled by other organizations that reside in your facilities but don't electronically interface with your systems?

If you find that you are the responsible manager for addressing any of these questions, then you will need written policies and procedures to address appropriate security measures for each situation. There are also technical security measures that you can employ to control and monitor the flow of data in and out of the enclave in order to defend your enclave boundary.

The objective for defending your physical and logical enclave boundaries should always be primarily to protect the confidentiality, integrity, and availability of your information and, in doing so, to protect your organization's reputation and customer trust. Understanding the system and network assets that make up your enclave and the risks to your enclave will help you to know how to apply additional safeguards to meet your desired level of protection.

The key to good security management of any network or host is to use a combination of safeguards as part of a deliberate security plan. Every technology has certain vulnerabilities that will not be entirely eliminated. Countermeasures can mitigate those risks. Using devices to control or defend an attack can create a strong barrier against attack, and tools can be implemented to reactively detect an attack or proactively identify weaknesses in network and host defenses.

Countermeasures are actions or entities used to reduce or eliminate one or more vulnerabilities or risks. Countermeasures may be either technical or nontechnical in nature. Nontechnical countermeasures include

> physical access control mechanisms, e.g., fences, doors, locks, and supporting infrastructures such as patrols; good system administration; and comprehensive training for both administrators and users. . . . Typical technical security countermeasures include detection/prevention, virus scanners, data link and network layer encryptors, security protocols, and tokens (IATF, 1999, p. 4.1).

The remainder of this chapter will take a high-level look at technical countermeasures within the Defense in Depth Layers: beginning with the network with its supporting infrastructure; followed by the enclave boundary; and finally, the computing environment as it affects people, operations, and technology.

The Network and Supporting Infrastructure

One of the first lines of defense in the protection of information is to ensure the use of confidentiality services (i.e., PKI, VPN, cryptographic communications, etc.) during transmission in order to protect the information from a passive intercept attack. Such attacks, if not encrypted, would allow an adversary to monitor communications; perform network traffic analysis; and steal user identifiers and authenticators (i.e., passwords). Network and infrastructure targets include voice, data, and wireless communications. Wireless networks include cellular, satellite, wireless LAN, and paging networks.

Many or all of these network communication paths are public switched networks [e.g., commercial Internet service providers (ISPs), plain old telephone service (POTS), Integrated Services Digital Network (ISDN), cellular, and satellite] and may be commercially leased. They are, therefore, subject to monitoring by the commercial owner. Sensitive organizational information could be flowing through network backbones and servers over which you have no control. Additionally, wireless communications broadcast the information over radio wave frequencies that can easily be intercepted by anyone with the right receiving equipment.

It is also important to remember that information passed during transmission is not only user files and electronic mail. Information about the addressing and routing of information, the status of network components, and other management traffic is also transmitted and must be protected from unauthorized modification. Simple Network Management Protocol (SNMP), Common Management Information Protocol (CMIP), Hypertext Transfer Protocol (HTTP), rlogin, and telnet are all examples of network management protocols (IATF, 1999, p. 5.0).

Encryption may stop an adversary from performing passive intelligence gathering operations against your organization's information. Active attacks on a network include attacking the integrity of security services: modifying or stealing information; introducing malicious code; or bypassing, straining, or defeating security mechanisms.

The Enclave Boundary

The enclave is the environment with personnel and physical security measures and under the control of a single authority. If the enclave has external connections, as most do, that entry into the enclave must be protected at the enclave boundary—the point where the external network's service layer connects to the enclave's network service layer. On the external end of the connection may be another entire network or a single remote or traveling user.

The key to defending the enclave boundary is to ensure that all boundaries (i.e., all points of entry into the enclave) are identified, controlled, and monitored. As elementary as identifying these boundaries seems, it is a step that cannot be overlooked. What good is tightly controlling one gateway into the enclave when a backdoor is left open and unattended?

Once the enclave boundary points are identified, they must be controlled and monitored. Network control measures include firewalls, routers, guards, VPNs, dial-in communications servers, identification and authentication (I&A), and access controls. Monitoring tools include intrusion detection systems (IDS), virus detection software, and vulnerability scanners. IDS usually comes in two forms: host-based and network-based. Host-based IDS is

software that monitors a system or application's log files, responding with an alarm or a countermeasure when a user attempts to gain access to unauthorized data, files, or services. . . . A network-based IDS monitors network traffic and responds with an alarm when it identifies a traffic pattern that it deems to be either a scanning attempt or a denial of service or other attack. It is quite useful in demonstrating that "bad guys" are actually trying to get into your computers (SANS, 2001, Items 2, 4).

Controlling IP Addresses

The person(s) responsible for dispensing Internet Protocol (IP) addresses for the organization should be able to provide a listing of the external connections to the enclave. The responsible Information Systems Security Officer should be preapproving these external connections anyway. In addition to the listing or network diagram that shows these connections, software is available to provide a current snapshot of the network to identify any other points of entry.

This protection approach of controlling and monitoring is known as perimeter-based security. While it focuses primarily on protecting the enclave from the outsider threat, it may also provide minimal protection against the malicious insider who launches an attack from inside the enclave or deliberately opens a door to allow access to an unauthorized outsider (IATF, 1999, pp. 6.0–1). For this reason, it is a good idea to routinely get a real-time picture of the network configuration or otherwise independently validate the network administrator's information to ensure that no backdoors go unreported. Independent verification should be used to verify that the enclave boundary (e.g., routers, firewalls, guards) is properly configured and that IP access control lists are complete and up-to-date.

Routers and Gateways

Within networks, there are network control devices that connect different networks together. These devices either forward data at the IP Layer or process data at the Application Layer. The former device is known as a *gateway*; the latter is called a *host*. A firewall is a host because it accepts and processes or discards data. In doing so, it severs the connection on the network and protects the enclave from external networks. Routers are hosts that forward IP packets between networks. Also known as Internet gateways, routers are sometimes distinguished from gateways in that routers move data between different networks, whereas gateways move data between different protocols. Access control lists (ACLs) should be implemented on routers to block unneeded protocols.

Firewalls and Guards

Firewalls have been a mainstay in the network defense arsenal for several years now. Generally speaking, firewalls are routing devices that provide walls between "us and them." They control access coming from a hostile, untrusted environment to a friendly, trusted environment (the organization's network enclave). As a control point for the enclave boundary, firewalls can broadly control access to the enclave by filtering the network traffic entering and leaving the enclave's network.

This filtering software consists of rule sets that "accept or reject packets of information, connection types or application specific communications attempting to cross the firewall" (CIAO, 2000, p. 33). For example, by analyzing certain packets, a firewall can determine and discard those that are possibly malicious, thereby preempting a potential denial-of-service attack. By blocking any traffic from the outside that claims to have originated from inside the network, a firewall can prevent IP spoofing attacks. Firewalls can also reject certain protocols used in penetration attacks. Firewalls designed to filter IP and protocol headers against a predefined rule set are also known as screening routers.

There are three common types of firewalls:

- Packet filtering firewalls screen data packets from source and destination transmission control protocol (TCP) and IP address headers and services. Since these firewalls use a very structured rule set, they can be an effective tool for blocking unneeded protocols.
- Proxy servers (also known as *application filtering*) apply a rule set to packets sent from outside (e.g., incoming electronic mail) and forward accepted packets to the appropriate internal application, thus allowing information to enter the organization's network without giving an external user direct connectivity.
- Some combination of the above.

One problem with firewalls revolves around cost: the cost of maintenance, because firewalls need to be upgraded every few months to stay relevant; the cost of operating them, in terms of the overhead needed to manually review logs; and the cost of performance, in the form of decreased network functionality.

Firewalls are weak in at least two other areas: they require proper configuration to be effective; and they may be ineffective for applications generating active content or implementing transaction-based Internet services. A firewall's effectiveness is dependent on how it is configured. Even if properly configured, firewalls can only provide limited protection against attacks carried in data that is authorized through the firewall into your network. For example, firewalls do not typically have the ability to analyze Java applets or provide the security mechanism necessary to allow or deny access to particular Web pages, applications, and databases on the basis of an ACL, user profile, or server authentication. Also, firewalls usually have inadequate auditing capability and cannot permit the use of strong authentication on incoming connections.

Guards employ stronger application filtering mechanisms, enabling the device to conduct content filtering. High-assurance guards (HAG) are commonly used between enclaves of different levels of sensitivity or classification.

The Computing Environment

Until now, we have concentrated on the protection and control of the information as it is transmitted throughout the network infrastructure — outside the enclave, and at the point where data enters the perimeter of the enclave, the enclave boundary. The computing environment addresses all information system assets within the enclave. This enclave is normally a physically protected area within the organization, but it could also be a laptop hosting a remote session from the hotel room of a traveling employee. Examples of items found within the computing environment include, but are not limited to:

- Stand-alone systems
- Communications systems
- Communications switching computers
- Video-teleconferencing equipment
- Network servers and clients
- Replication servers
- Process control computers
- Embedded computer systems
- Deployable computers
- Laptop/portable computing devices
- Personal Digital Assistants (PDAs), handheld computing devices
- Intelligent terminals
- Word processors
- Office automation systems
- Application and operating system software, including software libraries, source code, commercial and proprietary software, system utilities, etc.
- Associated peripheral devices and software (e.g., printers, scanners, monitors, tape drives, Zip drives, Jaz drives, external hard drives)
- Storage media (e.g., floppy disks, tapes, cartridges)
- Data repositories, including backup storage, data files, archived files, audit files, system logs, data directories, etc.
- Other office equipment (e.g., reproduction machines, facsimile machines, typewriters, dictation machines, tape recorders)

The computing environment includes the end user workstation, both desktop and laptop including peripheral devices; servers including Web, application, and file servers; applications such as intrusion detection, secure mail and Web, and access control; and the operating system (IATF, 1999, p. 1.2.6.3).

Whereas the network infrastructure and enclave boundaries are primarily concerned with data transmission, the computing environment focuses on the processing and storage of the information. To defend the computing environment, therefore, we must protect the confidentiality, integrity, and availability of information as it is moved between, and stored on, workstations and servers.

As we stated in earlier chapters, physically protecting the infrastructure (to include hardware) will mitigate the risk only of physical attacks, not of cyber attacks. There are different approaches to protecting the more virtual side of computers and networks, but none of these approaches is foolproof. Software invariably contains vulnerabilities that can be exploited. Using IDS alone or administrative security practices alone is not good enough. Only a combination of mechanisms will provide an adequate level of protection against attacks. Also, understanding these software vulnerabilities and other security issues surrounding information system software will assist management in developing applicable policies and procedures; determining levels of acceptable risk; and making informed security technology purchases.

It is imperative that the security officer or designee monitor and, if applicable, implement software patches and fixes. Sources of this information are provided in Appendix C and include Computer Emergency Response Team (CERT) advisories, security alerts, and updates/patches from software vendors.

SUMMARY

The DoD Defense in Depth strategy serves as a good example of how people, technology, and operations come together as the basic elements of IA. By examining how these elements interrelate we can develop a more holistic model that highlights the subelements of IA: physical security; personnel security; training and awareness; operational/administrative security; auditing and monitoring; indications and warnings; incident response; and contingency/recovery.

In addition to knowing what you are protecting, you also need to know the boundaries of this protection. Defining the physical and logical boundaries is paramount to knowing the limits of your security management responsibilities and legal jurisdiction. Once these limits are determined, a plan must be devised and implemented for protecting information in transit, defending the network boundary, and securing the computing environment.

REFERENCES

Critical Infrastructure Assurance Office (CIAO) Publication, "Practices for Securing Critical Information Assets" (January 2000).

Gardner, Dale, "ESM, ASAP!" *Information Security* magazine, ICSA.net (June 2000).

Garfinkel, Simon, and Gene Spafford, *Practical UNIX and Internet Security*, 2nd ed. Cambridge, MA: O'Reilly & Associates, Inc., 1996.

Information Assurance Technical Framework (IATF), Release 2.0.1 (September 1999).

Lane, V. P., *Security of Computer Based Information Systems*. Houndsmills: MacMillan Education Ltd., 1990.

National Security Agency (NSA) Systems and Networks Attack Center (SNAC), "The 60 Minute Network Security Guide (The First Steps Towards a Secure Network Environment)," version 1.0 (October 16, 2001).

System Administration, Networking, and Security (SANS) Institute, *Roadmap to Security Tools and Services*, 5th ed. (Summer 2001).

4. Determining IT Security Priorities

CHAPTER OBJECTIVES

- Identify what requires security protection
- Define the organization's Critical Objects
- Discuss the forms, types, and structures of information
- Address the fundamental issue of assigning value to information
- Identify the basic categories of organizational information that need to be protected by an IA function

IDENTIFYING YOUR SECURITY PROTECTION PRIORITIES

What Are You Protecting?

Until the organization identifies what needs protecting and why, there can be no associated risks assessed to determine if the protection is required nor can cost benefits be assessed to determine how much protection can be afforded.

> Despite the countless number of threats, there are really only five actual business risks you face: theft, fraud, legal liability, damaged corporate image, and lost revenue. Depending upon your organization, individual risks may be more or less important. Theft and fraud, for example, are typically high-probability risks for financial-services organizations. Web retailers, on the other hand, might elect to focus on lost revenue, while health care or insurance firms may position legal liabilities (for unauthorized disclosure of personal information) as the most significant risk (Gardner, 2000, p. 38).

Given that, when asked that most basic security question — "What are you protecting?" — at least three items should come to mind: your organization's reputation, its information, and the organization assets that sustain them. If your IA protection does not include these three items, then you are probably focusing your security efforts in the wrong direction. If your security initiatives concentrate only on protecting information without investing in safeguards for your people, facilities, and systems, your IA program is lacking. Your organization's credibility, information, and support assets all require protection because each is inextricably dependent on the others.

Reputation

Without the credibility and trust that a good reputation and public image brings, protecting information or other corporate assets may be futile. Public perception alone can make or break a business, regardless of the real situation. The job of maintaining a good reputation today cannot ignore safeguarding the information, systems, facilities, and people on which your organization's credibility depends. For example, inadequate safeguards for your publicly accessible Web site can result in hackers defaming your corporate name. Failure to restrict a disgruntled employee's privileged access may facilitate a denial of service attack. Failure to protect your organization's most sensitive information can cause public embarrassment, not to mention loss of competitive edge. Failure to protect the availability of your information assets could prove fatal to your business. Additionally, the cost of security investment to safeguard a good reputation pales when compared to the cost of lost revenues and the public relations to restore goodwill and customer confidence.

Support Assets

It would do no good to protect your organization's reputation or its information without also protecting its required assets: the people, facilities, systems, networks, and processes associated with your organization and its information. Whereas reputation and information are intangible concepts, your resources are tangible assets requiring both tangible and intangible security solutions. Information systems hardware, software, backups, archives, personnel records, audit logs, manuals, hardcopy output, peripherals, and communications fiber/wires and equipment are all examples of tangible assets. The key is applying the security safeguards across all these resources in the appropriate measure and proportions to effectively mitigate risk.

For example, if you spend all your security efforts investing in locks, fences, and guards, but don't secure your network connections, you may be already be a victim of electronic theft without realizing what has happened. If you have the best network security defenses in place but fail to control privileged (e.g., superuser, root, admin) access, you are ignoring your biggest threat: the privileged insider.

Information

Information has a quicksilver quality. It can't really be defined. If I try to grab the meaning, it splits, rolls away and joins up with other bits. People try to define it in order to capture it in words, try to draw distinctions between data and information, or knowledge and wisdom, but it still eludes capture. Information doesn't obey the normal law of physics. Information grows through sharing. It is not exclusive. I give you some information, and I still have it. Or you give me some information, and I don't get it. Then suddenly, after you have given up, I get it! Information can't be quantified. I can count the words in a book or the bytes in a computer file, but I can't count how much information I get out of reading a paragraph or a book or attending a seminar. Information is unlimited. As I study any phenomenon, there is more to learn—more to know. Information is not absolute. It depends on context. It is in the eye of the beholder. Looking across a flat Alaskan landscape, I see nothing. I see emptiness. An Eskimo hunter sees a wealth of information about animals that have crossed it, the thickness of the ice, and as many as seven kinds of snow. By the same token, I can call a computer an information technology; but if I lack the skills to use it, it is just a big rock (Whitney-Smith, 1996, p. 1).

Schweitzer identifies two ways to look at information in the context of IA: the enterprise view and the universe view. The enterprise view sees information as an integral part of the business process that demands the same emphasis on protection as any other business asset such as "employees, facilities, equipment, raw materials, product, and cash" (Schweitzer, 1996, p. 33). This approach helps justify an organization's annual IA budget, but no budget is large enough to adequately provide sufficient IA resources to equally protect all the organization's information.

The universe approach sees all information consisting of a spectrum of varying subcategories of information requiring different levels of protection according to the value, criticality, and sensitivity of the information. This approach provides a means of prioritizing the IA needs within the organization's enterprise. Management can now apply limited IA resources where they are most needed.

We see the enterprise and universe views of information as complementary. The former view identifies the important external relationship of IA to all other business assets. The latter identifies the internal relationship of information to other information. Both views are necessary to justify the need for IA resources and to prioritize the application of those resources. In addition, it is helpful to distinguish whether the information is sensitive or critical.

Sensitive information is data that would result in a "loss to the organization if it is accessed by or disclosed to unauthorized parties, or if it were improperly modified or updated" (Karabin, 1985, p. 1). Some information is so sensitive that unauthorized disclosure of the data could compromise the data's sources or collection methods and/or result in serious damage to the security of the organization. Although availability of this information is important, the emphasis is on data confidentiality and integrity.

Critical information is defined as data that the organization depends on to function normally. Any denial of or disruption to the availability of the information would result in a partial or complete loss of the organization's functionality (Karabin, 1985, p. 1). Although confidentiality and integrity are considerations, the emphasis is on data availability.

Not all information is created equal. The degree of sensitivity or criticality will vary among data. To that degree, the value of the information (and subsequent level of protection required) will be determined.

Critical Objects

Each organization has certain Critical Objects that require protection. These objects may vary, but generally, they fall into four categories or domains:

1. Information
2. The hardware and software that supports processing, storing, and transmitting the information
3. Communications
4. Logistics — the delivery of hardware, software, and information

Each of these domains is subject to attack and therefore represents different risks. Understanding these risks, in light of the value of the objects, will enable management to prioritize the application of limited security resources. Throughout this book, we will address ways to protect these Critical Objects;

however it is difficult to determine how much protection an object requires without knowing or assessing the value of the object.

Counting the Cost

The value of most Critical Objects can be quantified by adding up the various costs: initial procurement, licensing fees, operations and maintenance, technical support, leases, replacement costs, insurance, storage fees, delivery fees, etc. Objects such as hardware, software, communication lines, warehouses, and delivery services all come with price tags that can help determine the value of the object.

When it comes to information, what may be critical information to one organization may be worthless to another. Assessing value can often be more of an art than a science. The remainder of this chapter will be devoted to ways to take the guesswork out of determining the value of information.

Organization Information: Forms, Types, Structures, and Categories

Information exists throughout an organization of any size or mission. Information can have — that is, it can be represented in — a physical or logical form. A physical form would involve a newspaper, the printed output from a printer, CD-ROM disks, magnetic tapes, audio tapes, audio video media, and so forth. Information can be represented in a logical form (i.e., electrical signals or light signals) and stored, processed, and communicated by automated information systems.

Fundamentally, there are five universal types of information. This involves text (or written words), audio (spoken words), music (the sounds of musical instruments and/or spoken words), pictures (static images of objects), and audio–video (moving pictures combined with audio). The combination of two or more of these information types has been defined as multimedia.

From a structural perspective, the types and forms of information can be presented within seven Universal Information Organization Models as follows:

1. The Linear Information Organization Model structures in a sequential manner. Units of information are structured one after the other from beginning to end, like a presentation in a slide show.
2. The Hierarchical Information Organization Model organizes information in layers like a biographical family tree. Directory and file structures created by operating systems fall within this category.
3. A Web Information Organization Model organizes information as its name implies. Units of information are interconnected in a pattern. There are multiple interconnections and interactivity between the units of information throughout the Web. An interactive video game is an example of the Web Information Organization Model.
4. The Parallel Information Organization Model provides a means of displaying units of information in parallel in the manner of a closed-caption television session.

5. Units of information can be subdivided and organized in a matrix structure looking very much like a bingo card using the Matrix Information Organization Model.
6. The Overlay Information Organization Model provides a means of overlaying units of information, one on top of the another, like an X-ray or layered graphic.
7. The last model is the Spatial Zoom Information Organization Model. This model permits a discrete unit of information within a total displayed array to be magnified and effectively "zoomed" or displayed separately from the total display.

Automated computing, in contrast to print or broadcast media, can effectively provide information in each of the seven Universal Information Organization Models.

Chapter 1 ("IA and the Organization: The Challenges") provided a fundamental generic model for characterizing an organizational entity of any size or location, whether it operates within the private or public sector. All organizations are intended to meet needs within their defined geopolitical spaces. Organizational success is dependent on fulfilling these needs and not just on providing products or services. Inherent in any organization that emerges to fulfill needs are three fundamental tendencies or basic drives: to perpetuate its own existence (survival), to integrate the functions of its parts (coexistence), and to grow and develop (growth). The three tendencies manifest themselves as three interrelated, interconnected, and interdependent organizational components or "subsystems." These are the technical (i.e., production of goods and services), political, and cultural components of any organization. Organizational information can be categorized within the context of these organizational components.

Organizational Technical (Productive) Information Category

The organizational technical (productive) component's information is time-based because it involves information related to the current and intended future operations of the organization. Specifically, the information pertains to the purpose, activities, strategy, and expertise of the organization. The purpose of the organization could be reflected in legal documents such as the organization's charter, the minutes of the meetings of management bodies (i.e., the board of directors, board of trustees, committees, working groups, etc.), and in the electronic correspondence of organizational managers. Essentially, this information officially defines the direction in which the organization is moving, because it describes the needs that the organization wants to fulfill, how it plans to fulfill those needs, and the geopolitical spaces within which it wants to operate. Information about the organization's strategy includes such things as its goals, objectives, policies, rules, processes, mechanisms, procedures, and laws through which people perform the activities necessary to fulfill the purpose.

Information about organizational activities/tasks is broad and is related to people expending time, energy, and resources to achieve the organization's purpose. Generally, such information falls into four categories. The first is a functional or operational category. This includes information involving such functions as human resources, marketing, production, research and development, finance, logistics, and accounting. The second category involves information related to assessing the current internal position of the organization relative to the accomplishment of its defined purpose. This represents control information since it involves information necessary to monitor or control the functional or operational aspects of an organization. Such information includes cash flow and liquidity projections, inventory levels, productivity results, and resource-allocation information to manage the distribution of capital and people.

The third category of information related to organizational activities/tasks involves information about the geopolitical spaces within which the organization operates. This includes "business intelligence" as well as information about technology in one's own industry and others; about worldwide finance; about the changing local, national, and world economy; and customer surveys. Even the most uncertain organizational environments will contain strategically relevant information to help identify clear trends, such as market demographics, that can help define potential demand for future products or services. Organizations continuously try to collect information about the changing likes and dislikes of existing and potential customers and unique information about each customer. Information about past performance and customer tastes is analyzed and projections made of current trends. An organization needs to accumulate and analyze this information to understand its customers and to be able to reasonably predict and adapt to their changing needs. This is intended to produce reasonably predictable, favorable financial and operational results.

The fourth and last type of organizational technical component information concerns the competency or expertise of the people who work with the organization. Individuals are the ones who possess the knowledge and skills necessary to perform the activities in accordance with the strategy to fulfill the purpose. This information could be reflected in the form of performance evaluations, employees' training records, and employees' work histories.

Organizational Political Information Category

The organization's political component essentially empowers the organization's leaders to create a vision of what the technical component "is" and what it "could or ought to be." It is a mental image of what the technical component's purpose that has been fulfilled looks like — in behavioral and tangible terms. Information related to this vision could include an organizational vision statement, a strategic planning document, or the minutes of high level organizational bodies such as the Board of Directors or the Board of Trustees.

The needs and desires of individuals that perform the activities within an organization need to be clearly understood and captured. These needs and desires essentially determine the individual's own reasons and motivations for performing the activities to the maximum level possible. Such reasons and motivations constitute self-interest. Self-interest involves not only what people perceive they may gain but also may lose. Job satisfaction, work performance, employee conflicts, and the realization of the organization's vision are at risk. Generally, electronic employee surveys, minutes of group discussions, and records of supervisor to employee meetings provide information about the answers to three basic questions:

1. What do employees expect from the organization and think the organization expects from them?
2. Are employees getting what they expect, and do they think that the organization is getting what it expects from them?
3. What do employees think needs to change for them to get what they want?

Of course, the organization's expectations and needs should be compared to the input from employees. This information could be of great value to an organization. If people believe that the organization does not value them, recognize their achievements, or sufficiently reward their efforts, then the productivity and innovation of current and future operations could be at risk.

Also, within every organization of any size or type there exists a political network of people. In fact, organizations could be viewed as social networks — that is, a social system composed of social objects (people and groups) that are joined by a variety of relationships. It is this network of people who must share the organization's vision and whose actions are critical to the realization of that vision. This vision needs to be communicated as quickly and as consistently as possible to the people within this political network. The organization's IA baseline is a powerful tool for communicating and clarifying this vision through the use of bulletin boards, electronic mail, electronic newsletters and newspapers, notifications and minutes of briefings, shared directories, video teleconferencing (VTC), and the establishment of domains, communities of interest, and trusted relationships within the organization.

People need to be provided with the political entitlements required to proceed with the accomplishment of an organization's vision. These entitlements include such things as the authority, responsibility, and accountability to perform the activities needed to accomplish the vision. This information can be logically represented within the IA baseline as policy statements, job descriptions, letters of appointment, work plans, and organization charts. Also, IT can be a tool used within an organization for granting privileges to own and share information, applications, and network services.

Organizational Cultural Information Category

The third and last category of organizational information is that related to the cultural component of an organization. Organizations are in part held together by normative glue that is called culture. Culture consists of the values, objectives, assumptions (beliefs), and interpretations shared by organizational members. Each organization must decide the content of its culture, that is, determine what values should be shared, what objectives are worth striving for, what assumptions (beliefs) the employees should be committed to, and what interpretations of past events and current pronouncements would be the most beneficial for the organization. Once these decisions are made, the organization needs to communicate these values within the organization. Decisions about culture are often made implicitly, intuitively, and by trial and error. Also, especially within large organizations, there could be a number of subcultures with different sets of assumptions (beliefs) and values. For example, there could be one subculture that adheres to a more risk-taking approach, such as in research and development, and a more conservative one in the financial management part of the organization.

The organizational information of cultural significance involves the message or content of the intended core values of the organization. Sometimes these core values concern technical (productive) issues, such as the shifting emphasis on productivity and quality in order to survive competitively, or another organization's stress on having a long-term financial perspective. Often these core values are reflected in slogans that become important for organizational members, such as General Electric's "Progress is our most important product." An imbalance between the assumptions (beliefs) of organizational members and the message or content of a corporate culture could lead to conflict within the organization. From a cultural perspective, an organization only really has legitimacy when the environmental need and the technical (productive) output are congruent. Otherwise, issues arise among organizational members as to whether they are meeting the needs of their customers.

An organization can communicate the content or message of its intended culture through the use of artifacts such as special jargon, stories, symbols, rituals, and the creation of role models. This represents organizational information that can be created, processed, used, stored, and communicated by the IA baseline throughout the organization. Also, the IA baseline could inform employees about customer satisfaction and recognize those who exceptionally met that satisfaction. This would reinforce the legitimacy of the organization's purpose, vision, and technical (productive) output in the minds of employees.

Determining the Value of Information

Not all information is equally critical to the operational well-being of an organization. The organization must understand the value of its information in order to determine which is most critical and deserves the most protection. Without some kind of value system, management will have no basis for decisions regarding the prioritization and application of IA resources. For example, should an organization spend funds to develop contingency procedures to ensure the availability of certain information?

The real question is not the value of a given piece of information, but how we arrive at that value. How do we measure the value of information? In some cases the value may be easy to determine because it is easily quantifiable. Measuring the impact that a denial-of-service attack would have on software and databases used in a production line may be fairly easy. Calculating the loss of revenue, cost of system downtime, loss of productivity, etc., would be very possible.

In other situations, quantifying the value of information may not be possible or practical. What would be the impact of a denial-of-service attack on a critical government intelligence database used during air and ground operations during contingency operations? In this case, the value of the information would need to be expressed in terms of political or ethical impact, rather than monetary terms. A qualitative valuation would be called for, rather than a quantitative calculation.

In Chapter 2 ("Basic Security Concepts, Principles, and Strategy"), we discussed the practice of assigning a classification or handling instruction to information based on its sensitivity. In cases where this information is compromised, stolen, damaged, lost, or destroyed, the owners of the information must conduct an assessment to determine the severity of the damage. In the most serious cases, compromise of the information may lead to compromise of the sources and methods used to gain the information.

Other questions to consider when placing a monetary value on information are:

- How exclusive is the information? Are there alternative sources for this information?
- How useful is the information? Is it sufficient to achieve the goal? Will the information be available long enough to complete the project?
- What is the cost of reproducing or recreating the information?
- What are the legal liabilities if the information is lost, untimely, inaccurate?
- What does the information represent? How convertible or negotiable is it?
- What would be the operational impact if the information was unavailable, inaccurate, or compromised?

Selecting the appropriate technique(s) for information valuation depends on whether that value will be qualitative or quantitative. On the qualitative end of the spectrum are policies and regulations that dictate what the value of the information will be. On the opposite end are the techniques of accounting and statistics that look at real numbers or scientific samplings to determine the quantitative value. More in the middle of the spectrum are the less accurate methods of using checklists, questionnaires, the consensus of a small group of experts, or a combination of any of these to arrive at an estimated value for a particular body of information.

Any discussion of information and IA leads one to a topic that provides the point of intersection between the two—that is, the matter of the value of information and some means to determine this value. After all, if an organization's information were of no value, there would be little if any need to expend money to protect it. Also, one could argue that the protection of an organization's information with an effective IA function inherently preserves its value. Broad ranges of ideas have been expressed regarding how one defines the value of information.

The issue of "value" needs to be addressed. What determines whether any physical or logical object has any value?

In a pure economic sense, value results when a quantity of one thing will be given in exchange for another. Therefore, if two bushels of corn will exchange for one bushel of wheat, the value of corn in terms of wheat is one-half, whereas the value of wheat in terms of corn is two. The value of goods and services is basically expressed in terms of the standard medium of exchange, that is, the amounts of money for which they can be exchanged at any given time (i.e., the price). One may say that the exchange of goods and services results in an extrinsic value applied to goods and services. Also, from an economic perspective, there is the matter of "gross" value or worth versus "net" value or worth. The basic equation to derive this net value or worth involves the subtraction of the costs of producing the object from its market price. The market price represents the benefit to the organization by making the object available to the market. In other words, the price is what the organization receives from the market.

Some objects have what could be called intrinsic value. This involves a property or capacity that is assumed to be inherent in the object itself. It is often said that because bread has the capacity to satisfy hunger, it has an inherent or intrinsic value. However, from an economic perspective, if more bread were supplied than was demanded, the excess would have little or no value. The value of bread would depend upon its relation to unsatisfied wants rather than upon any inherent quality.

Another and more subjective aspect of determining value is the matter of what an object means to an individual or group of individuals — that is, the relevancy of the object. An old photograph of a beloved family member means a great deal to you and has value that can only be measured based on your emotional feelings, not the economic value of the photograph itself. If someone else sees the photograph and asks whose image appears in it, you essentially have to interpret the photograph's meaning by telling the other person who is in it and your relationship to that person (i.e., your mother, father, brother, best friend, etc.).

The value of an object is relational to time in both a positive and negative direction. An object can gain value over time or it can lose value, depending on a variety of circumstances. A stock share of a private sector organization is an example of how value can vary over the course of time.

We can measure the value of an object by its replacement, upgrading, maintenance, or damage repair costs. For example, the initial cost to purchase a machine may have been $100, but at current labor and material rates the current price may be $175 to replace it. Also, the repair, maintenance, and upgrading costs incurred over time not only preserved the "book value" of $100 but actually increased its value. One could argue that upgrades have transformed the object to the current "state-of-the-art" level and that its performance capacity has been historically dependable, and, therefore, predictable.

The value of an object can be representational. A Treasury bond or stock certificate represents some defined value and is legally relevant. One is guaranteed under law to receive this value (i.e., cash) when the Treasury bond or stock certificate is redeemed.

The current value of an object could be influenced by its ability to generate future value. A machine may cost a specified sum but be capable of manufacturing a product that generates more wealth for the owner of the business. The more machines the business purchases and operates, the more wealth will be generated over time. However, if the machines are not used, then the organization incurs an opportunity cost equal to the net profits (i.e., wealth) that could have been generated during the time the machines were not in use. This assumes favorable product demand conditions.

Value can be defined by an entity that has been granted the political authority to do so. That is, the executive, legislative, and judicial branches of a nation's local, state, and national political systems may determine what should be of value to its citizens. This would take the form of laws, executive directives, and judicial decisions. For example, each citizen should value the rights of other citizens. The rights of freedom of speech and to privacy are valued strongly in the United States.

Availability of objects could influence their value. An undersupply relative to high demand is one example that could increase the value of an object. Another would be object oversupply relative to a low demand that could decrease the value.

Finally, but certainly not least, is the issue of trust or credibility relative to value. In certain circumstances, one cannot have any value without some degree of trust. Trust is a concept that permeates every aspect of our lives. Would a specific Vincent van Gogh painting be valued at millions of dollars unless there was some degree of trust that this painting was original?

We are now at a point where we can address the matter of determining which information within an organization has value. This will help us better understand which information the IA function must protect and how we can develop a means of measuring the effectiveness of this protection (i.e., the IA Posture).

Information is an organizational asset. The value of information as an asset is strongly influenced by a few of the factors previously discussed. First, there is the matter of the availability of information and its relation to the issue of confidentiality. The value of information is dependent on the extent to which it is available to the appropriate individuals within an organization who can use it to generate benefits (financial or nonfinancial) for the organization. An organizational requirement or opportunity may call for greater sharing (i.e., availability) of information rather than limiting its dissemination in order to maximize benefits to the organization. An organization incurs an "opportunity cost" when people are not permitted to access information that influences the survival, coexistence, and growth of the organization. This cost can also be incurred if another organization obtains information that it uses to derive a benefit for itself. Therefore, the extent of the confidentiality of information influences the value of information.

Second, the value of the organization's information is affected by its meaning or relevance to the number of people within the organization who need to fully understand that meaning and perhaps act as a result of their understanding. This is where the matter of interpretation and clarity play such a part in determining and preserving the value of information. Essentially, information is relevant when it matters whether an organization has it or not.

Third, the credibility of information depends on its accuracy (i.e., integrity). A medical record, for example, has value only as long as the information is considered accurate. Such information would have no value to a surgeon — and potentially life-threatening implications for the patient — if the record's integrity were in doubt.

Fourth is the issue of the worth of the information relative to its cost. In other words, there needs to be some understanding of the additional benefits to be gained from the availability of the information compared with the costs of collecting, inputting, storing, processing, communicating, and outputting it.

Fifth, encapsulating these four factors is the matter of trust. There needs to be trust or a level of confidence in the following:

- The IA baseline that collects, inputs, processes, communicates, stores, and outputs information to ensure its availability and confidentiality
- The people, devices, and processes involved with the sharing of an organization's information
- The relevance or meaning of the information
- The credibility or integrity of the information
- The current and future worth of the information

The maximization of trust minimizes the risks to the organization — that is, the uncertainties as to its survival, coexistence, and growth.

There are two dimensions to understanding the worth of information within an organization: uncertainty and time. Organizations attempt to either reduce or manage uncertainty. There are three types of organizational uncertainty, which require management: technical, political, and cultural. Examples include uncertainty about markets, production capability, or future funding that will be legislated; uncertainty about candidates for success, power distributions, and the politics of reward allocations; and uncertainty about the appropriate value system for the organization, or the existence of conflicting value systems. An organization needs a capacity to produce information to reduce the uncertainty that it faces. Therefore, the worth of information can be linked to how much it can reduce the uncertainties that an organization considers significant to its survival, coexistence, and growth. Also, as previous discussions about the concept of value indicated, time is relative to value. Information may be considered valuable at present but worthless in the future because it would provide no means of reducing future uncertainty or it cannot generate future benefits to the organization. On the other hand, current or even past information may have an influence in generating future benefits.

MEASURING THE ACCOMPLISHMENT OF ORGANIZATIONAL IA NEEDS

IA is a major capability of any organization, like accounting, production, logistics, marketing, and so forth and plays a significant role in both its predictive and productive capabilities. The organizational IA function establishes an IA direction through the use of an organizational IA policy, acquires and maintains assets to create IA capabilities, builds and maintains the IA capabilities (prevention, detection, reaction, correction, and change), and employs IA assets to protect organizational technical (productive), political, and cultural information. These four components of the IA function strongly interrelate and affect the financial and operational performance of any organization.

Therefore, an organization requires a means of measuring its IA posture. In essence, IA management is responsible for aligning the IA function to achieve a posture at the level of risk acceptable to organizational management to achieve its IA needs. Traditionally, the effectiveness of IA has been measured by the use of risk assessment formulas. The concept of risk management will be discussed next, and then a more refined approach will be presented by which an organization can measure its IA posture.

SUMMARY

Every organization must determine what Critical Objects require protection. Critical information must be valued in order to determine the appropriate amount of protection to afford it. Additionally, it is important to note the context in which this information's value is determined — the technical, political, and cultural environments that shape the organization.

The concept of risk management will be discussed in Chapter 5 ("The Organization's IA Posture"). That chapter will provide a more refined approach for organizations to use as a means of measuring their IA posture.

An organization's credibility and survival can depend on how well it protects its information. Effective protection of information requires a comprehensive IA program to encompass the resources that access, process, store, and transmit this information in all its forms and attributes. Distinguishing what information is critical to operations from what is disposable will allow you to apply safeguards judiciously.

REFERENCES

Cook, V. G., Jr., and Fred Smith, *Influencing and Managing Change.* Monterey, CA: U.S. Naval Postgraduate School, 1986.

Gardner, Dale, "ESM, ASAP!" *Information Security,* ICSA.net. June 2000.

Information Systems Security Association (ISSA) G-11.01-93, *Information Systems Security Association's Guideline for Information Valuation,* April 21, 1993.

Karabin, Stephen. "Data Classification for Security and Control." *EDPACS: The EDP [Electronic Data Processing] Audit, Control and Security Newsletter* (December 1985; Volume XIII, No. 6).

Power, Richard, "CSI Special Report: How to Quantify Financial Losses from INFOSEC Breaches?" Computer Security Institute, *Alert* newsletter (October 1999; No. 199).

Schweitzer, James A., *Protecting Business Information: A Manager's Guide.* Boston: Butterworth–Heinemann, 1996.

Whitney-Smith, Elin. "War, Information and History: Changing Paradigms." Chapter 3 of Part 1: *Cyberwar: Security, Strategy and Conflict in the Information Age* (Campden et al., Eds.). Fairfax, VA: AFCEA International Press, 1996.

5. The Organization's IA Posture

CHAPTER OBJECTIVES

- Overall: to provide an understanding of the concept of an organization's IA posture and a practical means to measure and determine it for an organization of any size or purpose
- To provide an introduction that describes both the need for a process for determining an organization's IA posture and an overall description of the process
- To provide a description of each of the 10 steps of the process to show how the process can be practically and successfully used to reach a conclusion as to the organization's IA posture

INTRODUCTION

IA starts at the highest level in any public or private organization because it is at this level where the responsibility, authority, and accountability are placed to deliver predictable and favorable results for the organization as a whole. In the private sector, this responsibility lies with the owners of a private organization. For some private organizations, the owners may be directly involved with the organization's management and operation. In other private organizations, the owners may assign the responsibility, authority, and accountability to a Board of Directors or Trustees and a Chief Executive Officer (CEO) who represent them.

In the public sector, the responsibility, authority, and accountability begin at the CEO level of an executive, legislative, and judicial organization within a certain geopolitical space (i.e., cities, counties, states, nations). The CEO could be the president of a nation, governor of a state, mayor of a city, Chief Justice of the Supreme Court, Speaker of the House, and so forth.

The performance of the CEO of any private or public organization is measured based on his or her ability to deliver predictable financial and/or operational results with a reasonable assurance. The reasonable assurance and predictable aspects of such results play a significant part even in the case of financial and operational results that greatly exceed such estimated levels. There are the inseparable issues of risk and control. The CEO is ultimately responsible and evaluated for controlling organizational assets (people, material, information, facilities) to accomplish financial and operational results.

This responsibility involves having knowledge of the capabilities of these assets and directing their use toward the targeted performance to generate predictable performance. Any unreasonable divergence between the defined capabilities of those assets and the organizational performance may indicate that organizational capabilities were not sufficiently known and managed (i.e., controlled). The CEO's performance and reputation as an executive would be at stake.

Essentially, it is an issue of demand and supply. From an overall organizational perspective, risk management involves two basic things: first, minimizing the uncertainties associated with the demand for organizational products and services; second, sufficiently aligning and controlling the organization's technical (productive), political, and cultural components to produce the output to the maximum extent possible to meet the predicted demand.

IA is a major capability of an organization of any size or sector, in much the same way as accounting, manufacturing, supply, marketing, and so forth. The organizational IA function establishes an IA direction through the use of an organizational IA policy, acquires and maintains assets to create IA capabilities, builds and maintains the IA capabilities (prevention, detection, reaction, correction, and change), and allocates and employs IA capabilities to protect organizational technical (productive), political, and cultural information that is classified at various levels depending on its criticality and sensitivity (i.e., value). These four components of the IA function strongly interrelate and affect the financial and operational performance of any organization.

The effectiveness of the IA function is strongly related to the extent to which there is open and clear interpersonal communications between IA functional executives and the organization's executives. Also, there must be a clear understanding and appreciation of the differences between organizational executives and IA executives. Both types of executives require different skills and attitudes. Organizational executives have not only an entirely different set of perspectives, ambitions, and methods of communications but also an entirely different way of solving problems. In the IT and IA functions, there is a discipline that is founded upon the way machines work. This is infinitely more precise than the way organizational executives function, or for that matter, any human being. Generally, organizational executives seem willing to accept and tolerate levels of insecurity that IT and IA executives would find unacceptable. They are willing to do so because being secure is perceived as not being an absolute precedent to being profitable. Organizational executives must be bold and decisive by nature and IA managers must be cautious and imaginative by nature. Imagination plays a part since there is a need to continuously anticipate new ways in which organizational controls could be overcome either accidentally or maliciously. Organizational executives could be willing to accept x amount of insecurity because an organization can achieve y amount of profit, which they wouldn't have received if they waited to realize what the IA function would consider to be an acceptable level of risk. A good analogy involves a private sector retail organization and how it manages its inventory. Generally, each store has an annual inventory of its products. The organization's executives would be willing to accept, for example, a 10% "write-off" of the inventory due to inventory record inaccuracies, thefts of products from outside the organizations, thefts of products by employees, and so forth. Each store would be held accountable for any losses above this baseline of inventory write-off.

Clearly, there is a need for a common process to bridge the IA function with the overall operations of the organization. Such a process should represent a "point of intersection" between IA and organizational executives to permit common understanding, communications, and decision making. This "point of intersection" is the concept of uncertainty. IA managers and organizational managers must try to successfully define, control, and predict uncertainty. The extent of this uncertainty determines the degree of risks that an organization faces relative to its survival, coexistence, and growth.

The concept of uncertainty should not be viewed in a binary way — that is, to assume that the world is either certain, and therefore open to precise predictions about the future, or uncertain, and therefore completely unpredictable. Underestimating uncertainty can lead to decisions that neither defend against the threats that organizations face nor take advantage of the opportunities that higher levels of uncertainty may provide. Therefore, the ability to make systematically sound IA and organizational decisions under uncertainty requires an approach that avoids the binary view.

Executives rarely know absolutely nothing of strategic importance even in the most uncertain environments. It is more realistic to think of a continuum or scale that could be used to measure the extent of the uncertainty that an organization faces at any specific point in time. This continuum or scale of uncertainty is relevant to all organizational functions, including the IA function, and to the organization as a whole. An organization is technically (productively) effective to the extent that the uncertainty (i.e., risks) it faces matches its capacity to process information and to eliminate or reduce the uncertainty to the maximum extent possible. The uncertainty that remains at specific points in time can be defined as "residual uncertainty" or "residual risk." The greater the degree of this residual uncertainty, the greater the risks that confront an organization (Tichy, 1983).

Therefore, fundamentally there is a direct relationship between "security" and "certainty." Absolute certainty represents a state of absolute security. However, in the defense of an organization's information and IT resources there can rarely, if ever, be such a risk-free state. Realistically, security involves reaching an acceptable and reasonable relative state between risk (i.e., some degree of uncertainty) and certainty. Therefore, there needs to be a well-defined and effective methodology that provides a good alignment within an organization between its capacity to process the information necessary to reduce the uncertainties that confront it and the information necessary to reduce such uncertainties to an acceptable level. The organization's overriding goal is to achieve this level of acceptability as a result of the processing of the information.

The next section will describe a model of the methodology for determining an organization's IA posture. An IA posture represents the current state of an organization's security (i.e., certainty) relative to the confidentiality, integrity, and availability of the information that its IA baseline automatically stores, processes, and communicates. This posture provides the organization with a basic measure to understand the extent of its IA uncertainties (i.e., its risks) and its IA certainties relative to the achievement of its IA needs as defined in Chapters 3 and 4.

As previously stated, this process represents a model. A "model" is generally constructed to facilitate understanding and to enhance prediction by providing a simple representation of more complex forms, processes, and functions of physical phenomena or ideas. There are two fundamental features that characterize all models: form and content. It is possible to describe different contents by the same form of a model, and one content can be fitted into different model forms. The choice of form, which signifies here a form of representing the content, establishes the ease of manipulating the content and detecting errors of omission and commission. The choice of form, therefore, establishes the facility to refine and improve the model to better serve its purpose. There are three fundamental forms of models. These are verbal, mathematical, and analog. The model presented below is a verbal model. That is, it represents the process in words. Also, the model presented below must continuously be subject to validation to ensure its reliability and utility to the organization. This validation should involve a process of testing the results of the model as real events affect the organization. There may be a need to modify the model to improve its predictive capability and, therefore, its usefulness to the organization.

THE PROCESS FOR DETERMINING ORGANIZATIONAL IA POSTURE

Every organization requires five fundamental items to determine its IA posture. First, an organization requires sufficient knowledge that identifies the universe of potential threats associated with its IA baseline and its operating environments. Appendix A ("Listing of IA Threats") provides a description of basic threats. Second, an organization requires sufficient knowledge about the extent of actual threats that are currently confronting it. Appendix B ("Listing of Threat Statuses") provides a means of representing the status of threats that currently confront an organization. Third, an organization requires sufficient knowledge concerning the universe of potential vulnerabilities that could confront it based on its IA baseline and its operating environments. For example, the use of the various operating systems such as Windows NT, Windows 2000, or UNIX would involve unique vulnerabilities that require an identification and understanding. Fourth, an organization requires sufficient knowledge concerning vulnerabilities that currently exist within its IA baseline due to the lack of sufficient mitigating countermeasures and an estimate as to the exploitability of these vulnerabilities. Fifth, an organization requires sufficient knowledge about the nature and operational readiness of its IA capabilities. The IA capabilities of an organization must be at a distinct level of readiness in order to counter the threats and vulnerabilities that are confronting it.

Figure 5-1 depicts the 10 steps that represent a generic process for determining an organization's IA posture. The following sections provide a more detailed description of each of the 10 steps.

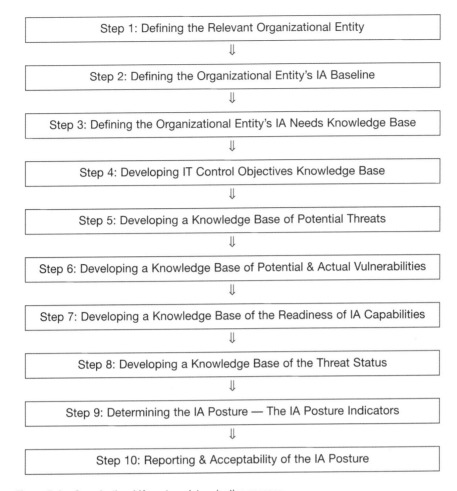

Figure 5-1 Organizational IA posture determination process.

Step 1: Defining the Relevant Organizational Entity

The process for determining IA posture starts with a clear understanding as to the scope of the organizational entity that will undergo the process. This scope could extend from the entire organization within its geopolitical environmental bounds to a variety of subsets of its components. These subsets could consist of branch offices, factories or inventory warehouses, operating divisions, regional offices, and so forth. For example, a major corporation may choose to use the process to determine the IA posture for the overall organization or to determine the IA posture for one or more of its operating divisions.

Step 2: Defining the Organizational Entity's IA Baseline

Once the organizational entity is determined, the IA baseline applicable to that entity needs to be defined. Chapter 3 discussed the concept of an IA baseline. From an IA baseline perspective, the IA posture could be determined for the entire IA baseline within the organization or a variety of subsets of this IA baseline.

These subsets could consist of the networks and supporting infrastructure, enclave boundaries, and computing environment. For example, it is possible to determine the IA posture of a stand-alone workstation, a database management system, a specific application, a local-area network (LAN) within an office or building, an organizational wide-area network (WAN), or the entire IA baseline within an enclave such as a manufacturing plant or warehouse.

Step 3: Defining the Organizational Entity's IA Needs Knowledge Base

The process for defining an organizational entity's IA needs was described in Chapter 4. The IA needs are the result of the evaluation of the relative importance of the organization's information to its survival, coexistence, and growth. There should be a clear understanding of the various forms, types, structures, and categories of organizational information that emerge from the definition of IA needs. Also, the process describes a means for identifying an organization's Critical Objects and determining the value that should be assigned to these objects.

Step 4: Developing IT Control Objectives Knowledge Base

This step requires an evaluation of the IA needs and the development of a set of IT control objectives. The development of the IT control objectives provides a means for an organizational entity to better focus its efforts on accomplishing its IA needs. In essence, IT control objectives are a finer level of granularity below IA needs and are obtained by stating how the IA needs will be accomplished. Also, IT control objectives provide a means of assisting in the determination of the organizational entity's IA posture (Step 9) since the knowledge of their accomplishment impacts the IA posture.

The *Control Objectives for Information and Related Technology* (COBIT) offers a means for an organization to have a predefined set of IT control objectives. COBIT was first published in 1996 by the Information Systems Audit and Control Foundation (ISACF). The initial impetus of the COBIT project was to update ISACF's 1992 *Control Objectives*. However, the scope of this project was soon expanded to provide a framework for control of information (and related) technology that would be authoritative, international and, most importantly, management oriented.

The resulting document's authority and international scope were achieved by aligning COBIT with 41 international standards, regulations, and practices for control of IT. This makes it an authoritative international set of generally accepted control objectives that is applicable to all platforms, and all sizes and types of organizations around the world.

The purpose of COBIT is to provide management and business process owners with an IT governance model that helps in understanding and managing risks associated with IT. COBIT helps bridge the gap between business risks, control needs, and technical issues. It is a control model to meet the needs of IT governance and ensure the integrity of information and information systems.

COBIT consists of the components described in the following sections.

Executive Summary

The executive summary consists of an *executive overview,* which provides a thorough awareness and understanding of COBIT's key concepts and principles. Also included is a synopsis of the *framework,* which provides a more detailed understanding of these concepts and principles, while identifying COBIT's four domains (Planning & Organization, Acquisition & Implementation, Delivery & Support, Monitoring) and 34 IT processes.

Framework Component

A successful organization is built on a solid framework of data and information. The framework component explains how IT processes deliver the information that the organization needs to achieve its objectives. This delivery is controlled through 34 high-level *control objectives,* one for each IT process, contained in the four domains. The framework identifies which of the seven information criteria (effectiveness, efficiency, confidentiality, integrity, availability, compliance, and reliability), as well as which IT resources (people, applications, technology, facilities, data), are important for the IT processes to fully support the business objective.

Control Objectives Component

COBIT's control objectives provide the critical insight necessary to delineate a clear policy and good practices for IT controls. Included are the statements of desired results or purposes to be achieved by implementing the 318 specific, detailed IT control objectives throughout the 34 IT processes.

Audit Guidelines Component

Organizations must constantly and consistently audit their procedures to achieve desired goals and objectives. The *audit guidelines* component outlines and suggests actual activities corresponding to each of the 34 high-level IT control objectives, while substantiating the risk of control objectives not being met. The guidelines function as a tool for providing management assurance and/or advice for improvement. As such, the audit guidelines serve as one tool for assessing compliance with the organization's IA policies as described in Chapter 14 ("Layer 9: IA Policy Compliance Oversight").

Management Guidelines Component

The union between organizational business processes and information systems must be effectively managed to ensure a successful organization. The *management guidelines* component is composed of *maturity models* to help determine the stages and expectation levels of control and compare them against industry norms; *critical success factors,* to identify the most important actions for achieving control over the IT processes; *key goal indicators,* to define target levels of performance; and *key performance indicators,* to measure whether an IT control process is meeting its objective. These management guidelines will help answer the question of immediate concern to all those who have a stake in organizational success.

Implementation Tool Set Component

An *implementation tool set* contains *management awareness* and *IT control diagnostics,* an *implementation guide,* frequently asked questions (FAQs), case studies from organizations currently using COBIT, and slide presentations that can be used to introduce COBIT into organizations. The tool set is designed to facilitate the implementation of COBIT, relate lessons learned from organizations that quickly and successfully applied COBIT in their work environments, and lead management to ask about each COBIT process: Is this domain important for our business objectives? Is it well performed? Who does it and who is accountable? Are the process and control formalized?

CD-ROM

The CD-ROM contains all of COBIT and is published as a Folio infobase (ISACF Web site: http://www.isaca.org/cobit.htm).

Step 5: Developing a Knowledge Base of Potential Threats

The organization will need to develop and continuously update a knowledge base of potential threats against its IA baseline that could prevent the organization from meeting its IA needs and IT control objectives. (Appendix A provides a description of basic threats.) A threat is an event or circumstance that has the potential to cause the loss of the confidentiality, integrity, and availability of organizational information. The universe of potential threats that an organization could face is quite large and it is not the intent of this book to provide a listing of all conceivable threats. However, this book will provide a means to understand the nature of threats and how to categorize them. Threat intents, sources, active versus passive, impacts, and mechanisms will be discussed. These subjects provide a means of developing a generic model to assist organizations in their determination of the threats that are posed to their survival, coexistence, and growth.

Traditionally, it has been considered necessary to provide the frequency of occurrence or estimated likelihood of the occurrence of threats. However, this has been a rather difficult undertaking since so many technical, human, and natural variables are involved in trying to provide such estimates. The emphasis has been centered around the probability of threats. If the probability of the threat is estimated to be high and if that threat can exploit a weakness in the IA baseline, then a vulnerability would exist. A risk could exist based on the extent of the control mechanisms that would be in place to mitigate the vulnerability. The portion of risk that remains after the application of control mechanisms has been termed the "residual risk."

However, it is no longer practical and realistic to think in terms of the probabilities of threats. There needs to be a shift toward a new approach, one that is centered more on vulnerability rather than on threats. The issue is no longer *if* a threat will occur. Rather, the real issue is *when* threats will occur, the extent of the organization's tolerance to such threats and their implications, and whether the organization is capable of preventing, detecting, and correcting such threats to accomplish its IA needs and IT control objectives.

Threat Intents

There are three basic types of threats depending on the extent of the intention to generate the threat. First, there could be a malicious intent to generate the threat. Second, a threat may result from accidental circumstances with no malicious intent. Third, a threat could result from a natural circumstance such as a flood or earthquake.

Sources of Threats

Threats can be initiated by natural events, by privileged and unprivileged authorized insiders, and by outsiders. An "authorized insider" is a person who is legally employed by the organization and could be approved to perform tasks within its geopolitical, physical, and logical boundaries. An insider could be authorized to perform privileged or unprivileged functions. Systems Administrator and Information Systems Security Managers (ISSM) are examples of authorized insiders who can perform tasks that need to be limited to a specified number of people.

An "outsider" can be divided into two categories. An "authorized outsider" is a person or organizational entity that is not legally employed by the organization but is bound to the organization as a result of contractual or operational circumstances. There may be requirements for such individuals to work within the geopolitical, physical, and logical boundaries of the organization. For example, such individuals may be authorized to perform tasks (e.g., cleaning, maintenance, inspection) within an organizational entity's office or buildings but not be granted an account to permit them to logically access organizational information available by the IA baseline. On the other hand, an authorized outsider may require access to IT resources to support the operations of the organization such as the performance of installation and maintenance of hardware and software resources. Consumers of the organization's products and services who interact with the organization by using its network can also be considered as authorized outsiders since there is an operational bind between organization (supply) and its customers (demand). An "unauthorized outsider" is a person or organizational entity that is not bound to the organization by employment, law, or operation. They should remain outside the physical and logical bounds of the organization, and it is the responsibility of the IA function working in unison with other security functions within the organization to keep them beyond these bounds.

Active versus Passive

A threat could be of an active or passive nature. That is, an "active" threat would result in the injection or modification of data while a "passive" threat does not inject or modify data but results in the release of data.

Impacts

Basically, a threat could negatively impact the confidentiality, integrity, and availability of organization information and IT resources. Confidentiality involves the securing of information from unintended disclosure. Assurance is provided that information is not disclosed to unauthorized persons, processes, or devices. Integrity means that information is secured against unauthorized modification or destruction and is, therefore, maintained in an unimpaired condition.

Availability involves the timely, reliable access to organizational information and information services (login, file transfer, e-mail, remote login, etc.) when needed despite problems such as outages, environmental disruptions, and malicious attacks.

Mechanisms

Mechanisms provide the means by which threats become a reality. There are five basic categories of threat mechanisms. The threat mechanism could be physical (e.g., fire, flood, personal destruction), software (e.g., trapdoors, Trojan horses, viruses, and other malicious software), communications (e.g., passive monitoring), operational (e.g., spoofing or deception through human interaction), or personal (e.g., illness, unauthorized absence). Appendix A provides a listing of a broad baseline of fundamental threats that can be modified over time.

Step 6: Developing a Knowledge Base of Potential and Actual Vulnerabilities

The organization needs to develop and continuously update a knowledge base of potential and currently existing vulnerabilities that are applicable to its IA baseline. That is, the organization must have a current and accurate understanding of the vulnerabilities that could be associated with and are associated with each of the IT resources installed and operational within its IA baseline. This step requires a number of tasks to successfully build and update this model of vulnerabilities.

We will begin the discussion by defining the meaning of the term "vulnerability" and its relation to a "weakness." A "weakness" consists of some inadequacy that relates to a control mechanism. Generally speaking, there are logical, physical, procedural, personnel, and information control mechanisms that are designed, installed, and operated to provide an output or response for a given input or stimulus. They are intended to create an actual output (response) equal to the desired response. A "security feature" of an automated information system (AIS) is a control mechanism such as physical and logical access controls, configuration control, or identification and authentication. A "weakness" can result from the nonexistence of any control mechanisms, the existence of an insufficient number of control mechanisms, control mechanisms that are inoperable, and control mechanisms that are not operating or functioning as required.

A "vulnerability" is a weakness in a control mechanism or hardware and software of IT resources that could be exploited by threats.

There are several means of categorizing vulnerabilities that exist in the hardware and software resources of the IA baseline. One approach is to categorize vulnerabilities as either algorithmic or probabilistic vulnerabilities. Hardware failures (including control mechanisms) and human actions in the operational environment that permit the occurrence of threats cause probabilistic vulnerabilities. Such vulnerabilities are system dependent and vary with the types of user services, the control mechanisms, etc. Design and implementation errors introduced during system development cause algorithmic vulnerabilities. Such vulnerabilities include missing and inadequate control mechanisms for preventing unauthorized access of IT resources.

Probabilistic vulnerabilities involve the following areas:

1. *Hardware failures.* Hardware failures in control mechanisms and related elements are probably the most common of the probabilistic vulnerabilities. Storage protection and file access control mechanisms can fail and thereby support accidental or deliberate threat attacks. Errors in communication devices that cause misrouting of information also support attacks. Components that constitute the source of such vulnerabilities should have fault detection, isolation, and automatic error recovery capabilities.

2. *Human operational vulnerabilities.* Since the proper functioning of an Automated Information System and its control mechanisms depend to some extent on human actions, the latter are a distinct source of unpredictable vulnerabilities. Leaving identifiers and passwords exposed for unauthorized use can introduce this vulnerability. A user's incorrect use of a system may also cause malfunctions in control mechanisms. Operational personnel may cause system failures that support threat attacks by unauthorized users. Deficient procedural controls may also allow this type of vulnerability.

Although identification of algorithmic vulnerabilities often involves a thorough understanding of design and implementation, there are also some obvious security deficiencies. Some of the more common and generic vulnerabilities are as follows:

1. *Residual data erasing.* Sensitive information left in temporary storage media is easily available for unauthorized access and removal. Such information might include authorized user passwords, identifiers, file names, and so forth. Therefore, residual data should be removed on all storage media before reallocation of the memory.

2. *Resource allocation control.* The misuse of resources may result from insufficient control over their allocation. For example, a process may request allocation of all available disk storage space, restrict central processing unit (CPU) usage, or involve repeated use of system services that can seriously degrade system performance. Another potential vulnerability is the ability of a subsystem to bypass normal resource allocation controls.

3. *Resource utilization synchronization.* Inadequate operating system synchronization of system resource use is a vulnerability that unauthorized users can often exploit. Inadequate control over simultaneous user requests for the same resource may enable an attacker to make requests that cause a system to go into a wait state, nullify a system lock on that resource, or distribute information within a storage medium.

4. *Implied sharing.* This involves an operating system sharing some of its work space with user programs. An example of this case is an operating system reading a list of system data sets and user passwords into a user memory area while authenticating that user's request for data sets. The passwords and other important data set information for other users is not

overwritten before the user who is sharing the work space accesses the memory area.

5. *Access control mechanisms.* Access control and other control mechanisms in AIS could contain design and implementation weaknesses that are easily exploitable. Such control mechanisms generally do not reflect a rigorous IA policy and are subject to unauthorized bypass. The distribution of access control mechanisms and the use of inconsistent design criteria contribute to the vulnerability.

6. *Isolation of system capabilities.* Existing operating systems are large, complex structures of interrelated components generally having more operating and control privileges than necessary. The improper use of these privileges by any one component, or errors in that component, can cause the failure or destruction of other components. System attackers can often exploit these weaknesses. The improper control of system-wide capabilities, such as provided by a privileged state, also provides an attacker who gains access to that state with almost unlimited capabilities to misuse components.

7. *Asynchronous interrupts.* This weakness results from the poor design of asynchronous interrupt handling capabilities. For example, if logon attempts are not correctly monitored because interrupt processing does not properly update the logon attempt, a user may generate an indefinite number of logon attempts and eventually guess a password.

8. *Incomplete parameter checking.* A major weakness in operating systems occurs at the interfaces between the system and the users. Users call operating system functions in a manner similar to subroutine calls, using many parameters and complex table structures. An example of incomplete parameter checking occurs when the system has passed two parameters, say, A and B. The system checks parameter A, changes it to another format if it is correct, and then checks parameter B. If both parameters point to the same address, it is possible to use the altered parameter for unauthorized access to the contents of the storage location.

9. *Inconsistent parameter checking.* In this category of vulnerability, the system has different validity checking criteria. Validity checking criteria for the privileged mode differ from user-mode criteria, or the parameters may have different criteria in different parts of the operating system. If the user routine passes the system routine check, it is then possible for the user to have the privileges of the system routine. These privileges may be sufficient to subvert control mechanisms.

10. *Asynchronous parameter checking.* This vulnerability has often been referred to as the time-of-check and time-of-use problem. When the parameters were initially checked by the privileged program, they were proper. But after the check and before their use, the user changes them to circumvent some control mechanism of the system. This attack is possible because systems can process input and output and relinquish control back to the user for concurrent processing.

11. *Non-unique identification.* This vulnerability stems from an operating system failure to ensure unique identity among users and system programs. If

a user can create a program with the same identifiers as a system routine and request loading, it may be possible to bypass a control mechanism or have control returned to the user in the privileged state. The system loading routine should have a mechanism for uniquely identifying all programs, both user and system.

An organization needs to develop the ability to continuously collect and update a knowledge base of information concerning potential and currently existing vulnerabilities applicable to its IA baseline as well as estimates of the potential exploitability of those vulnerabilities. Appendix C provides a listing of major sources of vulnerability information for a variety of hardware and software products. The organization's IA Policy Compliance Oversight function (Chapter 14) can provide the information concerning the potential exploitabilities of IA baseline vulnerabilities.

Step 7: Developing a Knowledge Base of the Readiness of IA Capabilities

Organizations need to have a complete and accurate understanding of their IA capabilities and the readiness of such capabilities. The IA capabilities of an organization can be defined based on two factors. The first factor involves the security services and security mechanisms described in the organization's IA Architecture layer (Chapter 8). The organization must maintain a current knowledge of the readiness of its IA architecture. This involves knowledge of the existence (in-place or not-in-place), operational status (active or nonfunctioning), sufficiency of numbers, and the effectiveness of the encryption, digital signature, access control, data integrity, authentication exchange, traffic padding, routing control, and notarization security mechanisms. The second factor involves determining the readiness condition of the 11 layers of the organization's Defense in Depth structure that are described in Chapters 6–16. These 11 layers essentially represent the technical and nontechnical infrastructure of the organization's IA capabilities. The total readiness of the organization's IA capabilities involves the sum of the readiness of both its technical IA architecture (Chapter 8) and the supporting nontechnical IA infrastructure (Chapters 6, 7, and 9–16).

The IA Policy Compliance Oversight function (Chapter 14) and Appendix I ("Information Assurance Self-Inspection Checklist") provide a means of assisting an organization in its effort to determine the readiness of its IA capability.

Step 8: Developing a Knowledge Base of the Threat Status

This step involves the organization's development and continuous updating of a knowledge base of information pertaining to the threats that have historically confronted it, the status of threats that are currently confronting it, and the threats that are expected to confront it. This knowledge has great significance in determining the IA posture of an organization. After all, a "posture" is a current position in time that is relatively measured compared to both historical performance and futuristic expectations (i.e., intended performance). The threat status essentially indicates the extent to which the organizational entity has experienced, is experiencing, or is projected to experience any threat activity and the scope and intensity of this activity.

Appendix B ("Listing of Threat Statuses") provides a means for describing the past, current, and projected threats to an organization at any point in time. The "Threat Category" column identifies the seven general categories of threats as described in Appendix A. There are specific threats associated with each threat category. The remaining five columns of Appendix B involve "Threat Occurrence," "Threat Detection," "Threat Prevention," "Threat Correction," and "Threat Impact." Each specific threat within a threat category should be mapped to each of these five columns to identify the status of the threat from past (historical), present, and projected perspectives. The following sections provide the information that must be identified for each threat within each of the seven threat categories.

Threat Occurrence Knowledge Category

- What threats have occurred that exploited IA baseline vulnerabilities? (Past)
- What threats are occurring to the IA baseline? (Present)
- What threats are expected to occur to the IA baseline? (Future)

Threat Detection Knowledge Category

- What threats were detected? (Past)
- What threats are being detected? (Present)
- What threats are expected to occur, be detected, or not be detected? (Future)

Threat Prevention Knowledge Category

- What threats were prevented from exploiting IA baseline weaknesses? (Past)
- What threats are being prevented from exploiting weaknesses in the IA baseline? (Present)
- What threats can or cannot be prevented from exploiting weaknesses in the IA baseline? (Future)

Threat Correction Knowledge Category

- What threats has the organization corrected or been unable to fully correct, and to what extent? (Past)
- What threats is the organization correcting and to what extent? (Present)
- What threats are expected to be corrected? (Future)

Threat Impact Knowledge Category

- What have been the impacts to the organization of threats? (Past)
- What are the impacts of threats to the organization? (Present)
- What could be the impacts of threats to the organization? (Future)

Change Knowledge Category

- What has the organization changed to enhance the detection, prevention, and correction of threats to the IA baseline? (Past)
- What is the organization changing to enhance the detection, prevention, and correction of threats to the IA baseline? (Present)
- What should the organization change to enhance the detection, prevention, and correction of threats to the IA baseline? (Future)

Step 9: Determining the IA Posture: The IA Posture Indicators

Three indicators can be used to provide any organizational entity with an understanding as to the status of its IA posture. The *first indicator* is a means to measure the sufficiency of the knowledge bases discussed in Steps 2–8, as shown in Table 5-1. The table depicts six levels of sufficiency, with Level 0 representing the lowest level and Level 5 representing the highest level (Russo and Shoemaker, 1989). For example, an organization that is uncertain as to what information it needs to accumulate and update relative to its IA baseline (i.e., Level 0) is operating at a higher level of risk than an organization that does have such certainty. Each level represents an indication of the extent of the certainty and uncertainty as to the sufficiency of information for each knowledge base. Therefore, the organization needs to continuously understand these levels of sufficiency in order to exercise some degree of control over its IA behavior and performance.

The *second indicator* is the extent of the organization's capacity to control and influence its IA behavior and performance. Step 4 addressed the subject of control and IT control objectives. The COBIT defines "control" as the policies, procedures, practices, and organizational structures designed to provide reasonable assurance that business objectives will be achieved and that undesired events will be prevented or detected and corrected. IT control objectives are developed to define the desired IA behavior and performance. The measurement of the organization's capacity to control its IA behavior and performance can be derived from an understanding of two categories of information. First, potential threats that could confront the IA baseline and IA needs must be identified (Appendix A). Second, threats that have historically occurred, threats that are currently occurring, and threats that are expected to confront an organization should be understood (Appendix B). The effectiveness of the organization's capacity to control its IA behavior and performance can be measured based on these results. The level of certainty as to the organization's capacity to control its IA behavior and performance will be higher the greater the certainty of sufficiency of knowledge bases, the more extensive the implementation of required IT control objectives, and the greater the existence and readiness of required IA capabilities.

The *third indicator* involves the predictability of the organization's IA behavior and performance. The extent of this predictability can be measured by comparing desired IA behavior and performance with actual results or performance (Appendix B). IT control objectives can represent desired IA behavior and performance. The greater the deviation between desired and actual IA behavior and performance over time, the lower the predictability of IA behavior and performance.

Table 5-1   Knowledge Sufficiency Levels

Level	Description of Level
0	Lack of an understanding of the organization's own knowledge needs. That is, the organization has no comprehensive understanding as to the information that it requires for a knowledge base area.
1	The organization understands the extent of its own knowledge needs. However, the organization is uncertain as to whether it has or has not the comprehensive information necessary in a knowledge base area.
2	The organization understands the extent of its own knowledge needs. However, the organization is certain that it does not have the information necessary to comprehensively understand its knowledge base area.
3	The organization understands the extent of its own knowledge needs and is certain that it has the information necessary to comprehensively understand the knowledge base area, but it is reasonably uncertain as to the validity and scope of the information.
4	The organization understands the extent of its own knowledge needs, it is certain that it has the information necessary to comprehensively understand the knowledge base, and it is reasonably certain that the validity and scope of all or a significant portion of the information are inadequate.
5	The organization understands the extent of its own knowledge needs, it is certain that it has the information necessary to comprehensively understand the knowledge base, and it is reasonably certain that the validity and scope of the information are adequate.

Step 10: Reporting and Acceptability of the IA Posture

The final step of the process involves two separate actions. First, the organization must define a formal approach for reporting assessments of the IA posture at prescribed periods of time to the right individuals within an organization. Chapter 16 ("Layer 11: IA Reporting") discusses a reporting process for an organization's IA function. Second, one or more individuals within the organization must have the authority to decide whether the IA posture is at an acceptable level. The results of this decision need to be sufficiently communicated within the organization in the event that corrective actions are required to change the risk to a level that is considered more acceptable.

SUMMARY

The IA posture is the "bottom line" for those responsible for IA within an organizational entity. Therefore, there is a need for some means of measuring it to provide organizations with indicators of the level of risk that confronts them. This chapter described a process for providing these indicators. Three indicators were identified and described. The first indicator is intended to measure the organization's certainty relative to the sufficiency of knowledge that it needs to continuously accumulate. The second indicator is intended to measure the organization's certainty as to its capacity to control its IA behavior and performance. The third indicator is intended to measure the organization's capacity to predict its IA behavior and performance. The extent of the certainties versus the uncertainties measured by these indicators can provide the organization with an understanding as to the current and projected state of the exploitability of its vulnerabilities. The scope and intensity of these exploitations determine the severity of the risk that must be considered for acceptance by appropriate organizational officials.

REFERENCES

Information Systems Audit and Control Foundation, COBIT—*Governance, Control and Audit for Information and Related Technology,* 3rd ed. (2001).

National Security Telecommunications and Information Systems Security Committee (NSTISSC), *The Insider Threat to U.S. Government Information Systems,* NSTISSAM INFOSEC/1-99 (July 1999).

Russo, J. E., and P. J. H. Schoemaker, *Decision Traps—The Ten Barriers to Brilliant Decision-Making and How to Overcome Them.* New York: Simon & Schuster, 1989.

Tichy, N. M. *Managing Strategic Change—Technical, Political, and Cultural Dynamics.* New York: John Wiley & Sons, 1983.

III: ESTABLISHING AND MANAGING AN IA DEFENSE IN DEPTH STRATEGY WITHIN AN ORGANIZATION

6. Layer 1: IA Policies

CHAPTER OBJECTIVES

- Provide the fundamental concept of policies and their distinction from other concepts such as standards, guidelines, and procedures
- Provide the intent and significance of establishing IA policies for an organization
- Provide the mechanics of developing, communicating, and enforcing IA policies within an organization
- Provide the basic structure and policy subjects for an organizational IA policy

THE CONCEPT OF POLICY

First, it would be beneficial to begin with an understanding of the concept of a "policy" and how this definition distinguishes it from other commonly used terms. A distinction will be drawn between the concepts of "policies," "guidelines," "standards," "practices," and "procedures." Generally, an organization of any size or profit motive has a "purpose" that defines its basis for existence; a "philosophy" that defines its fundamental or core beliefs relative to the achievement of its purpose; and "premises" which are the assumptions about its opportunities, threats, geopolitical space environmental constraints, strengths, and weaknesses. "Policies," "guidelines," "standards," and "procedures" provide a means for an organization to support accomplishment of its purpose.

"Policies" are management instructions indicating how an organization is to be run. They are high-level statements intended to provide guidance to those who make decisions. They typically include general statements of goals, objectives, beliefs, ethics, and responsibilities and are expressed in ordinary business language that does not address implementation methods. Importantly, policies are regulatory or advisory in nature and require special approval when a worker wishes to take a contrary course of action. In this they differ from guidelines, which are optional and recommended. Policies are mandatory and can also be thought of as the equivalent of an organization-specific law. Special approval is required when a worker wishes to take a course of action that is not in compliance with policy. Because policy is required, policies use definitive words like "do not . . . ," "you must . . . ," or "you are obliged to . . . ." The words used to indicate policies must convey both certainty and indispensability. For example, policies might be, "Every employee will have access to e-mail and calendaring applications." Or, "The Organization has legal and moral obligations to maintain the confidentiality of customers' personal information with respect to anyone outside the organization or anyone within the organization without a specific need."

Policies are distinct from "guidelines," which are optional and recommended. Replacing the word "must" in a policy statement with the word "should" creates a guideline. "Standards," like policies, require compliance. However, policies are higher-level statements than standards, providing general instructions that will last for many years. Standards make specific mention of technologies, methodologies, implementation procedures, and other detailed factors, and are thus likely to last for only a few years until conditions change. For example, a network-security standard might specify that all new systems must comply with the X.509 standard for public-key authentication — a requirement that may eventually become obsolete. The requirement for strong authentication will remain, however, and should be established as a policy.

"Procedures" are specific operational steps or practices that employees must take to achieve the goals that are defined in the policy statement. A policy, such as one on data backup, that grows too detailed or lengthy may become a procedure. Sample procedures might include such statements as:

> Employee mail accounts are named according to the following system: Firstname_Lastname. Duplicate first and last names are resolved by having the employees with the least seniority insert their middle name in this way: First_Middle-name_Lastname. Names not resolved by this method will be referred to the Chief Directory Officer for resolution. It is the user's responsibility to archive messages. The IT Organization will maintain backups of current messages (Steinke, 1998, p. 25).

Different organizations will have various levels of commitment to developing and maintaining documents related to policies, guidelines, standards, and procedures. Large, distributed enterprises with large IA baselines will generally have a greater need than smaller organizations for formally documenting uniform policies, guidances, standards, and procedures. For educational institutions, spelling out user responsibilities and prescribing consequences for abusive activities might have a high priority. Financial institutions will certainly have strong incentives to explicitly document the steps they take to secure information and prevent tampering. To minimize bureaucracy, every organization needs to determine which aspects of its business need to have policies, guidelines, standards, and procedures (Wood, 1997, p. 27).

THE INTENT AND SIGNIFICANCE OF IA POLICIES

IA policies have a clear purpose relative to the survival, coexistence, and growth of an organization. There will be a description of four significant purposes.

First, an organization's IA policies are intended to establish a general security framework and direction for the organization relative to its IA capability. The security framework and direction equate to the IA capability's mission and it is manifested in a purpose, a vision, and legitimacy. IA policies must define the purpose of the IA capability and be able to define the significance that the purpose will have in supporting the organization's efforts to fulfill its overall purpose. Also, IA policies provide a means of establishing IA performance expectations. They could provide a vision of what the organization's IA capability "is" and what it "could or ought to be." This vision involves what the IA capability's purpose would represent once it has been fulfilled — in behavioral and tangible terms. In regard to legitimacy, security policy is a statement of management support toward the organization's IA capability function. The organization's IA policies are a clear and definitive way for management to demonstrate that (1) IA is important, and (2) what behavior is and is not allowed. Policies can compensate for influences that may otherwise cause people to insufficiently protect information resources. They are a relatively inexpensive and straightforward way for management to define appropriate behavior, demonstrate its concern, and specify which behaviors are acceptable/unacceptable.

Second, IA policies ensure that controls are properly implemented. The COBIT, Third Edition, defines "control" as the policies, procedures, practices, and organizational structures designed to provide reasonable assurance that business objectives will be achieved and that undesired events will be prevented or detected and corrected. Therefore, properly defined and enforced IA policies are tools for management to influence organizational behavior and produce predictable IA results. This results from the IA policies' ability to control the total flow of material, people, and information into the organization, out of the organization, and within the organization.

Third, IA policies provide a means to avoid organizational liability. In addition to explicit statutes such as the U.S. Foreign Corrupt Practice Act (FCPA), an increasingly compelling body of case law is demonstrating that management and even technical staff may be held liable for inadequately addressing information security matters. The basis for this liability can be negligence, breach of fiduciary duty, failing to use the security measures found in other organizations in the same industry, failing to exercise the due care expected from a computer professional (computer malpractice), or failure to act after an "actual notice" (such as a compromise of security) has taken place. Discussions about liability exposure and the need for policies are often successfully used to gain additional management attention and support for information security efforts. It is advisable to consult with internal legal counsel prior to covering this topic with management.

Policies have been shown to be influential evidence in the eyes of the court that management has indeed been concerned about and done something about information security. If the policy writer's organization has not yet seriously addressed information security, it is important to promptly start work and to set the direction for future efforts.

Fourth, IA policies provide a means of defining who should be distributed IT resources within an organization as well as the extent and conditions of the distribution. Therefore, IA policies extend beyond the bounds of basic IA and have both political and operational significance for an organization. IA policies can be instruments of both sharing and constraint. For example, consider the use of software programs to help coordinate meetings and calendars on the organizational intranet. IA policies should address who gets access to the calendars employees are now required to post; whether everyone will also be able to schedule meetings themselves; whether a manager can block certain individuals in the organization from scheduling meetings; and, whether the manager can override someone's appointment and schedule a different meeting.

Appendix D provides a listing of Internet Web sites that can provide greater depth of information concerning IA policies.

THE MECHANICS OF DEVELOPING, COMMUNICATING, AND ENFORCING IA POLICIES

This section will discuss some of the practical aspects of developing, communicating, and enforcing IA policies within organizations.

The Development of IA Policies

There is a process for the development of IA policies. Four aspects of this process will be described. Appendix E provides an example of the basic structure and subjects of an IA policies document.

First, there needs to be a decision as to what information is required to initiate the development of IA policies — that is, what "input" is needed to the process of developing IA policies. Certainly, the IA needs of the organization are the starting point from which IA policies will undergo development. This represents precisely what information is important and what must be controlled by the organization.

Second, there needs to be a decision concerning who should be developing the IA policies. The development of the organizational IA policy could solely be the responsibility of IA management or the development process could involve a more politically diverse group of technical, operational, and managerial participants. The development of IA policies is a political endeavor and should not be limited to either the IA or technical staffs. There are a number of operational, technical, and managerial people who will be affected by IA policies. Therefore, these people should consider themselves participants to some extent in the development of policies that will affect how such policies could affect their contributions to the survival, coexistence, and growth of the organization. Larger, more decentralized organizations should consider the use of a formal working group to develop IA policies. This group could be chaired by an IA staff professional and include individuals representing the technical (systems administrators, systems developers, network management, and so forth), security, operational, and managerial aspects of the organization. In particular, the organizational elements that are considered the owners, originators, and users of organizational information should be represented on this working group. People who are affected by the IA policies should be provided an opportunity to review and comment prior to the policies becoming official. The resulting IA policies document should then be submitted to a higher organizational managerial person (e.g., Chief Executive

Officer, Chief Information Officer) or body (e.g., Board of Directors) for final approval. Smaller, more centralized organizations could place responsibility for the development of IA policies in the hands of the IA staff. However, it would be advisable to submit draft copies of IA policies for comments to those individuals within the organization who are considered essential to ensure the successful implementation of the IA policies.

Third, the developed base IA policies document may need to change for a variety of reasons. Some policies may need to be removed, modified, or added. There could be a number of reasons why such changes are necessary. Certainly, changes to the organization's IA needs will significantly indicate a need to change the organization's IA policies. Other considerations include the introduction of new technology such as wireless technology and mobile code. Also, there may be a need to adjust the IA policies to reflect the reality of its implementation. There may be instances in which a particular policy has been written and promulgated to influence organizational behavior. However, over time, the policy could be found to be impractical or unrealistic and in need of modification to ensure the achievement of its intended objective.

Fourth, a major factor influencing the development of IA policies is the principle of trust. Trust is the basis for determining access to organizational information and involves a balancing of organizational needs and potential IA threats. The granting of excessive trust could result in the realization of an IA threat. Also, the restriction of trust could impose limits on personnel relative to their access and understanding of organizational information and IT resources. This could have a negative impact on the accomplishment of organizational goals.

The Communication of IA Policies

The organization will need a process for ensuring that all individuals and organizations who are affected by the defined IA policies are made aware of their responsibilities to adhere to such policies. There are a number of means to communicate IA policies within an organization. Significant methods include organizational automated bulletin boards that permit access to the IA policies as well as frequently asked questions (FAQ), incorporating IA policies awareness as a part of employee orientation and training sessions, and providing refresher overview courses on IA policies once or twice a year. Employees could also be required to sign a statement or provide an automated response to designated individuals that verifies that they have fully read and understand the IA policies. The critical factor is that the communication of IA policies within any organization should be considered just a part of the organization's overall effort to communicate its objectives, policies, and procedures. The intent is to create an environment where the implementation of IA policies becomes as fully transparent and unobtrusive to employees as any other responsibility within the organization.

The Enforcement of IA Policies

The subject of the enforcement of IA policies does raise a fundamental issue that may confront many organizations. This involves the issue as to the responsibility for enforcing IA policies. One argument is that the IA staff is primarily responsible for the enforcement of IA policies, while another argument is that this is a supervisory/managerial responsibility. Perhaps the best way to describe this issue is to state that compliance with IA policies is the responsibility of all employees within an organization. The responsibility for the enforcement of the IA policies must be shared between the supervisors/managers of employees and the organizational function that is responsible for communicating and educating employees concerning IA policies. The IA staff is responsible for monitoring and evaluating organizational compliance with IA policies (Chapter 14) and reporting the results to organizational higher level management (Chapter 16).

Another significant point to emphasize is that IA policies are intended to influence the beliefs, attitudes, and behaviors of people within the organization. Therefore, it would be useful to consider the principles of human social behavior. There is a distinction that psychologists make between beliefs and attitudes. They indicate that beliefs require no emotional component. However, attitudes do. A person may have a belief that copying software without authorization is a felony while taking the attitude that breaking this law does not matter to anyone. There needs to be a recognition that people do not naturally desire policies and procedures. People tend to perceive policies as impediments to productivity and as measures to control behavior. Work environments tend to support freely sharing supplies, trusting co-workers to share information, and leaving documents and other material visible on desks. Our natural tendency is to trust co-workers and to be as supportive and polite as possible to potential and existing customers (Kabay, 1996, pp. 28, 30).

Personal views influence what is perceived and organizational employees need to have a consistent and favorable view of IA. People have a variety of views about the need for the limitations that could be imposed by IA. An organizational attempt to influence someone can result in one of three likely outcomes:

- *Commitment.* The other person becomes a "believer" and actively supports the IA policies.
- *Compliance.* The other person agrees with the IA policies but merely goes along with you. He or she does what is required but usually nothing more.
- *Resistance.* The other person disagrees and actively opposes the IA policies. There are a number of causes that could generate such resistance. There is a tendency in most people to resist measures that are perceived as impeding productivity.

Also, some people just strongly resist change and others just like to "rock the boat."

No matter what an organization does, not everyone will be enthusiastic about the IA policies. However, the organization should focus on defining whatever base of commitment exists and then undertake an effort to expand this commitment. The beliefs and attitudes of employees must be addressed when building their commitment. Employee beliefs can be derived from questionnaires, focus groups, and interviews. Attitudes can be learned or changed through something as simple as word association. For example, IA violations should not be portrayed using positive images and words. Also, reward and punishment can change attitudes. Even minor encouragement has an influence, so a supervisor or an instructor should praise any comments that are critical of IA violations or which support established IA policies. Employees who dismiss IA concerns or flout the IA policies should be challenged, not ignored. Attitudes can be changed by fear, but only if judiciously applied. Excessive emphasis on the terrible results of poor IA is likely to fail, with listeners rejecting the message altogether. The enforcement of IA policies is essentially one of persuasion and not the application of force. Also, there is a need for a consistency of enforcement of IA policies within an organization to avoid the perception of favoritism as well as a process and criteria for the handling of waivers and exceptions (Crouse, 1993, pp. 19–20).

SUMMARY

IA policies provide the first layer of an organization's IA Defense in Depth strategy. They provide a means for distributing access to organizational information and IT resources as well as establishing a vision concerning IA performance expectations. Therefore, there are political and operational considerations as well as the technical ones. The challenges that face an organization are to maximize the access to information and IT resources to the extent considered necessary to achieve organizational objectives while minimizing the resistance to such policies.

REFERENCES

Crouse, H. W., "How to Influence Users and Boost Security." *Infosecurity News* (May–June 1993): 19–20.

Kabay, M., "Psyching Out Infosecurity." *Infosecurity News* (January–February 1996): 28–31.

Peltier, T. R., "Designing Information Security Policies That Get Results." *Infosecurity News* (March–April 1993): 30–31.

Shim, J. K., A. A. Qureshi, and J. G. Siegel, *The International Handbook of Computer Security*. Chicago: The Glenlake Publishing Company, Ltd., 2000.

Steinke, S., "Lesson 121: Policy-Based Networking." *Network Magazine* (August 1998): 25–26.

Wood, C. C., *Information Security Policies Made Easy*. Sausalito, CA: Baseline Software, Inc., November 1999.

Wood, C. C., "Policies from the Ground Up." *Infosecurity News* (March–April, 1997): 24–29.

7. Layer 2: IA Management

CHAPTER OBJECTIVES

- Understand the need for senior management support
- Identify the characteristics of effective IA management
- Determine approaches to IA management
- Discuss challenges of managing IA resources
- Identify metrics for selling security to management

ESTABLISHING AN IA MANAGEMENT PROGRAM

Security Is an Integral Element of Sound Management

> There are two basic differences between your organization and its competitors: the value of products to customers, and their cost. If you can show you add value to the organization's products, then you will be making a contribution. If not, try to minimize security costs and at least break even on your investment (Kovacich, 1993, p. 25).

Security is not an end in itself, but it does provide a critical service and support function for the organization. As such, security is an integral element of sound business management that requires management support at the highest level. Yet despite a growing awareness of the need for IA among senior managers, many security offices still experience thin staffs, little or no budget, and insufficient tools. Senior managers need to understand that IA "magic" comes with a price tag, but, if handled properly, there is a return on investment (ROI). This chapter will discuss the personnel, resources, and responsibilities needed to perform effective IA management.

Defining Our Terms

Throughout the remainder of this book we will use the term "IA manager" as a generic term to describe the role and responsibilities of the person charged with the overall management of IA within the organization. In some circles, this individual might be called the Information Systems Security Manager (ISSM); Information Systems Security Program Manager (ISSPM); Information Systems Security Officer (ISSO); Information Technology Security (ITSEC) Manager; Chief Information Assurance Officer (CIAO); etc. In some cases, the roles and responsibilities described in this book may transcend the scope of any one individual. Regardless of the label, the IA manager, as the term is used in this book, is the individual(s) who is/are responsible for developing, implementing, and managing the organization's IA program; computer network defense strategy; and/or IA risk posture.

Reality Check

The IA manager today faces several IA challenges:

- Increasing complexity of systems, networks, and interconnectivity
- Profound reliance on information and information systems
- Ever-changing internal and external threats
- Competing demands
- Unavailable resources
- Decreasing assets
- Lack of experience
- Lack of available training
- Lukewarm support from management

Of all these challenges, the lack of management support could be the most troubling. In fact, an IA manager is only as effective as the support that he or she receives from senior management. It is key to the success of any organization's IA program.

> Sun Tzu, the ancient Chinese military philosopher, stated, "Leadership causes people to follow their superiors willingly; therefore, following them in death and in life, the people will not betray them." A successful security practice starts with the head of the company empowering a Security Manager and flows down through the security team members. Sun Tzu addressed the ability of the political authorities, "Which Lord has better leadership?" A company which internalizes security at its core, lays the foundation for a successful security practice. This internalization starts at the top (Miller, 2001, p. 1).

One reason why management support is needed is due to downward direction. People are more willing to enact change when they believe failure to do so could affect their career or livelihood. The person on the bottom rung of the ladder is not in a position to task his superiors. Even when authorized to act on behalf of management, attempting to implement change or enforce policy from the bottom up is a hard-fought battle. Senior management — top-down — support is imperative for a successful IA program because senior managers are in a position to provide both the downward direction necessary to enact policy and the deterrents or consequences necessary to enforce policy.

Another obvious reason is that the IA manager by himself/herself has no inherent authority; it is all derived from other sources. The IA manager can end up in a very tenuous position: without strong backing from management or enforcement from some outside agency, he or she may find forcing policy compliance impossible. The IA manager must have a direct conduit to the source of the authority on which his or her success depends.

IA Manager Positioning

As a result, the positioning of the IA manager within the organizational hierarchy is an important consideration that is often overlooked. The IA manager must have direct access to the responsible senior manager (e.g., president, director, CEO, CIO). This does not mean that the IA manager must work directly for that individual. It does mean that the person who is authorized to make day-to-day IA management decisions must have direct access to the person within the organization who is ultimately responsible for those decisions—the person who authorized the IA manager to make security decisions on his or her behalf.

Likewise, those responsible for enforcing security controls must be empowered and autonomous to perform unbiased reviews and evaluations. The IA manager provides a valuable checks and balances role. He or she must be given the positioning and support needed to maintain objectivity. The IA manager, for example, should not report directly to the audit department or the systems operations department, in order to eliminate any real or perceived conflict of interest.

The Art of Serving Many Masters

One of the most difficult concepts that both senior management and the IA manager must grasp is the difference between the organizational chain-of-command and the functional chain-of-command. It may not be possible or even practical for the IA manager to work directly for the person who ultimately underwrites the security of the organization. In some cases, that person may not even reside within the organization. For example, the Designated Approving Authority (DAA), responsible for system/network accreditation for certain government organizations, may be the director of the agency who owns the network backbone to which a local organization connects. The IA manager, in this case, functionally reports to the DAA or his/her designated representative while holding a position within the local organization's chain of command.

In other cases, the IA manager may report to an authority outside of the organization. Within the federal government, for example, the DAA role for some global networks may not be delegated below the agency director level. The IA manager at a field site may report to a local chain of command while being functionally responsible to directly report security-relevant information to the DAA (or designated representative) in another organization or agency.

Whenever the functional chain differs from the organizational reporting chain, it is important that all concerned parties understand the predicament in which the IA manager is placed. The IA manager may be given guidance by the DAA or certification authority that conflicts with the organization's plans. The IA manager should always attempt to satisfy both the organizational goals and security objectives, but this is not always possible. The organization's senior management must support the IA manager in these hard decisions. If not, the IA manager can be caught in a tug-of-war between the organization that pays his/her salary and the functional authority who accredits the system—not an enviable position.

Prerequisites for Being an IA Manager

As the resident expert on information security issues, the IA manager must be qualified and equipped to manage the organization's IA program and have adequate resources to perform the IA management functions (e.g., staffing, security tools). This book assumes a basic understanding of the roles and responsibilities of an IA manager. However, for a more extensive treatment of the subject, see Dr. Kovacich's *Information Systems Security Officer's Guide.*

It would be an interesting study to know how the average IA manager got into this career field. Perhaps they were the last person to show up for the meeting the day the organization decided to assign IA manager responsibilities. Maybe he or she was the only person in the office who knew anything about computers or the only one who volunteered when no one else spoke up. The selection of the IA manager should be based on the right mixture of personal qualities, skills, knowledge, experience, and education.

The IA manager should possess:

- Not only a working knowledge of the technical aspects of systems and networks, but the savvy to ask the right question when more information is needed and the ability to translate technical security requirements into an understandable language for both management and general users.
- Not only a textbook knowledge of security requirements, but the ability to interpret and apply security directives, regulations, standards, and policies.
- Not only an institutional knowledge of the organization, but an in-depth understanding of the organization's mission, objectives, strategic goals, and business processes to ensure that IA policies and procedures are enablers, not obstacles, to the accomplishment of the organization's mission. "The IA manager must understand organization's history, products, business environment, competition, long and short range plans, cost of business, and product value" (Kovacich, 1993, p. 321).

In reality, technology is becoming more complex and specialized, leaving the IA manager to be an expert in many different areas. Security guidance or directives often do not exist or are too ambiguous or high-level to be of any practical good; the IA manager then finds him/herself writing applicable policy for local business processes, if defined.

The organization may require a certain education level (e.g., minimum of an undergraduate degree in a technical discipline) or a certification (e.g., CISSP, CISA) to improve the likelihood of getting a better-qualified IA manager. As with anything in life, there are no guarantees that a person with these credentials is more qualified to be an effective security manager than someone who does not possess these qualifications. It would be more advisable to look for references and employment history than base a decision solely on the basis of education level or professionalization status. The intention is not to downplay the importance of education, but rather to keep the process flexible enough to allow for the exception to the rule. It would be a shame to eliminate an otherwise well-qualified candidate with years of real-world experience solely on the grounds of insufficient formal training.

Approaches to IA Management

There are three basic approaches to IA management: centralized, decentralized, and hybrid. All have certain advantages and disadvantages (see Table 7-1).

Table 7-1   Approaches to IA Management

Approach	Definition	Advantages	Disadvantages
Centralized	IA manager has a dedicated staff and all IA issues are handled by that office	Provides integrity (checks and balances; separation of functions); control; focus; specialization	Resource limitations; overhead costs; span of control constraints—hard to implement when geographically dispersed; redundancy issues; the larger the staff, the more time the IA manager will spend managing people problems
Decentral-ized	IA manager has no dedicated staff but depends on personnel within the workplace to perform required IA functions	No limitations to resources or span of control—geography not an issue; IA manager can focus solely on IA—no personnel management problems; little or no overhead	Dependency on other managers' assets; competing resources and priorities; staff is picked by other managers; communi-cation, coordination, and training challenges; requires buy-in from middle management; no checks and balances for integrity
Hybrid	IA manager has smaller and leaner dedicated staff but still depends on a decentralized workforce to handle routine IA functions as a collateral duty	Easier to sell to management since decentralized assets could be part-time; provides integrity checks	Still dependent on other people's people (but to lesser degree); training challenges

IA Management Staff

"The make-up of this [security] team is solely dependent on the company. Size, type of business, dependence on the Internet, and types of resources are all fac-tors that contribute to the make-up of the team" (Miller, 2001, pp. 1–2). The size of that team, as well as the actual mix of skill sets, grade structure of personnel, and amount of workload to be outsourced, must be tailored to the organization's unique business requirements. There is no cookie-cutter approach. If another organization is going to be held up as an example to follow, ensure that it is a positive example that adheres to best security practices.

Although, ideally, a manager would like to have great depth within an office — everyone able to perform all tasks with equal proficiency — to provide sufficient coverage at all times to allow for absences, vacations, and turnover; such depth is elusive. It takes a long time to train IA staff to be proficient in their assigned duties. The luxury of having all staff proficient in one another's duties, too, is usually precluded by the preoccupation of the staff with keeping up with their own workloads and the inevitable turnover of personnel that forces on-the-job training to stay focused on primary duties.

Workload can also drive the IA manager staff to become specialists by necessity. For example, for IA management of larger sites, there may be a full-time requirement for audit collection and review; monitoring and administration of security tools (e.g., enterprise security management, vulnerability scanning, intrusion detection tools); security training and awareness; account management (e.g., password issuing, group maintenance, certificate issuing); certification testing and evaluations; developing and maintaining IA documentation; and Webmaster for maintaining the IA Web site or data mining for IA-related topics. Even incident handling can be a full-time job.

Outsourcing

> Network security has become one of the most neglected aspects of network management, but for understandable reasons. Imposing security over a network of any size is exceedingly difficult, hard to understand, and time-consuming. Many companies do not have the skills onboard to handle the task; . . . [and] realize that it's hard to find, and keep, security specialists (Blacharski, 2000, p. 64).

Outsourcing some or all IA manager responsibilities has become a viable and increasingly popular alternative, since it is not always possible to maintain an adequate number of dedicated IA experts on staff. It may be even possible to outsource the IA manager position itself. However, this situation would only be effective if the individual was empowered to make security decisions, enact change, and represent the accreditation authority for the organization while at the same time being free from any real or perceived conflict of interest.

"Outsourcing costs far less and gives your organization ready access to a team of specialists who focus 24-by-7 on securing their client's networks," delivering a more complete security solution by providing constant enforcement from a skilled, full-time staff. The question to ask: "Is turning over the keys the best way to secure your [network] enterprise?" (Blacharski, 2000, p. 64). The particular insider threats that stem from a mercenary mentality are discussed elsewhere in this book.

Managing Resources

One of the biggest challenges the IA manager and staff will face is the effective use of time and manpower. The security business is very dynamic. The IA manager will be faced with more challenges than he or she can handle in a day. In those rare cases when business is slow, all one has to do is look; security issues are probably bubbling just under the surface.

One residual effect from selling the organization on the need for security involvement in all aspects of the organization is the demand to have security representation that a particular division or branch can "reach out and touch." Everyone will want his or her own personal security answer man. Although the

IA manager should not rule out involvement in these areas, he or she will need to look at current and projected manning levels in order to decide what impact a decentralized IA office would have on the synergy of the IA office and its ability to meet all other IA requirements.

Coordination

Communication is critical for the IA manager to successfully manage an IA program. The IA manager must be an effective communicator — able to translate highly technical and complex ideas into language that is understandable to a less technically oriented senior management. The IA manager must also be a good listener in order to read between the lines, clarifying the real requirements from what is being said.

One of the most overlooked communication traits is that of coordination — ensuring that anyone with a stake in the action is kept apprised of what is happening. The following potential coordination should not be ignored:

- Senior management
- Special security officers (SSO) (physical and personnel security)
- ISSMs, ISSOs, or IA managers at interconnected locations
- Certification and accreditation authorities
- Other security professionals
- Legal department
- Criminal investigators
- Project management offices and software developers, vendors, suppliers
- Integrators
- Configuration/change managers
- Systems/network administrators
- Audit department
- Disaster recovery/contingency planning staff
- Quality assurance office
- Budget and procurement office
- Training office
- Personnel/human resources office
- Facilities/physical plant office
- Logistics and supply personnel
- General users
- Other customers (internal and external)

Budgeting

The IA manager is probably going to be selected for technical comprehension as much as for management skills. It is one thing to expect an IA manager to have good people skills, to include being able to effectively manage people, but rarely do we think of the IA manager as a financial manager. Ideally, the IA manager will have a line item within the organization's annual budget in order to plan and execute the IA program.

Without this resource base, the IA manager may have to go head-to-head with the IT department in order to fight for limited monies for IA resources. The IA manager may also find him/herself budgeting for annual training and travel expenses.

Tips

- Learn from the budget and finance personnel about all available sources of income
- Look for monies earmarked specifically for IA initiatives
- Understand the terms under which the money may be obligated
- Examine the "O&M Tail"—the subsequent operational and maintenance costs
- Coordinate with the IT Department to ensure that IA software tools are compatible with existing software and do not duplicate existing capabilities
- Sell the IT Department on your vision for IA and enlist their help in selling senior management
- Be able to differentiate between what you want and what you really need (a lost art)

Salesmanship and the Need for Metrics

Management often views IA as an overhead expense rather than an integrated operational expense with a proportional ROI. Many managers do not understand the value of their organization's information and reputation or the relationship of security to their organization's business processes. Other managers do not understand the extent of the problem, wrongly assuming that a firewall or other single fix provides all the security necessary. Still others may choose to ignore the problem, hoping it will just go away.

> People at all levels say they're concerned about security, . . . but they don't spend very much on security in general. In most American companies, three-10ths of one percent of top-line revenue is spent on information security, according to Forrester [Research, Inc., Cambridge, MA] research, which also proves that most companies spend more on coffee than they do on security. . . (Ambrosio, 2001, p. 2).

Security comes with a price tag. Security tools, training, and especially people are expensive. Senior managers need to be sold on the merits of any resources invested in the cause of IA. Likewise, management will need to be resold on the need to continue or add to previous expenditures in IA resources. Sometimes the IA manager will feel that he/she spends more time justifying security than actually doing security. With limited money available to spend on IA, it is not enough to convince management of the need for IA improvements; getting a head-nod of concurrence to an idea may not make it materialize. The trick is to sell management well enough to have the IA initiative prioritized, programmed, budgeted, and realized.

> When investors decide whether to buy stock in a new company, they scan a document called a Red Herring (because of the color of its cover), which must list under the law, all

the risks the company faces as well as its opportunities for growth. Like a stock about to go public, IT spending is also an investment with very real potential benefits and very real risks — including, of course, security risks. But while some aspects of Web commerce are easy to quantify (i.e., how much business you do over the Web per day or week), doing a cost/benefit analysis for security is still a black art. Business managers often don't know how to estimate the risk (except to think it won't happen to them) or the cost (except that whatever it is will be too much) (Scheier, 2000, p. 1).

Cost is always relevant to value. In order to justify an expense, the cost should not exceed the overall value.

Some tips to selling security to management include:

- Put all proposal requests in writing. Ideally, all responses from management should also be written.
- Make the budget and finance personnel your friends. Get concurrence on the proposal from the audit and legal departments before it gets to senior management; this keeps everyone in the loop and gives senior management more confidence in their decision making, knowing that their financial and legal advisors concur.
- Sell management on the effects: why the benefits of implementing the proposal outweigh the disadvantages of not implementing the proposal.
- Involve management in implementation using realistic milestones and demonstrating how proposal costs actually translate into corporate savings (Powell, 1994, p. 28).

As a result, the IA manager must be able to concisely and graphically illustrate the organization's IA posture in order to sell a concept to management. Chapter 5, "The Organization's IA Posture," discusses the concept of an IA posture and presented an approach for measuring it. Also, Dr. Kovacich devotes an entire chapter to the subject of INFOSEC metrics management in his *Information Systems Security Officer Guide*. In doing so, he covers a variety a measurable events or actions that can be used as statistical support for "right-sizing" the IA office; justifying the expenditure of IA tools; or estimating the impact a decision will have on the organization's existing security posture. As good as metrics are, there are at least four shortfalls that the IA manager needs to bear in mind:

1. One challenge with metrics is not just measuring what gets done, but measuring what does not get done. While management is asking for tangible metrics (hours worked, number of certifications conducted; volume of audits reviewed, etc.), we also need to quantify what IA responsibilities are not getting done. Often the IA manager is overwhelmed with more responsibilities than he/she has resources to accomplish. The IA manager is faced with making choices on how to use the limited resources available and rationalizing what IA tasks will not get done. For example, audits may go unreviewed. The IA staff may be so busy reacting to current events that there is no time to be proactively testing for vulnerabilities, monitoring the network for anomalies, or conducting a self-inspection checklist assessment. Trying to explain to management the impact of not getting these

proactive activities done may be difficult unless a precedent for comparison has already been set, which leads us to the next shortfall.

2. Attempting to measure negative impact (e.g., what is not getting done) requires a benchmark either derived from your organization's historical documentation or borrowed from the current statistics of a comparable organization. Take the previous example of the inability to conduct audit reviews. If audit reviews have been conducted in the past, the IA manager can use that metric as the benchmark. If audit reviews have not been conducted in the past or if no metrics were documented, the IA manager may be able to use the metrics of another organization with similar audit requirements. For example, the IA manager could say, "This quarter last year we spent an average of six man-hours per day conducting audit review for X number of systems; today with X+n systems, we estimate we will need eight man-hours per day for this duty." Or "Organization Y, whose IT department mirrors ours, dedicates one person full-time to reviewing audits." Or, to take a different approach, "Last year we discovered 15 serious security violations through diligent review of audits. Based on those statistics, we estimate that up to five serious violations may have gone undetected already this year because of our inability to review audits with our current workload." Without an objective benchmark, predicting negative impact of unfilled IA responsibilities is simply conjecture.

3. Metrics may quantify things (e.g., users, systems, accounts), but they do not necessarily reflect specific level of effort or impact. For example, some new systems come with well-written documentation and all the pedigrees the IA manager or certifying authority needs to work a swift IA approval. Others systems may experience weeks of coordination and delays in fielding due to rewrites of inadequate documentation or correction of serious security findings. A graph depicting the total number of new systems that have been added to the IA baseline during a specified period does not express the painful ordeal of certifying any particular system. In this case, a graph illustrating the average time spent in certifying systems during a given period may be more effective, provided there is a track record on which to base comparisons. Also, metrics may not convey impact or severity. Numbers of incidents, for instance, do not reflect the loss of confidentiality, integrity, or availability that resulted from each infraction. For example, an organization may report five security incidents one month and only one incident the next month. While the numbers would seem to indicate a significant improvement, the severity of the single incident may have been more devastating than the previous five incidents combined.

4. Metrics do not normally consider institutional knowledge.

Productivity comes from knowledge capital aggregated in an employee's head in the form of useful training and company-relevant experience. . . . They are the people who leave the workspace every night (and may never return), while storing in their heads knowledge acquired while receiving full pay. They possess something for which they have spent untold hours listening and talking, while delivering nothing of tangible value to paying customers.

Their brains have become repositories of insights about "how things work here" — something that is often labeled vaguely as "company culture." Their heads carry a share of the company's Knowledge Capital, which makes them shareholders of the most important asset a firm owns, even though it never shows up on any financial reports. . . . The calculation of the management value-added makes it possible to count the worth of the people who possess the accumulated knowledge about a company. . . . The source of the energy that creates net information value-added is Knowledge Capital [which] equals management value-added divided by the price of the capital (Strassman, 2001, Part 3, pp. 2, 3).

Bearing in mind the shortcomings of metrics, the IA manager should utilize IA management when selling a concept to senior management. If you have not been keeping metrics in the past, the time to start is now. The more statistical and historical data that you can accumulate, the better off you will be when attempting to justify additional manpower, better tools, or a bigger IA budget.

Some examples of actions that lend themselves to metrics for any given time period include the following.

Systems and Network IA Management

- Number of major networks or local area networks (LANs) under IA management
- Total number of systems under IA management
- Number of new systems certified
- Average time taken to certify new systems
- Number of new systems under IA management versus legacy systems
- Number of remote systems or sites under IA manager's span of control
- Number of periodic IS reviews conducted
- Number of employees accessing network resources from home
- Number of policies written or updated
- Breakdown of expenditure of time (actual or average time spent doing administrative security, developing policy, conducting inspections, attending meetings, staffing actions, etc.)
- Number of IA staff on-hand
- Number of full-time IA staff versus number of staff augmenting the IA program as collateral duty

Administrative Security

- Average processing time for creating user accounts
- Number of new accounts and passwords issued
- Number or percentage of privileged users to general users
- Number or average of account suspensions or deletions
- Average number of visitor accounts requested
- Average number of uncleared visitor requests for escorted entry into secure areas
- Number of laptops or other portable computing devices in secure areas
- Number of digital certificates issued
- Number of systems using strong authentication versus static passwords
- Number of phone calls and walk-in customers served
- Number of support calls taken after hours

- Volume of audit reports reviewed
- Number or average of hours spent doing active monitoring
- Number of hours spent reviewing audit reports
- Average or actual number of anomalies detected during audit reviews
- Number of data transfer operations between different classification systems/networks

Incident Handling and Vulnerability Assessment

- Number of IA incidents identified or reported
- Breakdown of types of IA incidents
- Number of open investigations still pending action
- Percentage of security violations that ended in administrative or remedial action
- Number or percentage of employees discovered using system inappropriately
- Number or average of accesses on public Web site
- Number of false positives versus actual intrusions detected
- Number of probes detected
- Number of denial-of-service events
- Average system down time for denial-of-service events
- Number of viruses or other malicious code identified or reported
- Breakdown of types of findings from internal vulnerability testing
- Breakdown of types of vulnerabilities identified from red team penetration testing
- Breakdown of findings from random bag checks conducted upon facility entry/exit

Training and Awareness

- Total number of user briefed on IA education, training, and awareness (ETA)
- Average number of users briefed at each IA training session
- Number of system administrators certified
- Breakdown of methods used for security awareness (e.g., posters, videos, articles)

Contingency and Destruction Plans

- Number of times contingency or emergency response plans are exercised
- Number or percentage of systems being backed up daily, weekly, etc.
- Number of systems turned in for destruction (life-cycle replacement)
- Number of hard drives or nonremovable media removed for equipment turn-in
- Number of removable media destroyed

Budgetary Issues

- Breakdown of IA budget expenditures
- Projected IA budgetary needs
- Training budget for IA manager and staff continuing IA education
- IA travel budget (actual and projected)

MANAGING IA

Where to Begin

Publish a mission and functions statement. This establishes functions, defines responsibilities for the IA program, and sets the benchmark by which success of the IA program is measured.

Develop a long-term strategic plan (Kovacich, 1993, p. 26):

- Know the organization's current working environment, culture, and management philosophy
- Apply risk-management concepts
- Develop a process for internal and external communication and coordination
- Maximize available resources
- Where resources are unavailable, use least-cost approach to IA decisions
- Review and modify the strategic plan as required

Develop near-term tactical plans (Kovacich, 1993, p. 26):

- Review applicable regulations, policies, and the organization's existing information system security program
- Identify key team members including management and technical staff from IT, security, auditing, legal, and human resources
- Determine the status of the organization's current information security posture through physical and technical assessment of the organization's threats, vulnerabilities, countermeasures, and risks
- Analyze the differences between the current security environment and the security goals and objectives
- Establish action teams consisting of key team members to chart courses of action to meet the goals and objectives

The Importance of Daily Situational Awareness

"The greatest source of bad security is bad management, and the greatest source of bad management is not knowing what is going on. If nothing else, invest in audit (self-assessment) tools" (Rubin et al., 1997, p. 174).

The IA manager is supposed to be a risk manager. Most of us who do the job every day are not aware, in advance, of all the changes that are being made to our systems and networks. Even regarding the few changes we do know about, we are often hard pressed to say with any certainty what ripple effect those tweaks and changes will have on the overall IA posture of the network. We can only surmise what the aggregate effect of all the minor changes will be on the overall IA posture of the IA baseline.

Can any IA manager really say with any certainty what the real IA posture of their site is on any given day? If so, are they basing that assessment on a scientific formula or a gut feeling? And how do we know from day to day when that IA posture changes from acceptable to unacceptable risk? If we don't know what all these risks are, how can we possibly manage risk without some kind of automated security tools to identify what is on the network, what has changed, and what risks those changes pose to the accredited IA baseline?

IA managers need to rethink the way we approach IA management in general, and the certification/accreditation process in particular. Rapid insertion of new and emerging technologies is forcing us to evolve systems in the production environment. IA managers need the tools and manpower to shift focus from an initial look at each system to continuous monitoring of the network as a whole. Only when we know what is happening to our information systems and networks can we begin to be effective IA managers.

Dispensing Technical Guidance

The IA manager will spend much of his or her time dispensing security guidance only to find many of those decisions challenged. Management, developers, project officers, and system users are often simply looking for a security head-nod—some kind of confirmation from a security official that what is being proposed meets the minimum security requirements. If the proposal does not provide sufficient safeguards, the IA manager may be expected to instantly define all the security requirements that, once met, will result in security approval.

Ideally, the IA manager should be able to point to a written regulation, directive, or policy to back up every security decision or to validate every security requirement. When written guidance does not exist, historical precedence may be considered, but beware: a precedent does not necessarily connote a good security practice. When neither written guidance nor precedents exist, the IA manager may be required to make an unprecedented security decision.

In most cases, people will only tell the IA manager what they want him/her to know, leaving the IA manager to read between the lines. It is important to know how to ask the right diagnostic questions to get the whole story. Technical complexities make it more difficult to know what to ask. The wise IA manager will defer making a security decision when in doubt, in order to allow time to gather more information before laying down a precedent-setting decision.

Every security decision should be based on sound security concepts and principles. Remember: today's new precedent may be tomorrow's de facto standard. Each exception to the rule lessens the IA manager's ability to dispense consistent guidance and enforce security controls. If a policy does not universally apply to the whole organization, the security control that the policy supports is weakened. For example, an organization may have a policy requiring all employees to have unique user identifiers to enforce accountability. However, if the organization also permits system administrators to log into the system as the superuser "root"—providing no audit trail beyond the root login—what sort of accountability control really exists if the most privileged users do not have to abide by the organization's policy?

Every security decision should also be documented to avoid giving anyone the opportunity to misrepresent the original intent. Additionally, it is critical that all key processes to an organization's information be documented, communicated, and available to ensure consistency of operations during normal processing and to assist in continuity of operations when faced with system failure or personnel turnover. The documentation must reflect reality — that process actually being used — not the theoretical or supposed. If, in the course of documenting the process, you learn that policies are not being followed, either change the policy or change the process. Either way, ensure consistency between the process and the standard operating procedure it implements.

Legal Issues

It is imperative that the IA manager be familiar with applicable legal issues in order to know when it is appropriate and necessary to contact a law enforcement agency in the event of a security incident. It is also important for the IA manager to know where the legal boundaries start and stop to ensure that he/she does not overstep those bounds (e.g., in the case of monitoring).

The IA manager should be able to:

- Know local and federal laws that apply to computer-related crime; individual privacy rights; copyrights/patents; intellectual rights; trade secrets; employment contracts; work for hire; and software licensing
- Identify which agencies and offices are responsible for investigating IA incidents for your organization (NSTISSI 4014, 1997, p. A-20)
- Know who and how to contact within applicable law enforcement agencies, and under what conditions they should be contacted (NSTISSI 4014, 1997, p. A-20)
- Know when a search warrant is required and whom to contact to obtain one
- Understand how to protect a crime scene; seize and preserve evidence; and ensure that a chain of custody is maintained
- Know his/her legal and technical limitations for obtaining and examining computer forensic evidence
- Understand the procedures for interviewing a witness and who is authorized to conduct the interview (NSTISSI 4014, 1997, p. A-20)
- Know what constitutes entrapment and targeting techniques; understand the legal limitations and prohibitions (NSTISSI 4014, 1997, p. A-20)
- Know the organization's policy on employee firing practices and handling of disgruntled employees (NSTISSI 4014, 1997, p. A-20)

IA Management Essentials

- Determine what needs protecting and identify the threats; focus on real needs and real, foreseeable threats
- Decide on what priorities will be and what tradeoffs are willing to be made (e.g., constraints on operations)
- Know the value of your critical information; identify critical processes and systems, and know why (and how much) protection is required
- Promulgate realistic, written policies and procedures to ensure that all employees understand roles and responsibilities and expected security practices; review regularly for relevance

- Follow best practices identified by successful businesses
- Where possible standardize procedures, forms, and training
- Make security an enabler; sell management on the ROI that security can provide by protecting the organization's information, reputation, and continued operations

SUMMARY

Information assurance offers a growing opportunity for security managers who want a challenging career. The positioning of the IA manager within the organization and the amount of support that the IA manager receives from senior management will directly affect the effectiveness of the IA program. Likewise, the coordination, salesmanship, and management skills of the IA manager him/herself can directly affect the success of the program.

REFERENCES

Ambrosio, Johanna, Contributing Editor, "Security policies and budgets still lagging, survey finds." *Security News* (April 9, 2001).

Blacharski, Dan, "Outsourcing Security." *Network Magazine* (February 2000): 64–71.

Clark, Franklin, and Ken Diliberto, *Investigating Computer Crime.* Boca Raton, FL: CRC Press, 1996.

Ferdico, John N., J.D., *Criminal Procedure for the Criminal Justice Professional*, 6th ed. Minneapolis/Saint Paul: West Publishing Company, 1996.

Icove, David, Kark Seger, and William VonStorch*, Computer Crime: A Crimefighter's Handbook.* Sebastopol, CA: O'Reilly & Associates, Inc., 1995.

Kovacich, Gerald L., "The ISSO Must Understand the Business and Management Environment." *Computers & Security* (Vol. 16; 1997): 321–326.

Kovacich, Gerald L., "Congratulations, You're the New Infosecurity Officer!" *Infosecurity News* (July–August 1993): 25–26.

Miller, Matthew K., "Sun Tzu and the Art of (Cyber) War: Ancient Advice for Developing an Information Security Program," *SANS Institute* (April 2, 2001).

National Institute of Standards and Technology (NIST) Special Publication 800-12, "An Introduction to Computer Security: The NIST Handbook."

National Security Telecommunications and Information Systems Security Instruction (NSTISSI) No. 4011, "National Training Standard for Information Systems Security (INFOSEC) Professionals" (June 20, 1994).

National Security Telecommunications and Information Systems Security Instruction (NSTISSI) No. 4014, "National Training Standard for Information Systems Security Officers (ISSO)" (August 1997).

Powell, David, "Selling Aids: Eleven Hot Tips!" *Infosecurity News* (September–October 1994): 28.

Rubin, Aviel D., Daniel Geer, and Marcus J. Ranum. *Web Security Sourcebook*. New York: Wiley Computer Publishing, 1997.

Scheier, Robert L., "Security spending a necessary evil." *Executive Security Briefing* (December 22, 2000).

Strassmann, Paul, "Art of budgeting: How to explain spending on information security? (Part 1)." *Executive Security Briefing* (September 28, 2000); "Art of budgeting: How to ask for money for information security (Part 2)." *Executive Security Briefing* (December 11, 2000); "Art of budgeting (Part 3)." *Executive Security Briefing* (January 12, 2001).

8. Layer 3: IA Architecture

CHAPTER OBJECTIVES

- Provide a definition of an organizational IA architecture that will include its objectives, necessity, and relationships to the organization's IA baseline and the other layers of the organization's Defense in Depth strategy
- Provide a description of the basic components of a model of an organizational IA architecture
- Provide a description of the process for designing an organizational IA architecture and the issues associated with this design

THE OBJECTIVES OF THE IA ARCHITECTURE

The description of the IA architecture should begin with an understanding of the term "architecture." An architecture could be defined as a means of providing the foundation for building or designing an entity (e.g., buildings, bridges, public telephone system, automated information system) while promoting a common structure and a set of standards. There are components that comprise an architecture, interrelationships between these components, and principles and guidelines governing the architecture's design and evolution over time.

The objectives of the IA architecture are to ensure that at least the minimum level of interoperability and services is available to authorized users to securely perform their assigned tasks, to securely coordinate activities with other users, and to securely exchange information within the physical and virtual boundaries of an organization's IA baseline (Chapter 3). The IA architecture can achieve these objectives by integrating three levels of security to control the execution of transactions that result in the flow of information (i.e., in hardcopy and logical states), people, and IT material (i.e., IT hardware equipment such as workstations, servers, routers, cables, wires, laptop computers, CD-ROMs, disks, and tapes) through known access paths within the physical and virtual boundaries of an organization. These levels of security involve *physical security, procedural security,* and *logical* (i.e., *technical) security. Physical security* involves the protection of the facilities, hardware, and software of the organization's IA baseline from threats that could cause damage, theft, failure to operate, inappropriate modification, and misuse. *Procedural security* entails the establishment of officially documented and approved procedures for controlling the flow of information, people, and material. Procedures involving the proper hiring, processing, and assignment of authorizations to organizational personnel are aspects associated with procedural security as well as procedures for the proper accountability, classification, and labeling of information and material. *Logical security* is the technical level of security that involves the computer hardware and software that is responsible for controlling the flow of information in a logical (i.e., digitized) state within the organization's IA baseline and between the IA baseline and external entities (e.g., customers, suppliers, joint venture organizations, and public networks).

The remaining 10 layers (i.e., Layers 1, 2, and 4–11) of the Defense in Depth strategy are an infrastructure that provides direction, support, control, and enforcement for the IA architecture. The IA architecture basically provides a means to allocate and integrate technical and nontechnical controls within the organization's IA baseline to protect its Critical Objects as defined in Chapter 4 ("Determining IT Security Priorities"). The allocation and integration of these controls must produce an IA architecture that is an integral and seamless part of the IA baseline. The process for designing and building an organization's IA architecture involves having knowledge of certain significant information as well as the accomplishment of a number of actions. A description of this process follows.

KNOWLEDGE REQUIRED TO DESIGN THE IA ARCHITECTURE

The individuals responsible for the design and building of an organization's IA architecture need to have accurate, timely, and complete knowledge concerning a number of significant factors.

The Organization's Business Model

The organization's business model provides the basis for the development, operation, and security of the physical and virtual boundaries of its IA baseline. The IA architecture must be an integral and seamless part of this IA baseline and, therefore, the operational basis of the organization. As previously discussed in Chapter 1 ("IA and the Organization: The Challenges"), private and public organizations exist to provide products and services to meet the needs of their customers. Organizations formulate goals (policy) and develop business methods (procedures) to achieve the goals as well as measures of performance (control) to determine the extent of the accomplishment of the goals. Subsequently, organizations must determine the *operational events* that they need to implement (process model) and the *information* (data model) to sufficiently implement these events and achieve their goals. A *process* is a set of events. The physical and logical boundaries of the IA baseline contribute toward the performance of the operational events (process model) and the creation, collection, input, storage, processing, and communication of the information (data model). The extent of this contribution creates the dependency between organizational survival, coexistence, and growth and the IA baseline as well as the risks associated with this dependency. Also, the nonexistence or unpredictability of this contribution creates the greatest risk to the organization that the Defense in Depth strategy intends to mitigate.

IT Operational Events (Process Model)

IT operational events are associated with five objects. These objects involve organizational facilities, digitally converted information, IT devices, digitally converted executable instructions that can be executed within IT devices to input, process, store, output, and communicate information, and IT material (e.g., CD-ROMs, disks, tapes). The following is a list of the major types of IT operational events that are associated with information, hardware devices, executable instructions, organizational facilities, and IT material.

Information Operational Events

- Input (write) new information
- Store/save information
- View/display/list/output (read) information
- Delete information
- Manipulate information (e.g., sort, arithmetic-logic operations)
- Modify/change/replace existing information
- Join/append information
- Copy/replicate existing information
- Request for/search for/query for/find information
- Open and close containers of information (i.e., files, directories, subdirectories, files)
- Accept information
- Reject information
- Receive/retrieve information
- Send/transfer information
- Acknowledge receipt of information
- Acknowledge non-receipt of information
- Get (read) information about information (attributes)
- Set (write) information about information (attributes)

Hardware Device Operational Events

- Hardware device startup (i.e., device boot-up)
- Hardware device shutdown
- Add hardware device
- Remove hardware device
- Modify hardware device
- Repair hardware device
- Hardware device logon/logoff
- Hardware device configurations (system, security, and network configurations)
- Hardware device account establishment, modification, suspension, and disestablishment for individual, groups, and roles
- Hardware device request
- Hardware device release
- Hardware device read
- Hardware device write

- Set (write) information about device (attributes)
- Get (read) information about device (attributes)

Executable Instructions Operational Events

- Write instructions
- Store/save instructions
- View/display/list/output (read) instructions
- Delete instructions
- Modify/change/replace existing instructions
- Call instructions
- Load instructions
- Execute instructions (an executable instruction in execution is a "process")
- End the execution of instructions
- Abort the execution of instructions
- Suspend the execution of instructions for time
- Suspend the execution of instructions for events
- Join/append instructions
- Copy/replicate existing instructions
- Request for/search for/query for/find instructions
- Open and close containers of information (i.e., files, directories, subdirectories, folders)
- Accept receipt of instructions
- Reject receipt of instructions
- Receive/retrieve instructions
- Send/transfer instructions
- Acknowledge receipt of instructions
- Acknowledge non-receipt of instructions
- Get (read) information about instructions (attributes)
- Set (write) information about instructions (attributes)

Organizational Facilities Operational Events

- Enter into facility
- Exit from facility
- Modify the facility
- Repair the facility
- Clean the facility
- Renovate the facility
- Dispose of the facility

IT Material Operational Events

- Enter IT material into facility
- Remove IT material from facility
- Read IT material
- Write IT material
- Dispose of IT material
- Enter IT material into IT device
- Remove IT material from IT device

Information (Data Model)

Organizations must be capable of identifying all the information that they collect, create, input, store, process, and communicate. There are several qualities related to the concept of information that must be considered by organizations to adequately acquire this knowledge.

First, there are various types of information. Digital information can represent numbers, text, pictures (images), moving pictures (audiovisual), sounds, and executable instructions for computers.

Second, digital information can include both discrete and stream forms. The discrete form involves information with specific start and end points and includes such things as files, imagery, weather, maps, and messages. The stream form involves a continuous flow of information from such sources as the Cable News Network (CNN) broadcast, distance learning, or the universal clock.

Third, Chapter 4 ("Determining IT Security Priorities") indicated that the IA needs of an organization are based on the criticality and sensitivity of the information that the organization is dependent upon for its survival, coexistence, and growth. Therefore, information can be distinguished based on these levels of criticality and sensitivity. The result of this process is a knowledge as to the organization's Critical Objects that require protection.

Fourth, there is the factor of the timing of information. Information can be provided to its intended consumers in either real-time or non-real-time mode. This means that certain information can be provided to the intended consumers at the same point in time (i.e., real-time) at which the information was created. The other alternative is that information could be provided to its consumers at later points in time (i.e., non-real-time). For example, information that is generated as a result of sales transactions could be stored and then later retrieved for review.

Fifth, information can exist in structured and unstructured formats. The structured format involves information that is contained within a predefined record format. The record involves data elements that make up the record and that must be stored within it. The unstructured format is not restricted to a predefined set of data elements and could include textual information such as an electronic mail (e-mail) document as well as audio, video, voice, images, and graphical objects. They are basically "unstructured" because their exact content and organization are unpredictable. Therefore, by definition, unstructured information is any information type composed of content that doesn't fit a predefined descriptive model or arrangement. Each of these represents a static state for information. However, information within an organization is dynamically transitioning between the states as the organization itself is operating on a day-by-day basis.

Sixth, information can be defined relative to the overall functionality of the organization. Specifically, there are three broad categories to define organizational information. These information categories are policy, control, and operational. Policy information assists management when establishing goals and objectives and organizational direction. Operational information is necessary to perform the operational functionality of the organization. For example, operational information would include information associated with organizational marketing, procurement, production, financial management, accounting, customer relations, and so forth. Control information is necessary to monitor the basic operations of an organization with the intent of detecting and correcting the lack of achievement of organizational policy and operational functional areas.

Seventh, there is the matter of information ownership and the sharing of information. Generally, the owner of information should have the rights to deny access to anyone but himself/herself, to permit the accessibility of the information to select group(s) of individuals, or to permit the accessibility of the information to everyone. Also, there needs to be a distinction defined relative to the "originator" of information, the "possessor" (i.e., someone granted access) of information, and the "owner" of information. The organization should fully define these distinctions to all its employees as well as the rights of employees to grant or deny access to information. These distinctions are important both from an internal political perspective and from a legal perspective. For example, there may be a requirement that all marketing information that is generated within the organization is owned by the marketing department. The marketing department is responsible for ensuring that all marketing information is accurate, complete, timely, and secure. Also, the responsibility of ownership provides the marketing department the right to grant or deny access to this information.

Subjects and Objects

An organization must identify all its subjects and objects. First, NSTISSI No. 4009 defines a subject as consisting of individuals, groups of individuals, individuals represented by a single identity (i.e., a role such as a systems administrator or information system security officer), processes, and hardware devices. Individuals and groups of individuals could be the users of systems and the individuals that maintain the hardware and software of the systems. Also, individuals could assume the identity (i.e., the role) of a systems administrator. A systems administrator is responsible for configuring the system and performing account management. Processes represent instruction code that is in a state of execution within a hardware device. Generally, a process is identified by a unique process identification number that is directly associated with the user who initiated the process. A process could be clients, windows, daemons, and tasks. Devices involve such hardware as workstations, servers, routers, and firewalls.

Second, objects are essentially entities that are capable of containing, receiving, or providing information to subjects. The information could be in physical or logical form. Access to an object implies access to the information it contains and the information that it is capable of receiving and providing. There are separate categories of objects that involve facilities, IT material, information containers, executable instructions, and IT devices. The following represents examples of major objects under each of these categories:

Facility Objects

- Buildings
- Floors
- Rooms
- Offices/workspaces

IT Material Objects

- CD-ROMs
- Disks
- Digital Audio Tapes (DAT)
- Communications material (e.g., cables, wires, connectors, and so forth)
- System user manuals
- System administration manuals
- System installation/configuration manuals
- System or organizational security manuals
- Technical architecture drawings and data flow charts

Information Container (Addressable Memory) Objects

- Directory/subdirectory
- Directory trees
- Files
- Records
- Elements
- Databases
- Memory blocks
- Pages
- Segments
- Buffers
- Words
- Bytes

Executable Instruction Objects

- User and presentation interfaces (e.g., graphical user interfaces and command lines)
- Applications that are in a state of execution (e.g., client processes, server processes, and other application processes)
- Applications that are not in a state of execution (e.g., clients, servers, and other applications)
- Operating systems providing system and network services

IT Device Objects

- Workstations
- Laptop computers
- Personal Digital Assistants (PDAs)
- Servers (Web, application, file, database, printer, directory, proxy, network management, or security servers)

- Routers
- Bridges
- Repeaters
- Gateways
- Firewalls
- Printers
- Scanners
- Hard drives
- CD-ROM drives
- Disk drives
- Tape drives
- Monitors
- Keyboards
- Mice
- Input/output ports
- Input/output drivers
- Monitor drivers
- Disk drivers
- Tape drivers
- Consoles
- System clock
- Interprocess messages
- Interrupts
- Interrupt handlers
- Registers
- System calls
- System queues
- Schedulers
- Semaphores
- Complementary metal oxide semiconductors (CMOS)
- Communications ports
- Network interfaces
- Modems

Domains of Subjects and Objects

Organizations must identify the domains of their subjects and objects. Domains represent subsets of the total number of subjects and objects that have been identified for organizations. "Communities of interest" and "enclaves" are other terms that have been used to define the subsets of subjects and objects. Domains may be established in a variety of ways on a permanent or temporary basis as needs require. For example, a domain could be defined to consist of all the employees of an organization's finance or marketing departments. Also, a domain of subjects could be defined based on a specific project. In terms of objects, a subset of the organization's objects could be combined into a specific domain such as a domain of applications or file servers. There could be a relationship between domains of subjects and objects. A domain of subjects (e.g., marketing personnel) could be granted the ability to perform all or a limited range of IT operational events relative to a specified domain of objects (e.g., file and application servers) connected to a local-area network (LAN) or even remotely via the organization's wide-area network (WAN).

Access Paths

Organizations must identify all the access paths that exist or could possibly exist between subjects and objects. These involve physical and logical paths between subjects and objects through which flow people, information, and IT material as a result of an IT operational event. Therefore, there are physical and logical considerations associated with access paths.

The *physical* considerations will be discussed first. The complex network of telephone lines of the public telephone system offers a high-level example of an access path that physically interconnects people. This interconnection permits the flow of voice as well as other types of information between people. Also, computers use the "system bus" component to interconnect the other major components of the computer, consisting of the central processing unit (CPU), main memory, and the input/output subsystem. The interconnection of the three components permits the computer to input, process, store, and output information. The communications infrastructure of an organization transmits information using both cables (i.e., wire cable and fiber-optic cable) and air space (microwave, satellites, and radio). The cables use electrical signals for wire cables, light pulses for fiber-optic cable, or a variety of broadcast frequencies for wireless media through air space. Also, an access path could extend from the front door of an organizational facility to the various floors and rooms of the facility. The path could provide open access to organizational IT devices (e.g., workstations, servers, routers, CD-ROM drives, disk drives) and IT material (e.g., communication cabling, CD-ROMs, disks, and tapes). An unsecured door or window provides possible access paths that should be identified.

In regard to the *logical* considerations associated with access paths, the organization's communications infrastructure links subjects and objects into an integrated network. The communications infrastructure basically consists of IT devices that are interconnected using a variety of topologies (i.e., point-to-point, multipoint, star, ring, or mesh), nodes (i.e., bridge, switch, router, gateway, or multiplexor), and circuits. Circuits designate the physical (i.e., dedicated private line) and logical (i.e., permanent virtual circuit) links between the nodes. Several significant points related to the logical considerations associated with access paths should be emphasized.

First, an organization's communications infrastructure is divided up into paths along which signals can be sent. These paths are defined as "channels." Channels are controlled and allocated by many different types of concomitant processes (transduction, transmission, bunching, synchronization, duplexing, multiplexing, and switching). "Connections" are established within these channels to create logical access paths between subjects and objects. The duration of the connection between the subjects and objects is called a "session."

Second, the scope of an organization's communications infrastructure could vary as well as the extent of its interconnectivity beyond this infrastructure with external parties (e.g., suppliers, customers, and dealers). The following basically represents the scope of an organization's communications infrastructure. Interconnectivity with external parties is possible for each scenario that is stated.

- One standalone computer within an organizational facility
- Multiple standalone computers within an organizational facility with no interconnectivity between them
- Multiple standalone computers within an organizational facility interconnected with each other via an "air gap" using IT material storage media (e.g., disks, DAT) to exchange information
- A single LAN within an organizational facility
- Multiple LANs within an organizational facility with no interconnectivity between them
- Multiple LANs within an organizational facility that interconnect via an "air gap" using IT material storage media (e.g., disks, tapes)
- Multiple LANs within an organizational facility automatically interconnected with each other via a specialized security IT device that ensures the secure exchange of information. In the Department of Defense (DoD), this specialized device is known as a "guard"
- Organizational facilities interconnected via the organization's WAN backbone

Third, there are eight basic communication services that can connect subjects and objects through logical access paths. The output of each of these services corresponds to the previously defined types of information and could consist of text, numbers, pictures (images), sounds (voice), or moving pictures (audiovisual). The services and the types of information they provide are:

- Telecommunications (text, numbers, sounds, images, audiovisual)
- Radio (sounds, text, and numbers)
- Cellular communications (sounds, text, and numbers)
- Personal Communication Systems (PCS) (sounds, text, and numbers)
- Paging (text and numbers)
- Mobile satellite services (MSS) (sounds, text, and data)
- Very small aperture terminals (VSAT) (sounds, text, numbers, audio-visual)
- DirectTV (sounds and audiovisual)

Fourth, the direction of the flow or exchange of information through the channel could be one-way (i.e., unidirectional) or could involve a two-way exchange of information (i.e., bidirectional).

Fifth, there are four basic methods for generating the flow of information between consumers and suppliers of information. These methods are as follows:

- A *pull* approach involves the intended consumer of information actively participating in its access by directly activating a network service such as the File Transfer Protocol (ftp). An example involves a situation where information is posted to a central location such as a server and then pulled (transferred) by approved consumers.

- A *push* approach involves transferring data from one consumer to one or many other consumers using network applications such as an ftp or Simple Mail Transfer Protocol (SMTP). Examples include electronic mail (e-mail), forms, reports, customer orders, and manufacturing bills of material.
- A *tuning to channels* approach involves employees selecting preprogrammed stream data to view for a select period of time, such as broadcasts of CNN. Essentially, related information content is collected into channels (news, sports, etc.) and then the channels are broadcast to user desktop workstations.
- An *interactive* approach involves browsing (searching) for discrete information types (files, imagery, etc.). This method requires the consumer to directly interact with the presentation process such as an electronic survey or a project management flowchart that needs significant approval.
- *Profiling* is a more advanced approach than the interactive or browsing approach for accomplishing the awareness, access, and delivery of information since it is more of an automated rather than a manual process. Special tools (e.g., cataloging, metadata standards) are used to eliminate the dependence on "browsing skills." Basically, a profile of consumer information requirements is created and stored. This profile is useful for both the consumers and the providers of information and could be termed a "smart push–pull" approach. Consumers of information can become aware of available information by accessing information provider catalogs, and they can then subscribe to discrete or stream data types for automated, scheduled delivery from defined catalogs with automatic updates. Automatic-pull applications go to a predefined list of Web sites and download the information in advance. Automatic-push applications deliver information content to a consumer on a schedule determined by the software publisher. The information can be delivered in the form of e-mail or personalized Web pages.

Transactions

Organizations need to identify and account for all their possible physical and logical transactions. Transactions result in the flow of people, IT material, and information (i.e., in both physical and logical forms) through the physical and logical access paths of the organization. Basically, a transaction is a binding between a subject, an object, an IT operational event that the subject wants to perform relative to the object, and the access path through which the event will occur. There are physical and logical dimensions associated with transactions, as Table 8-1 indicates.

The table provides some examples of transactions. For example, the first case involves a person who wants to delete a file that resides on a specific server. The access path to accomplish this event involves a path from the individual to his or her client workstation to the specific server via the LAN where the workstation and server reside. An organization could use this approach for identifying the physical and logical transactions that it considers relevant. Each transaction could be assigned an "identification number" for accountability and control.

Table 8-1   Examples of Transactions

Subject	IT Operational Event	Object	Access Path	Number
Individual	Deletes	File XX on Server A	Individual on Client Workstation 1 connects to Server A on LAN I	1
Individual	Removes	Laptop	Individual in Room N to front door of Building Z	2
Role A	Configures	Server B	Role A directly connects to Server B using the console or performs remote configuration from Client Workstation 2 to Server B over the WAN using the telnet protocol	3
Process 1	Send/transfer Information	Process 2	Server D on LAN II sends/transfers information to Server G on LAN VII over the WAN using the ftp protocol	4
Group	Read Information	Shared directory d:// on Server F	Shared directory d:// on Server F connected to Client workstations of Group 7	5
Server J	Output/Print	Printer Q	Server J to Printer Q connected on LAN IV	6

Access Rights

Essentially, an "access right" is the authorization for a subject to execute an IT operational event on an object via a specific access path — that is, to execute a transaction. Therefore, the access path has to be open to permit the implementation of access rights. There are two aspects to the concept of access rights that need to be discussed from the perspectives of subjects and objects. Subjects are assigned "privileges" to execute IT operational events on various objects. For example, individuals who have been authorized to assume the role of systems administrator will be assigned privileges to control configuration settings for specific IT devices such as servers and routers.

On the other hand, objects are assigned "permissions." These permissions control access at the object level by defining which subjects are permitted to access the objects and the IT operational events that the subjects are permitted to execute relative to the objects. For example, accounts are generally created on IT devices such as workstations and servers. A subject who assumes the role of a systems administrator for a specific server may be the only individual who is granted permissions to establish, disestablish, or modify other user accounts or to establish, disestablish, or modify group accounts and group membership.

As previously discussed, domains of subjects and objects could be established. A domain represents a set of subjects or a set of objects. For example, an "object domain" could be created that includes a set of objects and the type of IT operational events that can be invoked on each object for specified access paths. Therefore, a subject such as an individual or a process could be defined to operate within this domain. Also, a domain of subjects could be established consisting of, for example, individuals, devices, or processes that are authorized to invoke IT operational events on individual objects or on a specific domain of objects.

THE DESIGN OF THE ORGANIZATION'S IA ARCHITECTURE

Up to this point, the organization should have completed a process that resulted in the accumulation of knowledge about the following areas:

- Organizational *information* including the criticality and sensitivity of the information as well as the originators, owners, and possessors of the information
- Organizational *IT operational events* associated with information, hardware devices, executable instructions, facilities, and IT material
- The *subjects and objects* and *domains of subjects and objects* that demand and supply information, hardware devices, executable instructions, facilities, and IT material
- The physical and logical *access paths* between subjects and objects through which IT operational events are executed
- The *transactions* that bind subjects, objects, IT operational events, and the physical and logical access paths
- The *access rights* of subjects and objects that establish *trusted relationships* between them and define the extent to which the transactions can be executed within the states of trust

This collection of knowledge serves as the "input" to the process for designing and subsequently developing the organizational IA architecture. The IA architecture design process consists of defining and integrating the information contained in the following sections.

IA Architecture Attributes

There are a number of fundamental security attributes that need to be considered during the design of the IA architecture:

- *Confidentiality*: Protection against unauthorized disclosure.
- *Integrity*: Protection against unauthorized modification.
- *Availability*: Protection against unauthorized loss/repetition.

- *Nonrepudiation*: The provider of information must have assurance as to the delivery of information and the recipient must have assurance as to the provider's identity. These assurances prevent the provider and recipient from later denying having processed the information.
- *Identification and authentication (I&A)*: Protection to determine identity and the validity of that identity.

Threats

Appendix A contains a description of some significant threats that could confront an organization and counter its effort to accomplish defined IA needs. These threats and the extent of the organization's vulnerability to such threats significantly influence the design of the IA architecture. The organization's survival, coexistence, and growth are at risk if it doesn't (a) identify all potential threats that could confront and the severity of the threats relative to the organization's survival, coexistence, and growth; (b) determine the threats that are actually confronting it, the sources of those threats, and the priorities that should be assigned to such threats; (c) assess the extent of its vulnerabilities relative to the actual threats; and (d) determine the extent to which it has the security services, security mechanisms, and the other layers of the Defense in Depth strategy (i.e., the countermeasures) in place and operational to adequately *prevent, detect, and correct* such threats (i.e., to mitigate the risks to an acceptable level).

There are four primary sources of threats. These sources involve natural or environmental events; the failure or lack of installation of organizational facility support systems; internal employees and other individuals who have been authorized to execute transactions (i.e., the insiders); and external organizations and individuals (i.e., the outsiders) who may pose a threat to the organization. Each of these sources of threats will be discussed.

First, natural or environmental events include such things as floods, thunderstorms, hurricanes, earthquakes, extremely high or low humidity, rainstorms, and windstorms. These events could result in the destruction or damage of organizational facilities and the computer systems within them.

Second, organizational facilities have internal systems that are intended to support their operations. For example, heat can cause electronic components to fail. Air conditioning is a support system that ensures that air can circulate freely. Backup electrical power should be available to ensure the functioning of air conditioning even if the primary power fails. Water could damage computer hardware as a result of floods, rain, sprinkler system activity, burst water pipes, and so forth. Water pipes should be identified within the organization to determine their locations relative to computer systems, especially areas where significant computer equipment is concentrated such as communication closets/rooms. Humidity at either extreme poses a threat. High humidity can lead to condensation. Condensation can corrode metal contacts or cause electrical shorts. Low humidity could cause the buildup of static electricity. Therefore, the floors of computer rooms should be bare or covered with anti-static carpeting. Humidity must be continuously monitored to ensure that it is at an acceptable level. Dust, dirt, and other foreign particles could interfere with proper reading and writing on magnetic medium IT material. No one should be permitted to eat or drink around computers. Air should be filtered and the filters replaced regularly. The lack of power due to electrical brownouts and blackouts could render all IT devices useless. However, voltage spikes are more common and could cause serious damage. Voltage spikes, such as those produced by lightning, may either damage equipment or randomly alter or destroy data. Also, a drop in line voltage can lead to malfunction of IT devices. Voltage regulators and line conditioners should be used to control the fluctuation of electricity.

Third, it must be fully understood that whenever access rights are granted to individuals, a *trust* is imposed on them along with the authority. Access rights are granted to employees and to those individuals who support the organization's survival, coexistence, and growth (e.g., suppliers, customers, and contractors who provide support services such as repair and maintenance of IT facilities and IT devices). Chapter 1 ("IA and the Organization: The Challenges") indicated that those "inside the castle" pose the greatest threat to an organization due to the authority of the access rights that are granted them along with the shield that the trust provides them. There are two aspects to this threat. An individual such as a systems administrator may be granted special privileges to execute IT operational events on IT objects. These privileges could provide the individual with the ability, for example, to improperly read or delete the information of other employees as well as to ensure that such actions are not identified with them. Also, the access rights that are assigned an employee could provide the basis for their attempts to rise to higher levels of access rights.

Fourth, external individuals and other organizations pose a potential threat to an organization. Hackers have repeatedly demonstrated their abilities and persistence in attempting to gain access to organizational IT objects as well as their success in doing so. Also, terrorists and organizations that directly compete with an organization pose threats that must be considered.

Also, an organization needs to perform an analysis of the potential threats relative to all the transactions that it had previously identified. There are three aspects to this analysis. First, transactions should only be executed by those subjects who are authorized to do so. Subjects who execute transactions for which they have no authority result in potential threats. The impact of each potential threat relative to the previously defined IA architecture attributes must be defined. The example transactions listed in Table 8-1 are used to illustrate this point in Table 8-2.

Table 8-2   The Impact of the Transactions Relative to IA Architecture Attributes

Transaction No.	Confidentiality	Integrity	Availability	Nonrepudiation	I&A
1			X		X
2	X		X		X
3	X	X	X		X
4	X			X	X
5	X		X		X
6	X		X		X

Each of the transactions listed in Table 8-2 is considered to be *unauthorized*. For example, Transaction 1 indicates that an unauthorized individual from a workstation (i.e., the subject) deletes (i.e., the IT operational event) a file (i.e., the object) that resides on a server (i.e., the IT device). The workstation and server are interconnected via a LAN (i.e., the access path). This unauthorized transaction negatively affects the availability of information and indicates a weakness related to I&A since an unauthorized individual was permitted to execute the transaction.

Second, there must be an analysis of the probable cause(s) for each potential threat. Appendix A provides useful starting information related to the causes of threats. A summary of the causes of potential threats is given briefly here.

Accumulation of Knowledge

Chapter 5 ("The Organization's IA Posture") indicated that the extent of the organization's knowledge of certain information has a direct impact on its IA posture. For example, if IA management employees are not aware of all the operating systems (executable instructions) that currently reside and function on its IT devices (e.g., workstations, servers, routers), then they will not have sufficient knowledge of the organization's vulnerabilities and the means to correct such vulnerabilities. The organization's IA posture will be adversely affected. On the other hand, if such knowledge becomes available to individuals who pose a threat, then the organization is at risk. There are physical and logical aspects to this issue.

The physical perspective involves the physical collection of information about the organization's facilities, IT material, information containers, executable instructions, IT devices (hardware and operating systems), and relevant security information (e.g., user identifiers, logon passwords, or information files). This collection of information can be achieved, for example, by searching the trash that is removed from organizational facilities (i.e., "Dumpster driving"), by searching the Internet, or even by making contact with organizational employees in person or as a result of telephone conversations (i.e., "social engineering").

The logical perspective involves the interception of a data stream through either direct monitoring or redirection. An *active interception* attack intercepts a message flow and performs analysis of the message content. Since there is knowledge of the message content, the attack can include alteration or fabrication of data, which is then redirected to either subvert existing information or produce some unauthorized effect. An example of an active intercept involves the unauthorized alteration of a Domain Name System (DNS) namespace. A *passive interception* is an attack that intercepts a message flow and performs an analysis of the characteristics of the data stream, not its content. Wire taps and network traffic analysis are examples of such interceptions.

Impersonation

Impersonation involves any form of attack that enables an intruding third party to intercede for one principal in the exchange of information or services without the knowledge of the other. *Active impersonations* involve a third party spoofing or faking the Internet Protocol (IP) address of one of the principals. The spoof impersonates either principal online without the other's knowledge. Essentially, an unauthorized person can impersonate or masquerade as a legitimate user (a spoof), an unauthorized user (a rogue user) can access unauthorized areas, or an unauthenticated user (a cracker or bogie) can totally subvert security systems. A *passive impersonation* does not directly target the connection or data stream but works indirectly to produce some unauthorized effect. Such an attack would involve the renaming of DNS namespace so that legitimate DNS lookup responses point to illegitimate hosts. Passive impersonation could also involve the creation of a secret trapdoor that allows unauthenticated, unauthorized access by a third party to system services.

Interference

This involves any form of security attack that renders an IT asset or service unavailable or unusable. An *active interference* attack specifically targets an IT asset or service with the programmed intention to either disable or destroy it. Examples of such attacks include the classic boot sector viruses that rewrite the master boot record on a local hard drive or denial-of-service (DOS) attacks (e.g., flooding) that overwhelm the capacity of a service provider, thereby rendering it functionally useless. *Passive interference* does not directly target the asset or service but works to subvert accessibility through indirect activities. The intent is to exhaust all local resources, thereby preventing access to or use of an IT asset or service through indirect means. Examples include a virus, bacterium, or rabbit.

Third, an analysis of the intents underlying the probable threats needs to be performed. There are four possible intents:

- An authorized user could be deliberately exercising their access rights improperly
- An unauthorized individual is trying to gain access rights
- A person or group intends to exceed the access rights that they were granted
- An authorized person or group could be improperly exercising their access rights by accident

Vulnerabilities

The organization needs to assess the extent of its vulnerabilities relative to the identified potential threats and their probable causes. Chapter 5 ("The Organization's IA Posture") provided an explanation of the concept of vulnerabilities. Chapter 14 ("Layer 9: IA Policy Compliance Oversight") provides information related to the means for assessing vulnerabilities.

Organizational facilities, IT material, information containers, executable instructions, and IT devices may have weaknesses in their design, configuration, management, or operation. Vulnerabilities are weaknesses that can be exploited by a potential threat. The exploitation of the weaknesses by the threats could prevent the successful execution of IT operational events and the flow of information, people, and IT material through the access paths. The vulnerabilities within an organization should be determined relative to the extent to which each threat that is associated with a transaction can be sufficiently *prevented, detected, and corrected*. For example, fire and water could damage or destroy an organization's IT devices and, therefore, pose threats. They must be prevented from initiating, or the access path between these threats and the IT devices must be blocked. A communications cable can be cut if there is an open path between an individual who poses a threat and the communications cable itself. From a logical perspective, threats that involve an unauthorized modification or reading of information can only occur if an open access path exists to the information. The end result of the assessment is knowledge concerning the extent of the vulnerabilities of the organization's facilities, IT material, information containers, executable instructions, and IT devices to the potential threats and their probable causes.

The next steps in the design of an organization's IA architecture are to identify the logical (i.e., technical) security services and their associated logical security mechanisms that are intended to counter the disclosed vulnerabilities. There needs to be a determination as to the allocation of the security services and security mechanisms relative to their physical and logical residence, intensity, and diversity as well as a means to manage these services and mechanisms. Finally, requirements for physical and procedural security need to be defined based on the threats and vulnerabilities. The integration of physical, procedural, and logical security makes up the organization's IA architecture.

Security Services

The security services that are listed below represent the logical (i.e., technical) services described in the International Standard Organization (ISO) International Standard 7498-2, Part 2, "Security Architecture." Five types of security services will be presented.

Authentication Service

This service provides for the verification of the identity of a remote communicating consumer entity and the provider of information. Authentication consists of two parts: peer entity authentication and data origin authentication. Peer entity authentication is used at the establishment of a connection to confirm the identities of one or more connected entities. Assurance is provided at the time of usage only that the corresponding entity is not attempting a masquerade or an unauthorized replay of previous connection messages. If the identity of the peer in a secure communications access path is not properly established, an unauthorized user (an adversary) could masquerade as an authorized user, leaving the information open to possible disclosure or manipulation by the adversary. Also, the data origin part of authentication provides corroboration to an entity in a particular Communications Layer that the source of the data is really the claimed peer entity it is supposed to be.

Access Control Service

Access control is concerned with limiting access to networked resources (hardware and software) and information (stored and communicated). The access control service provides protection against unauthorized use of resources via the Open System Interconnection (OSI). Such controls may be OSI or non-OSI resources accessed through OSI protocols. Access control can be applied to various privileges of access to a resource (e.g., read, write, or execute privileges).

Access control is the collection of mechanisms that enable an organization to exercise a directing or restraining influence over the behavior, use, and content of information systems. This control is used to achieve the organization's IA needs concerning the confidentiality, integrity, and availability of information. Generally, access controls are either rule-based or list-based, and there are several current approaches to the employment of access controls:

- *Discretionary access control (DAC).* DAC is a rule-based approach and focuses on the integrity of information. Access is restricted based on the identity of subjects and/or groups to which they belong. The controls are discretionary in the sense that a subject with a certain access permission is capable of passing that permission on to another subject. Essentially, the granting/revoking of access privileges is left to the discretion of the individual users, without the intercession of a systems administrator or security personnel.
- *Mandatory access control (MAC).* This represents a higher level of access control than DAC and is based on multiple defined levels and categories of information with a focus on the confidentiality of that information. MAC has also been referred to as "rule-based access control" since a subject's access to objects is based on a set of predefined rules. Access to objects is restricted based on the sensitivity of the information contained in the objects (represented by labels) and the formal authorization of the subjects to access information of such sensitivity (e.g., user's clearance). MAC permits read access only if the subject dominates the object (the person has the same or higher clearance) and allows write access to an object only if the subject and object clearance are equal. Only administrators (not owners of information and other objects) may change the category or classification of an IT resource, and no one may grant a right of access that is explicitly forbidden in the access control policy.
- *Role-based access control (RBAC).* Access control decisions are based on the "job role" a user is tasked to perform within the organization. The users are not permitted to pass access permissions on to other users at their discretion. This is the fundamental difference between the RBAC and DAC approaches. Basically, roles are sets of allowed access permissions and transactions. RBAC permits high granularity even within transactions. An example is where a database file on a client is brought up for certain users without personal data visible, such as social security numbers, or where separation of duties is enforced. The allocation of privileges to a role is not so much in accordance with discretionary decisions but rather in compliance with organizational-specific guidelines. For example, an incoming employee is simply granted the "profile set" that has been pre-established for the job he or she has been hired to fill. RBAC is also known as non-discretionary access control.

Data Confidentiality Service

This security service provides for the protection of data from unauthorized disclosure. There are four subservices:

- *Connection confidentiality.* This service provides for the confidentiality of all (N)-user data on an (N)-connection.
- *Connectionless confidentiality.* Connectionless confidentiality provides for the confidentiality of all (N)-user data in single connectionless (N)-Service Data Units (SDUs). SDUs are the units of data that are to be transmitted.
- *Selective field confidentiality.* This service provides for the confidentiality of selected fields within the (N)-user data on an (N)-connection or in a single connectionless (N)-SDU.
- *Traffic flow confidentiality.* This service provides for the protection of the information that could be derived from observation of traffic flows.

Data Integrity Service

The data integrity security service provides for the integrity of all user data or of some selected fields over a connection or connectionless data exchange. This service is intended to detect any modifications, insertions or deletion of data. There are four subservices:

- *Connection integrity with recovery.* This service provides for the integrity of all (N)-user data on an (N)-connection and detects any modification, insertion, deletion, or replay of any data within an entire SDU sequence (with recovery attempted).
- *Connection integrity without recovery.* The intent of this service is the same as connection integrity with recovery, but with no recovery attempted.
- *Selective field connection integrity.* This service provides for the integrity of selected fields within the (N)-user data of an (N)-SDU transferred over a connection and takes the form of determination of whether the selected fields have been modified, inserted, deleted, or replayed.
- *Connectionless integrity.* This service, when provided by the (N)-layer, provides integrity assurance to the requesting (N + 1)-entity. The (N + 1)-entity represents a communications layer at the next higher level. It provides for the integrity of a single connectionless SDU and may take the form of determination of whether a received SDU has been modified. Also, a limited form of detection of replay may be provided.
- *Selective field connectionless integrity.* This service provides for the integrity of selected fields within a single connectionless SDU and takes the form of determination of whether the selected fields have been modified.

Nonrepudiation Service

This service can take one or both of two forms:

- *Nonrepudiation with proof of origin.* The recipient data is provided with the proof of the origin of the data. This proof will protect the recipient against any attempt by the sender to falsely deny sending the data or its contents.

- *Nonrepudiation with proof of delivery.* The sender of data is provided with the proof of the delivery of the data. This proof will protect the sender from any attempt by the recipient to falsely deny receiving the data or its contents.

Security Mechanisms

The ISO 7498-2 identifies eight security mechanisms that are associated with the previously discussed security services.

Encryption Security Mechanism

Encryption is also known as *encipherment* and can be located within a number of Communications Layers. However, the focus has tended to be at Physical and Data Link Layers. There are two basic types of encryption: link-by-link and end-to-end encryption. Individual links are protected by link encryption. All information that is passed to the physical link is encrypted. End-to-end encryption involves an encryption at the sending node and a decryption at the receiving end.

Encryption does provide confidentiality of either information or traffic flow. This mechanism provides the means and methods for the mathematical transformation of information in order to conceal its content, prevent alteration, disguise its presence, and/or prevent its unauthorized use.

There are two categories of encryption algorithms: symmetric or asymmetric.

In a symmetric encryption algorithm, the encryption key is secret, and knowledge of the encryption key implies knowledge of the de-encryption key and vice versa. The sender and receiver both use the same key. On the other hand, in an asymmetric algorithm, the encryption key is public and knowledge of the encryption key does not imply knowledge of the de-encryption key or vice versa. The two keys are referred to as the private key and the public key, respectively. When the two keys are to be used, one key may be made public, and the process is called Public Key Encryption. The sender uses the destination's published public key to encrypt the message. The de-encryption of the message can only take place by the destination using the private key.

Encryption is a security mechanism that can be used to support the authentication, data confidentiality, and data integrity security services.

Digital Signature Security Mechanism

The digital signature mechanism provides data integrity as well as confidentiality. That is, it provides the guarantee that data has not been altered or destroyed in an unauthorized manner. The *digital signature* is data appended to (or is a transformation of) a data unit or frame that permits a recipient to prove the source and integrity of the data. The entire encrypted message is referred to as the digital signature in a public key environment. On the other hand, the Message Authentication Code (MAC) is called the digital signature in the secret key environment. The MAC is a cryptographic checksum added to the data.

There are two different processes that are represented by these security mechanisms. First, there is the "signing" process that uses information that is private (that is, confidential to the signer). The signer's private information as a private key is used either to encrypt the data unit or to generate a cryptographic check-value of the data unit. The second process is the verification process. This involves using the public procedures and information to determine whether or not the signature was produced with the signer's private information. The significant fact about the signature mechanism is that the signature can only be produced using the signer's private information. After the verification of the signature, it can subsequently be proven to any third party that only the unique holder of the private information could have produced the signature.

The digital signature security mechanism can be used to fully support the authentication and nonrepudiation security services as well as the connectionless and selective field connectionless aspects of the data integrity security service.

Access Control Security Mechanism

This mechanism uses the authenticated identity of an entity, its capabilities, or its credentials to determine and enforce the access rights of that entity. The access control mechanisms ensure that only authorized users have access to information and IT resources. Access control mechanisms could be applied at either end of a connection or to a connectionless communications exchange of data. The following five access control mechanisms will be described:

- *Access control lists (ACLs).* ACLs are posted centrally and implement access by representing the columns as lists of users attached to the protected objects. The speed of ACL searches can be increased by the use of user groups and wildcards. Also, groups make the management of ACLs easier. Access to the ACLs need to be controlled as tightly as the objects themselves or they can be manipulated.
- *Capabilities.* This involves the assignment of a required capability set to an object (file, directory, process, and so forth) such that only those subjects (users or processes) who possess all of the required capabilities are permitted to access the object. Essentially, users (subjects) are assigned capabilities (sets). The objects have lists of required capabilities that users must have in order to access them. This noncentralized approach makes tracking and administering permissions difficult, particularly in revocations, since it is difficult to know who has access to what objects and they can still pass access on to others.
- *Profiles.* Profiles are posted with users and implement user access to an object only if it falls within the user's profile. However, since object names are not consistent or amenable to grouping, they cannot be reduced. Also, if a user has access to many protected objects, his or her profile can get long. Another problem is change. That is, if an object's path/location changes, all user profiles accessing it must somehow be located and changed. Again, the lack of a centralized permissions list makes tracking and administering difficult.
- *Protection bits.* Protection bits are posted with the objects. The protection bits represent attributes that are associated with the objects to represent access permissions. For example, in the UNIX file system, attributes indicate its owner, plus group and world permissions. The access to the object itself (e.g., the file) is controlled by similar protection bits on the directory tree above it. Again, there is the difficulty in tracking and maintaining all user permissions.

- *Password protection.* Passwords are posted with the objects and involve placing password protection controls on each object. Users must have password lists since each file they want to access is protected by a different password (although they can be context grouped).
- *Credentials.* This is data that is passed from one entity to another that is used to establish the access rights of the requester entity.
- *Labels.* These involve tokens (labels such as Secret or Top Secret) that are possessed by a user and confer specified access rights. Such labels are used to grant or deny access according to a defined policy.

The basis of access control is authenticated identification. Generally, a user claims an identity of a person or process, and then the identity needs to be proven. In manual systems, a common piece of proof is a credential carrying the photograph and signature of the individual. Authentication information must be verified before the user identification is accepted through comparison of known and presented information. The access control security mechanism only supports the access control security service.

Data Integrity Security Mechanism

This mechanism ensures that data has not been altered or destroyed. It involves either the integrity of a single data unit or field, or the integrity of a stream of data units or fields. Generally, different mechanisms are used to provide this integrity. The determination of the integrity of a single data unit involves a process at the sending entity and a process at the receiving entity. The sending entity needs to append to a data unit a quantity that is a function of the data itself. This quantity could be supplementary information such as a block check code or a cryptographic check value and may itself be encrypted. The receiving entity generates a corresponding quantity and compares it with the received quantity to determine whether the data has been modified in transit. This security mechanism alone will not protect against the replay of a single data unit. Therefore, detection mechanisms that reside within appropriate OSI layers may lead to recovery action (for example, via retransmission or error correction) at that or a higher layer.

In regard to connection-mode data transfer, protecting the integrity of a sequence of data units (i.e., protecting against incorrect ordering, losing, replaying, and inserting or modifying data) requires additionally some form of explicit ordering such as sequence numbering, time stamping, or cryptographic chaining. For connectionless-mode data transfers, time stamping may be used to provide a limited form of protection against replay of individual data units.

The data integrity mechanisms support the data integrity security service and the nonrepudiation security service.

Authentication Exchange Security Mechanism

This security mechanism provides corroboration that a peer entity is the actual entity being claimed. Examples of such mechanisms include authentication information, such as passwords, provided by a sending entity and checked by the receiving entity, and cryptographic means. The mechanism may be incorporated into a communications layer in order to provide peer-to-peer entity authentication.

Peer entity authentication is the only security service supported by the authentication exchange security mechanism.

Traffic Padding Security Mechanism

This mechanism provides a generation of spurious traffic and/or filling of protocol data units (PDUs) to achieve constant traffic rates or message length. Traffic padding can provide various levels of protection against traffic analysis. However, such a mechanism is only as effective if protected by a data confidentiality service. Traffic padding only supports the traffic flow subservice of the data confidentiality security service.

Routing Control Security Mechanism

This is a mechanism that provides for the physical selection of alternate routes that have a level of security consistent with that of the message being transacted. Such mechanisms ensure that the routes used by the data across the network are those that have been specified.

It is possible to choose routes either dynamically or by prearrangement so as to use only physically secure subnetworks or transmission links. The initiator of a connection or the sender of a connectionless message may specify routing instructions. Such instructions request what particular subnetworks or links are to be avoided. The routing control mechanism can direct the network service provider to establish a connection via a different route if persistent attacks on the initial route are detected. Data carrying certain security labels may be forbidden by the defined policy to travel through certain subnetworks not cleared at the appropriate level.

Routing control supports the connection, connectionless, and traffic flow subservices of the data confidentiality security service.

Notarization Security Mechanism

Notarization provides the needed assurance that the properties about data communicated between two or more entities, such as their integrity, origin, time and destination, are what they are claimed to be. A third-party notary provides assurance that is trusted by the communicating entities and that holds the necessary information to provide all the required assurance in a testifiable manner. Each communication channel can use digital signature, encryption, and integrity mechanisms as considered appropriate to the service being provided by the notary. The data is exchanged between the communicating entities via the protected communication channels and the notary when the notarization mechanism is invoked. Notarization only supports the nonrepudiation (origin and delivery) security service.

ALLOCATION OF SECURITY SERVICES AND SECURITY MECHANISMS

This step of the IA architecture design process involves a determination as to the allocation of the security services and security mechanisms relative to where they reside from physical and logical perspectives, their intensity or strength, and the extent of their diversity.

The Physical and Logical Residence of Security Services and Security Mechanisms

First, the residence of security services and security mechanisms can be discussed from physical and logical perspectives. From a physical perspective, security services and security mechanisms could reside within an IT device and function as a *subcomponent* of that device. An example would be an access control list (ACL) within a router device or a password file or security certificate that resides within a user workstation. Security mechanisms could reside within an IT device uniquely dedicated to performing security functionality. Firewall or encipherment (i.e., encryption) devices are examples since they are primarily dedicated to performing security functionality. There may be needs from the other less sensitive LAN(s) within the enclave to access this information. A self-protecting security device could be used to mediate the trusted transfer of this information across the two security boundaries. Within the DoD, this device is referred to as a *high-assurance guard (HAG)*. From an external perspective, the enclave should protect its boundaries from remote users, public networks, and the organizational WAN with the use of firewalls. A firewall will restrict possible enclave entry and exit by filtering based on source and originator IP addresses, network service ports, and network service applications.

From a logical perspective, the ISO 7498-2 defines a means of allocating security services and their associated security mechanisms within the OSI Reference Model.

The OSI Reference Model represents the process of communications between computing devices as consisting of seven layers. Each of the seven layers of the OSI Reference Model will be briefly described.

The Applications Layer

The Applications Layer manages the interaction between the user and the network application itself, taking commands from the user, returning error codes to the user, and passing along information retrieved from across the internetwork. Essentially, the Applications Layer generates the "output" to the consumers of information as text, numbers, pictures (images), sounds, and moving pictures (audiovisual). Applications generally fall into one of the following categories:

- *Remote computing.* Remote computing basically consists of the Telecommunications Network (telnet) Protocol. A telnet client application is used by remote users to connect to hosts executing a telnet server application. There is a conversion by the telnet client of input from the local keyboard into standardized "virtual keystrokes" on a network virtual terminal (NVT) that are interpreted by the telnet server software on the host. There is a translation for the NVT of data passed by the host to the client so the local client application can convert it into the appropriate screen output.
- *File transfer.* The ability to manage files on remote systems is one of the most basic network applications. There are two file transfer protocols in general use. These are the File Transfer Protocol (ftp) and the Trivial File Transfer Protocol (TFTP).

- *Resource sharing.* Resource sharing involves the ability of network users to share computer resources, mostly networked disk storage. For example, the UNIX-based program lpr permits the sharing of printers across a network.
- *Communications.* Generally, these communications applications relate to intersystem communication — that is, getting access to data and resources across an internetwork. Examples of such applications include electronic mail and network news (Usenet news), which support interpersonal communication — people send messages to other individuals (e-mail) or to people sharing an interest (news). Additional communication protocols, such as Internet Relay Chat and various "talk" applications, permit direct, real-time interaction between two or more individuals.
- *Data publication.* The publication of data across the Internet (or within a private intranet) is made possible by the Gopher application and especially the World Wide Web (WWW). The publication of information over a Web server has greater immediacy and accessibility than files that must be transferred from an ftp server.
- *Network management.* Network management involves a wide range of subjects: anything from workstation configuration and assignment of IP addresses through network design, architecture, and topologies. Network management functions can be generally considered as providing network service without interruption; resolving network service interruptions; avoiding network service interruptions or degradation; and deploying and maintaining network systems, hardware, and software (Loshin, 1997, pp. 72–83).

The Presentation Layer

This layer is concerned with the syntax and semantics of the information that is transmitted. That is, the layer functions as a place to translate information from disparate systems into information that all network hosts can correctly interpret. For example, there could be a need to encode data in a standard, agreed-upon way. User programs do not generally exchange random binary bit strings. They exchange items such as individual's names, dates, amounts of money, and invoices. Such items are represented as character strings, integers, floating-point numbers, and data structures composed of several simpler items. Different information systems have different codes for representing character strings (e.g., ASCII and EBCDIC), integers (e.g., ones complement and twos complement), and so on. In order to make it possible for information systems with different representations to communicate, the data structures to be exchanged can be defined in an abstract manner, along with a standard encoding to be used "on the wire." The Presentation Layer is responsible for managing these abstract data structures and converting from the representation used inside the information system to the network standard.

The Session Layer

This layer permits users on different machines to establish "sessions" between them and manages the flow and timing of a connection, determining whether information is being sent and received by the processes. A session permits ordinary data transport, as does the Transport Layer, but it also provides some enhanced services useful in some applications. A session, for example, may be used to permit a user to log into a remote time-sharing information system to transfer a file between two machines.

The Transport Layer

The basic function of this layer is to handle the interaction between processes on the destination and source hosts, mediating how the information is being sent, often doing error detection and correction on information being sent and received and determining whether information has been lost and needs to be retransmitted. The Transport Layer accepts data from the Session Layer, splits it up into smaller units if necessary, passes these units to the Network Layer, and ensures that the pieces all arrive correctly at the other end. This activity must be performed in a way that isolates the Session Layer from the inevitable changes in the hardware technology.

The Network Layer

The Network Layer actually delivers bits of information between physically connected nodes on the network and in turn supports the connection of Transport Layer processes.

The Network Layer controls the operation of the subnet. A significant issue involves how packets are routed from the source to the destination with the use of router devices. Routers could be based on static tables that rarely change. Also, the routers could be determined at the beginning of each session, such as a terminal session. Finally, routers could be highly dynamic by determining a new path for each packet based on the current network load. It is significant to note that at the Network Layer and below, there is no concern with the contents of the packages of information being moved around the network. The basic concern is with transmitting data between two network nodes. However, above the Network Node, there is no concern with the delivery of data between nodes. Instead, beginning at the Transport Layer, information is passed between programs (or processes) running on two hosts.

The Data Link Layer

The Data Link Layer is responsible for adding reliability and retransmission functions, for example, with the Ethernet specification of how electrical impulses are encoded with data and supports the connection of Network Layer entities. This is accomplished by taking a raw transmission facility and transforming it into a line that appears free of transmission errors to the Network Layer. The sender breaks the input data up into data frames (generally a few hundred bytes), transmits the frames sequentially, and processes the acknowledgment frames sent back by the receiver. The Data Link Layer is responsible for creating and recognizing frame boundaries since the Physical Layer merely accepts and transmits a stream of bits without any regard to meaning or structure.

The Physical Layer

The Physical Layer transmits raw bits of information over a communications channel. Essentially, this layer handles the transmission and reception of electrical impulses (or another appropriate signal, depending on the medium). This is accomplished, for example, on an Ethernet network by the network itself and network adapter (network interface) cards that are attached to each network device. Information is passed physically from one interface to another, and the Physical Layer provides the means to create links between data link entities. Issues here are how many volts should be used to represent a 1 and how many for a 0, how many microseconds a bit lasts, whether transmission may proceed simultaneously in both directions, how the initial connection is established and how it is disconnected when both sides are finished, and how many pins the network connector has and the use of each pin.

The Transmission Control Protocol/Internet Protocol (TCP/IP) is another model that defines the communication process. The TCP/IP does not follow the ISO standard because neither a presentation layer nor a session layer is individually defined. TCP/IP applications provide the services of these two layers as necessary. In regard to the data link and physical layers, TCP/IP does not provide any specific protocol but instead interfaces with whatever protocols are available.

Security services could be allocated at each of the seven layers of the OSI Reference Model as indicated below:

- *Application Layer.* All of the previously specified security services could be allocated and reside at this layer.
- *Presentation Layer.* Connection data confidentiality, connectionless data confidentiality, and selective field data confidentiality could be allocated and reside at this layer.
- *Session Layer.* No security services are applicable.
- *Transport Layer.* Authentication (peer entity and data origin), access control, connection data confidentiality, connectionless data confidentiality, connection integrity with and without recovery, and connectionless integrity could be allocated and reside at this layer.
- *Network Layer.* Authentication (peer entity and data origin), access control, connection confidentiality, connectionless confidentiality, traffic flow confidentiality, connection integrity without recovery, and connectionless integrity could be allocated and reside at this layer.
- *Data Link Layer.* Connection confidentiality and connectionless confidentiality could be allocated and reside at this layer.
- *Physical Layer.* Connection confidentiality and traffic flow confidentiality could be allocated and reside at this layer.

The Intensity of the Security Services and Security Mechanisms

The organization's IA architecture could consist of a wide range of security services and security mechanisms. However, the services and mechanisms could be used at varying levels of intensity based on the severity of the threat and the criticality and sensitivity of the object that is threatened. For example, authentication could be at a basic level that consists of a user identifier and password. However, if justified by the threat and sensitivity and criticality of an object, authentication could involve using, for example, digital certificates, cryptographic algorithms with long key lengths, and biometric methods. Also, security service and security mechanism intensity could be increased by using them in granular ways. For example, an access control mechanism could be used to control access at the workstation, network, directory, file, and file element levels.

The Diversity of the Security Services and Security Mechanisms

From an IA perspective, security services and security mechanisms should exist within a broad range of organizational IT devices rather than being concentrated in one or a few devices. Diversity is the basis for the Defense in Depth strategy. This diversity can be achieved by the allocation of security services and security mechanisms within workstations, servers, routers, firewalls, and HAGs. Also, Chapter 3 ("Determining the Organization's IA Baseline") discussed the concepts of physical and virtual boundaries of organizations. There needs to be a consideration of the allocations of security services and security mechanisms relative to these boundaries to achieve diversity as indicated below:

- *Organizational WAN boundary protection.* The boundaries between the organizational WAN and any public networks require protection. This would involve the use of firewall and encipherment devices as well as security services and security mechanisms within router and switch devices.
- *Organizational enclave boundary protection.* An *enclave* is an organizational facility. The boundaries of an enclave can be addressed from both internal and external perspectives. Internally, enclaves may want to isolate their multiple LANs from one another. For example, one LAN may be authorized to store, process, and communicate highly sensitive organizational information.
- *Organizational computing environment boundary protection.* Workstations and servers residing within the enclave need to be individually protected from threats from both within and outside the enclave. Therefore, security services and security mechanisms need to be allocated to these devices, such as authentication and access control.

Security Management Component

IA architecture should include a means to manage the security services and security mechanisms that reside within the organization's IA baseline. Generally, this involves the establishment of procedures to configure and to control the access to security mechanisms such as ACLs, firewalls, routers, switches, auditing, virtual private networks (VPNs), certificates and key distribution, and virus scanners.

The Integration of Physical Security, Procedural Security, and Logical Security

Up to this point, the organization has addressed the design of its logical (i.e., technical) architecture. However, the IA architecture must be designed to integrate three levels of security to control the execution of transactions that result in the flow of information (i.e., in hardcopy and logical states), people, and IT material (i.e., IT hardware equipment such as workstations, servers, and routers) through known access paths within the physical and virtual boundaries of an organization. Two additional levels of security need to be developed. These involve physical security and procedural security.

Physical security involves the protection of the facilities, hardware, and software of the organization's IA baseline from threats that could cause damage, theft, failure to operate, inappropriate modification, and misuse. Procedural security entails the establishment of officially documented and approved procedures for controlling the flow of information, people, and material. Procedures involving the proper hiring, processing, and assignment of authorizations to organizational personnel are aspects associated with procedural security as well as procedures for the proper accountability, classification, and labeling of information and material. Logical security is the technical level of security that involves the computer hardware and software that is responsible for controlling the flow of information in a logical (i.e., digitized) state within the organization's IA baseline and between the IA baseline and external entities (e.g., customers, suppliers, joint venture organizations, public networks, and so forth).

THE IMPLEMENTATION OF THE ORGANIZATION'S IA ARCHITECTURE

The IA architecture can be implemented within an organization by using a process consisting of three steps. First, the goal IA architecture must be developed. This is likely to be an iterative process with trade-offs among functionality, performance, security, operational risk, and technological risk. Candidate architectures will be evaluated against one another based on IA requirements, costs, and policy. Iterations of the IA architecture will be developed until a balance has been achieved. The output of this effort is a written IA architecture. This output will be used as input to the system development or acquisition program.

Second, after the establishment of a goal IA architecture, a strategy must be developed that will allow the organization's IA baseline to transition to the goal IA architecture. The transition strategy is a set of interim, achievable incremental steps toward the goal IA architecture. This strategy should be based on projections of the available technology and the current and projected statuses of the IA baseline.

Third, an enforcement mechanism should be developed to manage and control changes to the goal IA architecture and to provide a means for the goal IA architecture and transition strategy to evolve to accommodate changes in requirements, threats, and technology. There are two approaches to consider for managing the configuration of the organization's IA architecture. One approach is to incorporate configuration control of the IA architecture into the organization's overall configuration management process as described in Chapter 10 ("Layer 5: Configuration Management"). The organization's IA management would participate as a member of whatever group was responsible for

Configuration Management but would not necessarily have full authority in terms of managing the changes to the IA architecture. The other approach is to establish a separate and distinct configuration management process for the IA architecture. This approach differs from the other approach in that IA management would have complete responsibility for controlling changes to the IA architecture. The basic objective of both approaches is to control changes to the goal IA architecture as well as review appropriate system development efforts to assure that changes to these systems would not be inconsistent with the goal IA architecture.

SUMMARY

The IA architecture is critical to the security of an organization since it provides its IA capabilities in the form of security services and security mechanisms that are then allocated throughout IT devices within the physical and virtual boundaries of the organization. This allocation of security services and security mechanisms provides a significant approach for the implementation of an organization's Defense in Depth strategy. The ISO Standard 7498-2, Part 2, "Security Architecture," provides the standard for building the IA architecture.

REFERENCES

Graham, B., *TCP/IP Addressing—Designing and Optimizing Your IP Addressing Scheme,* 2nd ed. San Diego: Academic Press, 2001.

International Standards Organization, *Information Processing Systems—Open Systems International—Basic Reference Model, Part 2: Security Architecture.* ISO 7498-2.

Loshin, P., *TCP/IP Clearly Understood,* 2nd ed. San Diego: Academic Press, 1997.

Minoli, D., "Building the New OSI Security Architecture." *Network Computing* (June 1992): 136–148.

Nichols, R. K., D. J. Ryan, and J. J. C. H. Ryan, *Defending Your Digital Assets Against Hackers, Crackers, Spies, and Thieves.* New York: McGraw-Hill Companies, 2000.

Press, B., and M. Press, *Networking By Example.* Indianapolis, IN: Que Corporation, 2000.

Schein, P. G. *Windows 2000 Security Design.* Scottsdale, AZ: The Coriolis Group, 2000.

Taylor, E. *The Network Architecture Design Handbook.* New York: McGraw-Hill, 1998.

9. Layer 4: Operational Security Administration

CHAPTER OBJECTIVES

- Recognize various types of information system users
- Describe examples of rules of behavior
- Understand security issues associated with general users
- Understand the insider threat associated with privileged users

ADMINISTERING INFORMATION SYSTEMS SECURITY

Introduction

A fairly comprehensive checklist is provided in the Appendix of this book as a mnemonic for the IA practitioner. Anyone can follow a checklist to secure a system. The real challenge is obtaining (and maintaining) a level of system security while it is managed, maintained, and used by people.

People

The *good* news is that a successful IA program depends upon the involvement and cooperation of people. The *bad* news is that a successful IA program depends upon the involvement and cooperation of people. These people come with varying backgrounds, experience, skill levels, and capabilities; unique personal issues; and even different moral values. The challenge for the organization is to take all these uniquenesses and channel them into a cohesive team that works together to achieve common objectives. It is sometimes likened to herding cats.

An effective security training and awareness program is essential to ensuring that the organization's IA policies and procedures are understood. You can't expect people to follow rules when you do not first explain what those rules are. This training should be relevant and tailored to the various roles that people take in regard to the use of information systems.

General Users

All personnel with any level of access to the computing environment fall under the category of "general users." The organization must explicitly state the policy for the general use of all information system assets. This policy should unequivocally state:

(a) What the general user is authorized and/or required to do
  - Using the system for only official or authorized purposes
  - Protecting the system from unauthorized use by others
  - Protecting their authenticator (i.e., password)
  - Ensure proper handling, marking, controlling, storage, and destruction of information
(b) What behavior or activity is unauthorized
  - Exceeding authorized roles and privileges
  - Introducing malicious code or unauthorized software or hardware
  - Circumventing, straining, or defeating security mechanisms
  - Relocating or modifying equipment or connectivity
(c) What disciplinary action will result from failure to comply with the policy
(d) How and to whom to report security incidents

Rules of Behavior

Each user needs to understand and acknowledge the good security practices and expected behavior that the organization demands regarding a variety of conditions. These rules should be written and should conclude with an acknowledgment statement. Each employee should be required to read the rules of behavior and sign the acknowledgment statement. This should be done as a condition of employment, prior to receiving system access, and administered at least annually thereafter. These rules should address:

- Individual accountability
- Official use and authorized purposes
- General and privileged users
- Incident reporting
- Internet access
- Working from home
- Traveling employees
- Dial-in access
- Copyright and licensing

Remote and Deployed Users

The term "user" is often used to describe anyone that has access to an information system, but rarely do all users fall into one general category. Some employees may conduct official work from home; some may travel on temporary duty assignments requiring access back to the organization's servers from their hotel room; still others require complete administrator privileges to conduct on-line maintenance from a remote location. As the workplace and its support functions become more virtual in nature, new challenges are created for the IA manager.

Policies must address rules and procedures for:

- Establishing a modem connection
- Working from home, if authorized
- Establishing a remote account
- Remote privileged access, if allowed

Privileged Users

A privileged user is a user who has been authorized to control, monitor, or administer an information system. He or she may have "superuser," root access, administrator, operator, isso, or equivalent access that allows total or near-total control of an information system. In some cases, the privileges may allow only execution of select root-level commands (e.g., to perform backup or a system reboot) or only be allowed for certain periods (e.g., during periodic maintenance or a system installation). Examples of privileged users include:

- System administrators
- Help desk personnel
- System developers and integrators
- Security administrators/ISSO/ISSM
- Webmasters
- Maintenance personnel

Privileged users represent the biggest insider threat to any information system or network, simply by virtue of their access and the resultant damage that could occur through inadvertent or malicious misuse. For this reason it is imperative that these individuals be properly screened and trained and their privileged use properly monitored.

Screening. A skilled resume writer can embellish or fabricate work experience, training, and educational credentials, making a below-average system administrator appear to be a technical wizard. In the same way, few applicants will voluntarily disclose derogatory information from their past. It may be prudent to conduct a security background check or, at minimum, a security screening interview or other suitability investigation to help identify behavioral patterns that would categorize a prospective employee as an unacceptable risk.

Most applicants only furnish references that will be complimentary. Check out the references that the applicant provides; then ask those references for additional names of individuals who could shed some light on the character of the applicant, and so on. After going down three layers or more into this process, you may begin to put together a more complete picture of the applicant's behavior patterns than the original references would have provided.

These checks should, obviously, be done before the individual is given full access to any sensitive position or authorized role that enables him/her to bypass security controls. Thorough background checks take time, however. If it is not possible to totally restrict access to a system before the background investigation is completed or before all prerequisite training can be administered, restrictions must be placed on the individual's access to prevent unrestrained or unlimited privileged access to system or network devices.

Screening is important not only during the hiring phase, but afterwards as well. For national-level security clearances, for example, the U.S. government requires a periodic review every five years. Some organizations also require periodic or random polygraphs. Such reviews or examinations serve as both integrity checks to reveal existing behavior problems and deterrents to discourage the employee who is contemplating misbehavior.

Below are personnel actions that are reportable and should require a management decision to permit continued access to systems or networks with sensitive or classified information:

- Serious unlawful acts
- Indications of emotional, mental, or personality disorders
- Unreported foreign travel
- Close and continuing association with non-U.S. citizens
- Alcohol or drug abuse
- Unexplained affluence or financial irresponsibility
- Willful violation of security regulations
- Coercion, blackmail, or recruitment attempts
- Unauthorized disclosure or news leaks

Training.   Training is critical for privileged users — not only for security training to ensure that policy is understood, but to obtain a working knowledge of the systems themselves. Too often, users are granted privileges to perform functions for which they are inadequately trained. The organization should consider a policy to establish and certify minimum training and experience levels as a prerequisite for additional privileges. An understanding of security policy requirements, technical security mechanisms, and operational security procedures should be a part of the certification standard. This is especially important as advances in technology have opened up privileged access IT roles (e.g., Webmaster) that may or may not be located within the traditional IT department.

Least Privilege and Separation of Roles.   Most operating systems enforce some kind of separation of roles between a general user and a privileged user. The privileged role (i.e., root access) often enables the superuser complete control of a host and the ability to circumvent security mechanisms. For example, the privileges required for a system administrator to back up a server may also allow the same administrator the privileges necessary to read a user's mail.

Some OSs, however, provide for further separation of privileges within the superuser role. By allowing a systems administrator to execute only the superuser commands required and by preventing execution of all others, the principle of least privilege is enforced and a type of compartmentation has occurred. In the first case, the systems administrator receives only the privileges necessary to perform his or her duties and is, thereby, theoretically limited to a subset of all commands; in the latter case, the compartmentation forces a separation of duties or functions that could provide necessary checks and balances. A system administrator and security administrator, for example, would perform complementary, but distinctly different, roles. Such separation of functions becomes more crucial as the level of trust in the system increases.

Prevention. In addition to separating roles and limiting access in an effort to avoid giving a system administrator carte blanche privileges, vulnerability assessment software can also be used to prevent unauthorized access. These tools can help identify weaknesses in operating systems and applications that, if exploited, would enable a user to exceed authorized access. Such vulnerabilities should be mitigated, preferably through technical countermeasures. When procedural security measures are used to mitigate risk, the IA manager will find that effective enforcement is greatly dependent upon review of reliable audits to identify offenders, followed by swift and decisive action by management.

Limitation. The number of privileged users should be limited to the absolute minimum number required to perform the duties. This is often a big challenge for the IA manager. For example, systems operations will want to ensure that sufficient numbers of administrators have superuser privileges in order to provide quick on-site response to system issues without resorting to on-call support. For the IA manager this may mean having to authorize more privileged user access than desired to accommodate shift workers, maintenance personnel, etc. Regardless, the IA manager must determine the threshold of his/her ability to control and manage privileged access; ensure that the system and network operations people understand that limitation; and work with management to either keep the numbers of privileged users within that manageable number or increase IA resources to accommodate additional privileged users.

Accountability. Privileged users should be held accountable at any and all times for use of their access. Limitations on overt access must be defined and enforced. For example, privileged users should not be allowed to log onto the system using a generic account (e.g., "root," "admin," "isso") but should log onto the system with a unique identifier. If possible, technical measures should be taken to ensure that all privileged access is audited. If a system administrator executes root privileges from within a shell, the events may not be audited.

Detection. Unauthorized use must be detected. It does no good to collect audits without review and analysis of reliable and nonrefutable audit records. Random or periodic screening interviews may act as a deterrent for the user who would contemplate misuse of privileges. Regardless, all privileged use should be regularly monitored; system administration logs and audits of privileged use should be reviewed daily. The collection of audits should be centralized and correlated for analysis.

Deterrence. Privileges must be used to perform authorized actions only. The degree to which an organization responds to abuse of privileges will set the precedent for all other users. Ignore the problem or deal inconsistently with abusers, and your ability to enforce proper use of privileged access will be severely hampered. The abuse of privileges should be taken seriously and dealt with harshly. A bored system administrator, for example, who abuses his privileged access by snooping through the CEO's mail should not be tolerated any more than a janitor who rifles through file cabinets and desks just because he has a key to the office. Sharing or compromising a privileged account or password is also something that should be dealt with severely.

Outsourcing Concerns.   The increasing dependence upon outsourcing contractor support has also complicated security management and added to the insider threat.

> The American workplace is undergoing tremendous social and technological changes. Increased pressure to minimize costs has led both the private and public sectors to reduce full-time personnel and outsource many functions previously handled in-house. This has resulted in an increasingly disgruntled and transient work force, and provided "insider" access privileges to many people who are not direct employees of the organization. Technological advances have created opportunities for further cost savings, enabling interconnection of critical information systems and networks among government agencies and businesses and their contractors, vendors, and customers. In this environment, it is increasingly difficult to distinguish one's own facilities, networks, and information systems from those of contractors, vendors, customers, and business partners. It is even more difficult to know who has been authorized to access facilities or systems — an organization may have unwittingly given access to someone they just fired, and who now works for their vendor. As a consequence, critical information systems may be more vulnerable to individuals who can use their physical or electronic access to attack or exploit information systems — employees as well as vendors, contractors, customers, and business partners (NSTAC NSIE, 1998, p. 2).

As some organizations realize the difficulty of keeping trained and qualified IA staff, the demand for outsourcing managed security services has grown. Such companies can attract highly qualified security professionals and provide a range of services to include 24/7 monitoring of their clients' networks. The risk in this approach is the organization's dependency upon the service provider. In one case, a network security service provider suddenly went out of business, leaving their 200 customers without security services. These customers included a well-known publishing operation, "several large health-care institutions and banks" (Berinato, 2001, p. 1).

Security Operations

Security Administration Essentials

- Employ the least privilege principle; limit privileged access to the absolute minimum privileges and number of individuals necessary to accomplish the job.
- Electronically display a legally approved warning banner stating the terms for system access and the potential ramifications of misuse.
- Assign and train a security point of contact for each system or set of systems.
- Keep antiviral software definitions and vendor patches up-to-date.

- Keep operating systems and applications current with latest updates (e.g., patches, service packs, hotfixes).
- Stay abreast of known system and networking vulnerabilities.
- Regularly perform host-based and network-based vulnerability scans and penetration testing on "clients, servers, switches, routers, firewalls, and intrusion detection systems" (NSA SNAC 2001, p. 8).
- Ensure that audits are operational and collecting required events for operating systems and server-level applications.
- Force frequent password changes and good password selection; periodically run password cracking programs against password files to identify easily guessed passwords.
- Train users to "not open e-mail attachments or run programs unless the source and intent are confirmed and trusted" (NSA SNAC, 2001, p. 7).
- Disallow anonymous, guest, shared accounts and multiple logons.
- Configure the system to implement security features, tighten security controls, and turn off vendor default settings/accounts (e.g., guest accounts).
- Eliminate all unnecessary network protocols and connections; disable unneeded services (e.g., Web, mail, print, file sharing); block e-mail attachment types that may carry malicious code threats (e.g., .bas, .exe, .vbs).
- Review system logs and audit trails for anomalies; review logs of privileged access daily.
- Monitor and filter for active content.
- Prohibit unauthorized monitoring and use of sniffers.
- "Explicitly block the printer ports at the boundary router/firewall and disable these services if not needed" (NSA SNAC, 2001, p. 8).
- Check periodically for unauthorized modem connectivity.
- Prohibit read–write access via Simple Network Management Protocol (SNMP) and disable SNMP where it is not needed.
- Provide security training and awareness for general and privileged users to include security incident reporting and emergency response.
- Control, label, and protect removable media; where possible, limit the use and proliferation of access to removable media drives (e.g., floppy drives, CD-ROM drives).
- Implement automated and manual procedures for screen saving the monitor during periods of nonuse when still logged on.
- Implement security tools to help flag security problem areas: Enterprise security management/administration, enterprise security policy enforcement, intrusion detection, etc.

Operational Security Checklist

See Appendix I ("Information Assurance Self-Inspection Checklist").

SUMMARY

The primary ingredient in the success (or failure) of operational security administration is people. Computer users come in all shapes and sizes but for security purposes are usually divided up according to privileged access: general users and privileged users. The latter group represents the largest insider threat to the confidentiality, integrity, and availability of your organization's information. Training, least privilege, and separation of roles help mitigate the risk that privileged users bring because of ignorance or negligence. Accountability and detection can be used as a deterrent for those users whose disdain for security would cause them to contemplate malicious acts. The risks of outsourcing administrative security services must be carefully weighed because of the prerequisite privileges and dependencies. Regardless, good security administration practices are imperative for improving and maintaining the IA posture of any organization.

REFERENCES

Berinato, Scott, "Security Outsourcing: Exposed!" *CIO Magazine* (August 1, 2001).

Johnson, John D., "Building Information Assurance." SecurityPortal article (www.securityportal.com) (December 7, 2000).

Letteer, Ray, "Information System Security Education, Training, & Awareness for Web Administrators — An Integral Part of Defense in Depth." Article from SANS Institute Resources Information Security Reading Room (September 16, 2000).

National Computer Security Center, "A Guide to Understanding Configuration Management in Trusted Systems." NCSC-TG-006-88 (March 1988).

National Security Agency (NSA) Systems and Networks Attack Center (SNAC), "The 60 Minute Network Security Guide (The First Steps Towards a Secure Network Environment)," version 1.0 (October 16, 2001).

National Security Telecommunications Advisory Committee (NSTAC) Network Security Information Exchanges (NSIE) Insider Threat Workshop After-Action Report: "The Insider Threat to Information Systems: A Framework for Understanding and Managing the Insider Threat in Today's Business Environment" (June 18, 1998).

SANS, *Roadmap to Security Tools and Services*, 5th ed. (Summer 2001).

10. Layer 5: Configuration Management

CHAPTER OBJECTIVES

- Provide an understanding of the necessity of establishing a formal structure and process for managing changes to the configuration of the organization's IA baseline
- Provide a basic formal approach for managing changes to the configuration of the organization's IA baseline

THE NECESSITY OF MANAGING CHANGES TO THE IA BASELINE

Chapter 3 ("Determining the Organization's IA Baseline") defined the concept of an organization's IA baseline in terms of its physical and virtual boundaries. Five significant factors could result in changes to the organization's IA baseline.

First, there are frequent changes in organizational IT equipment and facilities. In terms of IT equipment, the organization replaces its existing hardware and software with upgraded versions of currently installed products or completely new products. For example, at the time that this book was written, organizations were replacing Windows NT with Windows 2000 and XP. In terms of facilities, the interior and exterior of existing organizational facilities undergo changes over time. These changes could result in the movement of people and IT equipment to new locations within the facilities. Also, organizations acquire or construct new facilities to better achieve their objectives.

Second, changes in the organization's business process model may necessitate changes to the IA baseline. The organization's technical (productive), political, and cultural subsystems will change over time. For example, as the organization expands or reduces the bounds of its geopolitical operational environment, its IA baseline must change accordingly to meet new requirements for information and services.

Third, the discovery of security vulnerabilities will require changes to existing hardware and software within the IA baseline. For example, software patches are made available by software vendors to correct discovered vulnerabilities.

Fourth, generally, the technical knowledge of people expands over time. More and more people are capable of writing software programs such as scripts and possibly entering them into the IA baseline. The Internet provides people with an ever-expanding source of free software that could be downloaded either at employee homes or within the organization and entered into the IA baseline. Also, employees could be sharing these software products with other employees within the organization. There is a risk that malicious software could be entered into the IA baseline.

Fifth, organizations have substantially increased their use of commercial "off-the-shelf" software products. Such software could be a source of malicious code if proper controls are not taken to control its entry into the IA baseline. Also, there is the issue of what has been termed "outsourcing." Organizations have become increasingly dependent on other organizations to administer and operate their IA baselines and to develop and install new applications. This dependency does result in cost savings but also introduces risks that need to be considered.

As indicated in Chapter 5 ("The Organization's IA Posture"), the extent of the organization's knowledge concerning the existence of the physical and logical boundaries of its IA baseline does directly affect its IA posture. An organization is operating with a lower IA posture when it has little or no accurate information concerning its IA baseline. Therefore, there is a need for a structured process that will provide accountability by identifying, documenting, and controlling changes to the organization's IA baseline.

CONFIGURATION MANAGEMENT: AN APPROACH FOR MANAGING IA BASELINE CHANGES

Configuration management can provide a process for managing changes to the organization's IA baseline by applying technical and administrative direction and oversight to the following:

1. Identification and documentation of the functional and physical characteristics of each element of the IA baseline
2. Control of changes to those characteristics
3. Recording and reporting of change processing and implementation status

The intent of configuration management is to:

1. Provide a mechanism to ensure the documentation of all changes
2. Anticipate the effects of changes on cost/schedule as a basis for informed approval/disapproval of proposed changes
3. Maintain the integrity of the schedule
4. Maintain up-to-date documentation on the statuses of proposed changes
5. Ensure that all changes are communicated to the appropriate organizational personnel

The National Computer Security Center has published a document that provides a guide for understanding configuration management. This document is entitled "A Guide to Understanding Configuration Management in Trusted Systems" (NCSC-TG-006). Its focus is configuration management at the individual information system level. However, the document's concepts and methodology can also be applied at the organizational level.

Organizational configuration management can be defined from structural and functional perspectives. Structurally, a body of qualified individuals will need to be formed to provide overall management of the organization's configuration management process and to render decisions related to configuration changes of the IA baseline. This body is generally called a Configuration Control Board (CCB). Functionally, configuration management consists of configuration identification, configuration control, configuration status accounting, and configuration auditing.

Configuration Control Board (CCB)

The CCB is responsible for the overall management of changes to the IA baseline. This board is headed by a chairperson, who is responsible for scheduling meetings and for giving the final approval on any proposed changes to the IA baseline. The membership of this body can vary and include technical as well as nontechnical individuals. At some point, the functional requirements; initial and ongoing operational and maintenance (O&M) costs; staffing and administrative overheads; and training prerequisites must be weighed when considering additions or modifications to the IA baseline. The organizational IA manager must be a voting member of the CCB and render the IA position as to the security implications of proposed changes.

The configuration control process begins with the documentation of a need to change one or more IA baseline elements. As will be subsequently discussed, this need results from a "Request for Change" (RFC) or a discrepancy report. These documents should include justifications for the change, all of the affected items and documents, and the proposed solution. The RFC and the discrepancy report should be recorded in order to provide a way of tracking all proposed changes to the IA baseline and to ensure that duplicate RFCs and discrepancy reports are not processed. When these documents are recorded, they should be distributed for analysis by the CCB, who will review and approve or disapprove the documents depending upon whether or not the change is viewed as a necessary and feasible change.

Once a decision has been reached regarding any modifications to the IA baseline, the CCB is responsible for prioritizing the approved modifications to ensure that the most important are implemented first. Also, the CCB is responsible for assigning an authority to perform the change and for ensuring that the configuration documentation is updated properly. From an IA perspective, there must be a specified number of individuals that have been formally approved to change the components of the IA baseline.

Upon the completion of the change, the CCB is responsible for verifying that the change has been properly incorporated and that only the approved change has been incorporated. Testing may be required to ensure that the functionality of the IA baseline is not adversely affected after the change is completed. The CCB should review the test results and then render a final decision.

Configuration Identification

Chapter 3 defined the concept of an IA baseline. The basic function of configuration identification is to establish accountability for the facilities and IT equipment (hardware and software) that form the physical and virtual boundaries of the organization's IA baseline. The facilities and IT equipment should be assigned unique identifiers (e.g., serial numbers, names) for purposes of identification. This assures the proper accountability for IA baseline items. Configuration items may be given an identifier through a random distribution process, but it is more useful for the configuration identifier to describe the item it identifies. Selecting different fields of the configuration identifier to represent characteristics of the configuration item is one method of accomplishing this. The U.S. social security number is a "configuration identifier" we all have that uses such a system. The different fields of the number identify where we applied for the social security card, hence describing a little bit about ourselves. As the configuration identifier relates to the IA baseline, one field should identify the item (printer, CPU, monitor, and so forth), another field the version the item belongs to, the version of software that it is, or its interface with other configuration items. When using a numbering scheme like this, a change to a configuration item should result in the production of a new configuration identifier. This new identifier should be produced by an alteration or addition to the existing configuration identifier. A new version of a software program should not be identified by the same configuration item number as the original program. By treating the two versions as distinct configuration items, it is possible to perform line-by-line comparisons.

Configuration Control

Configuration Control involves the systematic evaluation, coordination, approval, or disapproval of proposed changes to the organization's IA baseline. The methodology for controlling changes to the IA baseline will be discussed from two perspectives. First, there may be requests from within the organization to change the IA baseline. These requests could be formally recorded and submitted using a "Request for Change" (RFC) form. Second, discrepancy reports could be generated within the organization concerning the adverse condition of IA baseline elements such as printers, operating systems, and monitors. Change requests and discrepancy reports will be separately discussed.

Change Requests

Three aspects of change requests will be described. These involve a means of classifying change requests, a means of defining the various elements of the IA baseline that are subject to change, and a means of prioritizing changes.

Change Classifications

There should be a method for classifying the RFCs so that changes can be appropriately assessed in terms of technical impact, cost, and time. Three classes could be used for the RFCs. A judgment will need to be made as to whether the IA baseline is affected by the change. If not, the RFC is classified as either Class I or Class II. The classes are defined as follows:

- *Class I.* A Class I RFC is a change having major direct impact on the organization's resources and/or user functionality and user operations. Examples of Class I changes are:

  Organizational level IT architecture and standards

  Intersystem and interapplication interfaces

  IT policies

- *Class II.* A Class II RFC is a change to automated information system (AIS) network operational documents, operational hardware and software and communications, operational policy, and requirements. Examples are as follows:

  Operational source code

  Operational AIS configuration

  Operational infrastructure configuration

  Commercial software registry and license management

  Operating system or application anomalies

  Organizational IT architecture baseline drawings/database

- *Class III.* Class III RFCs refer to issues that do not fall within the Class I or Class II criteria. Class III RFCs do not affect the AIS network or users within the AIS network. Examples include:

  Changes to documentation that do not change functionality or the configuration of a system or baseline (administrative changes)

  Changes to hardware settings or software variables that do not affect the operation or function of the hardware, software, or communications, or supporting documentation

  Changes to drawings, sketches, or software code headers that correct information already present in the document or program

  Installing or configuring new equipment or software that does not affect the interface characteristics with other configuration items

Change Categories

In addition to classifying RFCs, a categorization of the changes must also be accomplished. RFCs are placed into one of the seven categories listed below:

(a) *Design.* Applies to the design of the system or software
(b) *Requirement.* Applies to the functionality or performance of the system or software
(c) *Software.* Applies to Operating Systems or applications
(d) *Database.* Applies to a database or data file
(e) *Interface.* Applies to inter-system and inter-application interfaces
(f) *Documentation.* Applies to design, development, user, or other support manuals
(g) *Communication.* Applies to network configuration items, such as bridges, routers, gateways

Prioritization of Changes

The changes that affect an organization's IA baseline can be categorized in a variety of ways. The intent of the categorization is to provide a means of prioritizing identified requirements for change. These requirements for change can be recorded using a predefined Request for Change (RFC) form. Basically, there can be three priorities of change that could affect the configuration of the organization's IA baseline. Each of these priorities of changes will be individually discussed below:

Emergency Changes.   A change is prioritized as emergency if any of the following apply:

(a) Change must be made to the IA baseline which, if not accomplished, would seriously affect organizational operations.
(b) A situation which is preventing the operation of the organization or has the potential to prevent its operation must be corrected.
(c) A hazardous condition which may result in fatal or serious injury to personnel, or extensive damage or destruction to equipment must be corrected. (A hazardous condition usually will require withdrawing the configuration item from service temporarily, suspension of operation, or discontinuing of further testing or development pending resolution of the condition.)
(d) Change must be implemented as soon as possible.

Urgent Changes.   A change is prioritized as urgent if any of the following apply:

(a) If not accomplished expeditiously, the change may seriously compromise the mission effectiveness of the organization.
(b) The change will correct a potentially hazardous condition, the uncorrected existence of which could result in injury to personnel or damage to equipment. (A potentially hazardous condition compromises safety and embodies risk, but permits continued use of the affected item within reasonable limits provided the operator has been informed of the hazard and appropriate precautions have been defined and distributed to the users.)
(c) The change is needed to meet significant contractual requirements.
(d) The change must be implemented within five days of initiation.

Routine Changes.   A change is prioritized as routine when the criteria of emergency or urgent are not applicable. Routine changes are processed under normal operating conditions.

Discrepancies/Corrective Actions

The IA baseline could also change as a result of reported discrepancies. However, depending on the nature of the discrepancy, an IA baseline change may not be required. If an IA baseline change is required, a corrective action is identified. A corrective action is a change that does not meet the RFC criteria specified under Class I, II, or III. The following are examples of discrepancies:

- Hardware or communications failure affecting functionality (repairs)
- Inoperative CPU, printer, monitor, transceiver, or cable as a result of a trouble ticket
- Operating system failure affecting functionality
- Correction of document anomalies such as incorrect spelling or inaccurate information

Discrepancy reports are assigned categories based on the initiator's need for corrective action implementation. Categories are required in order to effectively manage the use of resources (people, equipment, money, etc.) and to implement the recommended corrective action. There are four categories identified for discrepancies.

- *Category I (Emergency).* A hardware or software problem that prevents users from accessing or using AIS network resources and cannot be resolved using standard operating or recovery procedures, or that has a severe operational impact. These problems must be corrected immediately.
- *Category II (High Priority).* These involve a hardware or software problem that:

    Prevents users from accessing or using IT resources, but can be resolved using standard operating or recovery procedures, and that occurs frequently (daily or every few days) for short durations, causing severe degradation of services to the user.

    Interrupts processing for users and occurs frequently (daily or every few days) for short durations, or any problem that damages the integrity of user data. This type of problem does not have a workaround and causes severe degradation of services to the user.

    Jeopardizes AIS network operations.

    Category II problems must be corrected as soon as possible with the corrective action implemented on an emergency basis.
- *Category III (Priority).* The same as Category II, except the problem occurs less frequently (less than once a week for short durations) causing minor degradations of service to users. Category III discrepancies should be corrected as soon as possible but no later than three weeks after initiation.
- *Category IV (Routine).* A discrepancy that is minor, does not fit into Categories I through III, and has an easy workaround. Category IV discrepancies are corrected under normal operating conditions and only after discrepancies of a higher priority have been corrected.

Change Controls

From a security perspective, there are potential vulnerabilities associated with the implementation of both the change request and discrepancy reporting methods of changing the organization's IA baseline. Therefore, some degree of control needs to be maintained over these changes. For example, operational software (versus software in a state of development) that appears to be both error-free and meeting user needs is often modified to meet new requirements. Strict administrative and organizational controls must be employed during this modification process to ensure that such modifications are properly requested, approved, coded, tested, documented, and authorized for the operation. Such controls will also help to prevent unauthorized and potentially fraudulent changes. Each step in the modification process (from initiation, design, programming, testing, and documenting through implementation) requires its own procedures and rules to protect the integrity of the software. There are risks associated with making changes to the organization's IA baseline. These risks include undocumented changes, untested changes, and the inclusion of unauthorized changes. There are recommended controls for mitigating such risks.

Proper Authorization

There should be written evidence that the requested change has been properly initiated and approved by the appropriate user department. This reduces the possibility of authorized requests being submitted through normal modification channels. Two signatures should be a requirement — those of the initiator and a supervisor who has been authorized to approve such modifications. Another person could be responsible for the coordination of all change requests. A change request procedure with a single focal point helps to ensure that two people are not initiating incompatible changes. A master change schedule should be maintained and used both to manage changes and to minimize the number and severity of problems and disruptions. Requests should be prioritized based on technical and operational impact considerations.

Independent Testing or Verification of Modifications

There is a need for an independent or "third party" review of the modifications that are intended for the elements of the IA baseline. For example, in terms of software maintenance, the integrity of source code changes can be improved if programmers are required to submit their debugged source program changes to an independent party such as a Quality Assurance (QA) function after they have been tested and approved by the user. The QA group reviews the changes and applies them to copies of the production source programs. Also, QA maintains an audit trail of changes for inclusion in the program documentation folder. Although the QA group cannot review and understand all program changes, its presence minimizes the likelihood that unauthorized code will be inserted in production copies of source programs. Whenever a program is moved into the production source code library, a compiled object listing of that program should be moved to the production object code library. The optimal procedure automatically compiles an object code module whenever a source program is moved into production.

Documentation Control

QA should be responsible for reviewing documentation updates resulting from changes to the IA baseline. Prior to implementation of the modification, all required changes to documentation must be submitted and approved by QA. Without this formal acceptance of updated documentation, the modification to the IA baseline should not be considered complete.

Independent Implementation

The required change to the IA baseline should be implemented by an independent party. This party should be separate from the initiator, tester, and recorder of the change.

Configuration Status Accounting

Configuration status accounting involves the preparation and maintenance of manual lists or automated information to identify the initial, approved IA baseline and record, monitor, and report all changes to the established IA baseline. The configuration accounting system will provide the ability to trace all changes related to the IA baseline and may consist of tracing through documentation manually to find the status of a change, or it may consist of a database that can automatically track a change. The intent is to rapidly locate all authorized versions of an IA baseline configuration item, add together all authorized changes with comments about the reason for the change, and arrive at either the current status of that configuration item or some intermediate status of the requested item. The status of all authorized changes being performed should be formulated into an organizational IT Baseline Status Report that will be presented to the organization's Configuration Control Board (CCB).

Configuration Auditing

Configuration auditing involves checking for top-to-bottom completeness of the organization's IA baseline configuration information to determine that only authorized changes have been made and that the capabilities of the IA architecture have been maintained. Configuration audits should be performed periodically to verify the configuration status accounting information. The configuration audit minimizes the likelihood that unapproved changes have been inserted into the IA baseline without being detected and ensures that the status accounting information adequately demonstrates the validity of the configuration management assurance. Therefore, there is an assurance that the configuration control procedures of the configuration management system are being followed. The assurance feature of configuration auditing is provided through reasonable and consistent accountability procedures. Also, there are automated configuration auditing tools that have been designed to detect and report changes in the configurations of systems. For example, an automated tool could detect and report the Internet Protocol (IP) addresses of any new devices that are connected to a communications network.

SUMMARY

The IA baseline of an organization will undergo technical and nontechnical changes over time. The organization needs to have accurate and timely knowledge and control of its IA baseline to ensure its security. Configuration management provides a structured and formal process to achieve this knowledge and control. The organization's IA management needs to fully participate as a member of the CCB to assess the security implications of proposed changes to the IA baseline.

REFERENCES

Dart, S., "Webcrisis.com: Inability to Maintain." *Software Magazine* (September 1999; Vol. 19, Issue 2): 50–57.

Leon, A., *A Guide to Software Configuration Management*, Boston: Artech House, 2000.

National Computer Security Center. *A Guide to Understanding Configuration Management in Trusted Systems*. NCSC-TG-006 (March 28, 1988).

11. Layer 6: Life-Cycle Security

CHAPTER OBJECTIVES

- Understand IA concerns during each phase of the system life cycle
- Understand system certification and accreditation (C&A)

SECURITY THROUGHOUT THE SYSTEM LIFE CYCLE

Introduction

We often hear the phrase "cradle to grave" used when speaking of the extent to which security affects each phase of the system life cycle. As true as this is, it does not go far enough. What we are dealing with is really a "conception to grave" responsibility. Security should be included in the inception and planning of the system; integrated into the system's design; only implemented with required security features installed; always operated with security features despite changes to configuration; and, at the end of its life cycle, disposed of in accordance with established procedures. Security is involved in each stage of the system's life cycle.

Initiation

Security is not an end in itself; therefore, the operational requirements that drive the initial idea for the system may not be security related. Nevertheless, an assessment at this stage is necessary to determine the feasibility of the concept. For example, there is no point in expending time and money designing a system to perform a function prohibited by laws or regulations. Considerations include:

- Sensitivity of the information (e.g., degree of required confidentiality, integrity, availability, and accountability)
- Threats to the system or information
- Location of the system (i.e., environmental concerns)
- Interdependencies (e.g., other systems, networks, or processes)
- Legal or regulatory restrictions
- Organizational policy, procedures, and precedents

Note: The IA manager's job is not to find every reason why an operational requirement cannot be accomplished; rather, his/her job is to determine how a required operational function can be accomplished in a secure manner.

Definition

The function of the system, along with the considerations during the initiative stage, will determine the security requirements. These requirements need to be identified and defined to ensure that they are factored into each subsequent stage of the system life cycle. For nonnegotiable requirements (i.e., laws, regulations, standards) the requirement may be already defined. For more negotiable requirements a risk analysis or cost–benefit analysis may conclude that certain security features would not be necessary or cost-effective.

Design

Once defined, the security requirements must be integrated into the system design. Too often, security features are simply afterthoughts. It is imperative that security be engineered into the very fiber of a system or application's software design. "It has long been a tenet of the computer community that it costs ten times more to add a feature in a system *after* it has been designed than to include that feature in the system at the initial design phase" (NIST Handbook, 1998, p. 74). Adding security features after a system has already been developed and implemented is like trying to put the eggs or flour into a cake after it has been baked. The IA manager must ensure that all architectural and engineering proposals and designs incorporate security control requirements. For large projects, critical design reviews (CDRs) may need to be scheduled at intervals during the design phase to keep security requirements on track.

Security considerations at this stage of the system life cycle include:

- Required technical and operational security controls
- Security specifications
- Benchmark standards and test criteria for verifying security controls
- Personnel security requirements (e.g., certification and training; background checks)
- Security documentation requirements
- Validation requirements

Acquisition

The IA manager should ensure that only reliable sources are used for software procurement. The technical market drives much of what is available, procured, and supported in hardware and software today. Federal government as well as industry is marching to the beat of commercial off-the-shelf (COTS) solutions for information systems needs. This situation brings its own risks as buyers are forced to accept software that may contain malicious code. The practice of hiring third-party programmers to provide software fixes for events such as Y2K and the Euro conversion also raises concerns about possible backdoors, Trojan horses, and other malicious code that may be implanted into software under the guise of a software fix.

Development

During the development stage, the security controls are built into the system. For larger systems, in-progress reviews (IPRs) aid management in understanding how a system's development is progressing relative to pre-agreed budget and schedule milestones.

Integration of software during the development phase should be conducted in a development environment. Yet, one of the challenges that the IA manager faces today is fast-track technology with pressure to place prototype and experimental systems in the production environment, where the systems can evolve.

Implementation

At the end of the system's development, but before the system is allowed to operate, a security test and evaluation (ST&E) should be performed. This formal testing can provide the basis for system certification: the validation that the system meets the applicable security criteria and requirements. Certification looks at system vulnerabilities in light of technical and procedural countermeasures. A risk assessment looks at threats in relation to nontechnical countermeasures. The residual risk not addressed by mitigating factors is the risk that management must assume in the formal authorization and assumption of risk, called accreditation. All systems should be accredited before allowing the system to operate.

1. *Risk management.* The IA manager is responsible for evaluating the organization's IA posture with regard to its vulnerabilities, determine if additional safeguards are needed, and develop and maintain a plan to improve the organization's IA posture, considering the most economical way of providing the needed protection. Additionally, the IA manager determines if a risk analysis is required for each information system prior to certification. The IA manager periodically tests the IA posture of the system by employing various intrusion/attack detection and monitoring tools in accordance with applicable regulations and laws. The IA manager then analyzes the results of the testing and recommends or requires appropriate countermeasures to mitigate risk.
2. *C&A process.* In England, each automobile must be annually inspected to ensure it meets the minimum standards for roadworthiness. The test is only a snapshot in time, but serves as an indication of how well the vehicle complies with regulations. Secondly, there is a requirement for someone to underwrite the secure operation of the vehicle, so proof of insurance is a prerequisite for operation of the vehicle. Finally, before one can drive on British roadways, the government (the road owners) requires proof of certification and insurance (along with the obligatory tax) prior to granting approval to operate the vehicle on their roads.

    This analogy parallels the C&A process. A new system must undergo a ST&E, which certifies the "roadworthiness" of the system as it complies with regulations and standards. Where certification is an inspection, accreditation is a management decision. This decision may be partially based on the results of an objective certifying inspection, but, as with the auto insurance company, the decision is more likely to be based on the good record of the "driver." In some cases, the network service provider will also require C&A proof before granting network connection approval, thus allowing the system to traverse their information highway.

3. *Certification* is the comprehensive evaluation of technical and nontechnical security features of an information system or network and other safeguards, made in support of the accreditation process, to establish the extent to which a particular design and implementation meets a set of specified security requirements. System ST&E may be performed by the certifying authority (or designee) and/or IA manager (or designated representative) prior to any new system being used operationally. Recertification testing of any IS should be performed at the discretion of the IA manager or certifying authority upon evaluation of any changes to the system that may affect security accreditation (see Accreditation).

    If a program management office (PMO) or other external organization is sponsoring a system, they may perform an independent security certification prior to fielding the system. In these cases, the IA manager may choose not to undergo a full-fledged ST&E, seeing such testing as redundant, provided the system version and configuration mirror the one already evaluated. However, the IA manager must remember that the delivered system and/or configuration do not always match those tested; the system may be integrated as an application within an existing baseline; and configuration changes may occur in the process of integrating the system. Regardless of how well the system may be evaluated prior to integration into the security baseline, the IA manager is responsible for ensuring that any newly integrated system undergoes security testing and evaluation to make sure that security features are functioning and security requirements are met within the environment in which the system operates.

4. *Approval to operate.* Upon successful security evaluation of the system, the certifying authority or IA manager recommends to the appropriate designated accreditation authority (DAA) and network service provider that approval, or interim approval, to operate should be granted. *Interim approval to operate* (IATO) is a *temporary* approval to operate the system pending an accreditation decision. It is intended to allow operations to begin/continue while awaiting a final approval to operate by the DAA. IATO is also used to allow a site time to satisfy security-relevant findings within a specified time limit, with the goal of meeting final approval criteria.

    IATO does *not* constitute an accreditation or final approval to operate and should not preclude a "get-well plan" for bringing the information system into full compliance with security requirements. IATOs should not automatically be extended or constitute long-term approval to operate outside of security requirements. Failure to bring a system into security compliance should result in application of stringent actions: revocation of IATO, the termination of information systems operations by the DAA, and/or the termination of network connectivity by the Network Service Provider.

5. *Accreditation.* Each information system should be certified by an approved certification authority and accredited to operate in accordance with a DAA-approved set of security safeguards. The IA manager or Information Systems Security Officer/Manager acts as the organization's focal point for C&A actions.

   (a) Accreditation is a formal declaration by a DAA that an AIS or network is conditionally approved to operate:

   - In a particular security processing *mode of operation*
   - With a prescribed set of administrative, environmental, and technical safeguards
   - Against a defined threat and with stated vulnerabilities and countermeasures
   - In a specified operational environment
   - Under an accepted *concept of operations (CONOPS)*
   - With stated interconnections to other systems
   - And at an acceptable level of risk for which the DAA(s) has/have formally assumed responsibility

   (b) Any changes to the conditions of accreditation for any information system or network could require accreditation and approval to operate. Determination of whether reaccreditation is warranted will be a joint decision between the IA manager and the certifying authority.

   (c) Normally an accreditation is only valid for a limited time. Even if no significant changes occur in the system that would warrant a reaccreditation sooner, a reaccreditation would need to be accomplished before the original accreditation expiration date.

Complicating factors. In today's interconnected world, it is not unusual to have connectivity to a network accredited by another DAA. In these cases a memorandum of agreement (MOA) or interconnection service agreement (ISA) between the DAA for each of connecting system and the DAA responsible for the network may be needed to formally outline the understanding and responsibilities for each of the parties.

Operation and Maintenance

Once the system has been certified and accredited to operate, the security responsibilities do not stop. The tendency in some organizations is to view the C&A as an event, not a process. Once the system has been turned on for operational use, the security of the system must still be scrutinized to verify that it continues to meet the terms of its accreditation and to ensure that appropriate countermeasures address any new or changing threats.

Security tools (e.g., enterprise security management software, intrusion detection system software; network vulnerability assessment software; audit reduction tools) are becoming indispensable in identifying common anomalies to the IA manager. Though a manual review is still required to separate real security incidents from benign hits, these tools are helpful in flagging problems that previously could only be found through a laborious review of reams of audit logs — a needle-in-the-haystack search.

These tools can also be useful to shorten the ST&E process and assume more risk in allowing a new system to function in an operational environment. The challenge of the C&A process is to ensure not only that the system initially meets minimum security requirements, but that those security standards are upheld throughout the operational life of the system. This requires a robust change management process, as defined in Chapter 10. It is also imperative that changes to the system be anticipated.

Maintenance of the system brings its own challenges: remote maintenance, personnel clearances, nondisclosure agreements, and so on. Policy should spell out the organization's position on issues such as remote maintenance, remote diagnostics, and remote configuration management (i.e., pushing new version releases). Policy and escort procedures must also exist for on-site and off-site maintenance by individuals without appropriate clearances.

Destruction and Disposal

At the end of the system's life cycle, the IA manager must ensure that information processed and stored in the system is not inadvertently compromised because of improper destruction and disposal. Computer systems contain both volatile and nonvolatile memory.

Volatile memory is lost when the machine is powered off [e.g., random access memory (RAM), active processes and displays, and active network connections]. Nonvolatile memory remains until deliberate action is taken to erase it [e.g., digital or analog data written to persistent storage media such as hard disks, floppy disks, zip disks, and magnetic tapes, as well as read-only memory (ROM), programmable ROM (PROM), or erasable PROM (EPROM) and their variants].

To better understand the procedures contained herein, it should be understood that overwriting, clearing, purging, degaussing, and sanitizing are not synonymous with declassification. Declassification of magnetic media or the system itself is the documented removal of all classified data from the media. Such declassification of a system or medium is different from the declassification of information within a document, also known as downgrading, that takes place when classified data is removed from a document, reducing or eliminating the need to protect the document at the level of the original classification.

Additionally, the following definitions should be reviewed:

- *Clearing* is the process of eradicating the data on the medium by overwriting or degaussing in order to provide an acceptable level of risk that the data previously on the medium cannot be recovered under normal operations. Laboratory techniques may allow retrieval of the information.
- *Degaussing* (i.e., demagnetizing) is a procedure that applies a reverse magnetic field on magnetic media, reducing magnetic flux to virtually zero. If sufficiently strong, the degausser will wipe the medium clean of previously stored data, rendering that data unreadable even under laboratory conditions.

- *Overwriting* is the process of overlaying a character pattern upon previously written data in order to render the data unreadable under normal operations.
- *Sanitizing* (also called *purging*) is the process of removing the data on the medium through the use of degaussing to the point that laboratory techniques cannot recover the information.
- *Destroying* is the process of physically damaging the medium to the point that it is no longer usable and all data previously stored on the medium is unretrievable. Often when the strength of the degausser (measured in oersteds) is sufficient to sanitize the medium it will destroy the medium's timing track and render the medium unusable. Physically destroying the medium, in this case, may not be necessary.
- *Declassification* is an administrative or management declaration that the previously classified media no longer requires protection as classified information.

Procedures should identify the required process for destroying different forms of media (e.g., floppy diskettes, hard drives, disk packs, magnetic tape) and should clearly state the destruction steps.

For example: "When destroying, remove the media (magnetic Mylar, film, ribbons, etc.) from any outside container (reels, casings, hard cases or soft cases, envelopes, etc.) and dispose of the outside container in a regular trash receptacle. Degauss the media, cut the media into pieces using a crosscut chipper/shredder, and then dispose of the pieces in a regular trash receptacle."

Procedures should address what types of the organization's hardware and software require destruction and how that destruction and disposal must be carried out, to include:

- Central processing units (CPUs)
- Printers and laser toner cartridges
- Video display units
- Computer cabinets and housings
- Magnetic media
- CD-ROMs

Life-Cycle Management Essentials

- Ensure that security is planned and developed into any prospective new system.
- Certify that security features are performing properly before allowing the system to operate.
- Approve and track configuration changes to the IA baseline, verifying that the changes do not affect the terms of the system's accreditation.
- Assess the status of security features and system vulnerabilities through manual and automated reviews (i.e., simple scans and self-inspection audits).
- Destroy and dispose of hardcopy printouts and nonvolatile storage media in a way that eliminates possible compromise of sensitive or classified data.
- Keep system documentation current, reflecting patches, version upgrades, and other baseline changes.

- Track hardware and software changes through a process that ensures changes are approved and tested before installation and operation; ensure that the IA manager or representative is part of that approval process.
- Control privileges and authority for modifying software.

SUMMARY

Often security is thought of as an event rather than a process, as a stitch in time rather than a thread that runs throughout each phase of a system's life cycle. Security is often not considered during the initial planning, design, and development of the system. Attempts to retrofit security into the system after it is developed are typically more expensive and less effective than if it is incorporated from inception. Likewise, security does not end once the system has been accredited and approved to operate under certain conditions. Throughout the system's operational and maintenance phase, the system's compliance with the terms of its accreditation must be verified. Even when the system's life cycle is over, security policies and procedures must govern the secure destruction and disposal of the system.

REFERENCE

National Institute of Standards and Technology (NIST) Special Publication 800-18, "Guide for Developing Security Plans for Information Technology Systems" (December 1998).

12. Layer 7: Contingency Planning

CHAPTER OBJECTIVES

- Understand the importance of contingency planning
- Discuss the need for backups
- Identify the need for an emergency action plan
- Provide a contingency planning list

PLANNING FOR THE WORST

Introduction

The dichotomy between users and certification and accreditation (C&A) authorities was once explained as follows: C&A authorities want to protect the information's confidentiality; ensure data integrity; and, if possible, see that the information is available when users want it. Users want the information available when and where they want it, without corruption, and, if possible, in a secure manner. The IA manager is left in the middle trying to appease both extremes.

The organization's dependence on IT as an integral part of the business process means that when systems or networks are unavailable, business processes fail. As a result, availability is one of the primary concerns of users, to include management. Managers are briefed daily on system downtime. Scheduled downtime is coordinated well in advance with all affected departments. Improved software tools now allow IT departments to predict system outages and network faults before they occur, in order to take preventive action before experiencing operational downtime.

Availability is the focus of contingency planning—the multifaceted approaches to ensure that critical system and network assets remain functionally reliable. Contingency planning accounts for an emergency response, backup operations, and post-disaster recovery as a set of comprehensive, consistent, documented, and tested procedures. When services are interrupted, adequate backups ensure that security functions and user data are continuously maintained. When data is modified or destroyed, proven actions allow recovery upon detection. When a natural disaster renders the organization inoperative, documented procedures are implemented to facilitate continuity of operations.

Backups: What and How Often to Back Up

Frequent backups of critical data and system files must be performed and stored off-site. Backups are useful for at least two reasons: to restore data when normal data storage is unavailable and to force proper online storage management. Not all data needs to be online or available at all times. Archiving inactive data is a viable and practical option. Additionally, the storage of data should be centralized (e.g., network files) to facilitate centralized backup procedures. Storage of critical information on the local workstation should be prohibited.

The IA manager should develop backup plans specific to the organization's needs. The plans should consider data-production rates and data-loss risks such as:

1. *Immediate losses of services.* Develop policy and procedures to ensure that the risk of a power failure and the resulting loss of data is minimized at the time of power loss. For example, if a user was creating a word-processing document when power loss occurred, the document would be lost if the user or the application, itself, had not made periodic "saves." Some word-processing systems allow the user to make periodic saves automatically (for example, Word for Windows). Most applications do not have this capability, and the users must be made aware of this potential problem.

2. *Media losses.* Develop a local procedure that reflects this risk. If a hard disk were dropped or contaminated in some way, the disk backups, coupled with periodic incremental backups between full backups, would allow you to restore the data almost to the condition it was in before the loss. Keep "active backups" for disks that contain often-used applications.

   Procedures must be specific enough to address how (which media) and how frequently backups will be done. For example, how often will complete ("zero-level") backups be accomplished? Will incremental backups be done all other times? What media will be used for backup storage? Will backups be stored off-site?

3. *Archiving inactive data.* Develop procedures to manage the disk space. For example, old correspondence might be put onto a disk for archiving purposes. Thus, you could create a list of all files and file descriptions that could be returned to the active users. Security audit files need to be retained for a set length of time (e.g., six months, one year, three years) according to established policy. These files may be archived to tape or compact disk (CD) in order to free room on the operational system.

Preparing for the Inevitable Power Outage: UPS

The acronym UPS in this case is not the parcel delivery service but "uninterruptible power source/supply." These battery backups automatically provide an alternative power supply to critical systems and servers in the event the primary power source is lost. The alternate power supply may keep a system running from a period of minutes to hours, depending on the capability of the UPS device itself.

Emergency Action Plan/Disaster Recovery Plan

Major disasters could occur at any time, without warning and with the potential to destroy the organization's capability to carry out normal operations at its current location. In the event of an emergency, immediate action must be taken to safeguard and minimize property damage or loss and to prevent loss or compromise of classified information. Additionally, procedures must be developed and exercised to ensure that a capability exists for recovering from a disastrous event.

Every facility should have an emergency action plan that addresses the following procedures:

- Emergency destruction procedures
- Emergency evacuation procedures
- Duress situation procedures
- Fire protection
- Bomb threat procedures
- Natural disaster procedures
- Clandestine device notification procedures
- Sabotage or terrorist attack procedures
- Riot or civil disorder procedures
- Loss of utilities procedures

The primary concern in the event of any emergency is the safety of people. Protection of information should always be secondary to the safety and protection of personnel. Safeguarding of classified material, for example, should never be used as authority to bar or otherwise obstruct firemen, medical personnel, rescue workers, or any other emergency personnel. In these circumstances, safeguard sensitive or classified material by assigning enough personnel in or around the vicinity of the facility to provide sufficient surveillance to determine whether sensitive or classified material has been exposed to non-cleared or authorized personnel. In such cases, identify the personnel coming in contact with the material; ensure that classified material is not removed; and determine if administering an inadvertent disclosure oath is necessary.

Continuity of Operations Plan (COOP): What Is Plan B?

In the case that an event renders the organization unable to perform its normal operations at a certain location, it is imperative to have a continuity of operations plan (COOP). The COOP can establish written procedures and a formal relationship between two sites in the event of a contingency or disaster. For example, Site A can be the contingency site for Site B, and vice versa.

The key to writing a good COOP is allowing management to identify and prioritize all critical systems. When an event occurs that causes normal operations to cease, the COOP allows support personnel to know the prioritized order in which to restore systems to full operational capability.

SUMMARY

Contingency planning can help maximize the availability of information and information systems when disaster strikes. Frequent backups of your data will minimize the loss of information in the event of service interruption. The preparation needed to respond to an emergency or unscheduled outage will provide a return on investment in the event of a real contingency.

REFERENCE

National Institute of Standards and Technology (NIST) Special Publication 800-12, "An Introduction to Computer Security: The NIST Handbook." U.S. Department of Commerce, 1995.

13. Layer 8: IA Education, Training, and Awareness

CHAPTER OBJECTIVES

- Provide an understanding of the necessity of IA education, training, and awareness within the organization
- Provide organizations with a basic process for developing a program to provide IA education, training, and awareness

THE IMPORTANCE OF IA EDUCATION, TRAINING, AND AWARENESS

An organization should consider the IA education, training, and awareness of its employees as a significant investment. The significance is equal to that of any other investment that an organization must make to achieve its objectives and meet the needs of its customers. This results from the extent of the operational dependency that organizations have on their IA baselines for their survival, coexistence, and growth. The significant growth of electronic commerce (e-commerce) provides the best case supporting this fact. The lack of sufficient IA education, training, and awareness for employees could actually result in a loss of productivity and revenue for organizations. In essence, if an organization doesn't sufficiently expend resources for the IA education, training, and awareness of its employees "up front," then it may have to expend even more resources at a later point because of the lack of employee knowledge or misunderstandings. IA incidents, and thus costs to organizations, could result from such a situation.

IA education, training, and awareness encompasses all individuals within an organization who work directly with the IA baseline, such as system administrators, as well as those who directly or indirectly receive information from the IA baseline. Employees need to fully understand the necessity of IA and its contributions to the survival, coexistence, and growth of the organization and what is expected of them in terms of these contributions. As employees come to fully understand what is expected of them, their morale improves and the number of security incidents could be minimized. Also, employees need to fully understand the IA mechanisms that are in place and how to correctly and thoroughly use the IA mechanisms. Therefore, employees require initial, periodic, refresher, and revised sessions when new mechanisms and controls are introduced into the IA architecture. All employees require IA awareness, some employees require training in the use of IA mechanisms or controls, and a few employees require much more in-depth security knowledge and are thus candidates for IA education.

IMPLEMENTATION OF ORGANIZATIONAL IA EDUCATION, TRAINING, AND AWARENESS

The model for implementing an organization's IA education, training, and awareness consists of several components. First and foremost, the fundamental concepts and principles described in Chapter 2 ("Basic Security Concepts, Principles, and Strategy") should be incorporated into all organizational training disciplines. This permits security to be transparent to the employee in much the same way that seatbelts permit safety to the driver and passengers of an automobile. The use of seatbelts is generally a standard feature of any automobile and so widely accepted that it becomes a matter of routine to attach them before the automobile moves. The effectiveness of IA education, training, and awareness is enhanced the more it becomes integrated within the organization's overall training and awareness program. The objective is to minimize to the greatest extent possible people's belief that security is a function outside the normal operations of an organization and that security is an impediment to successful operations. Employees must come to understand that security is everyone's responsibility. For example, organizations may provide indoctrination for new employees concerning their rights, benefits, authorities, and responsibilities. This indoctrination may involve briefings, presentations, films, and a copy of an employee handbook. IA should be incorporated into this indoctrination by informing the employee concerning his or her IA responsibilities, processes, points of contact, and organizational IA policies.

Second, the objectives of IA education, training, and awareness need to be defined. These objectives can involve the following:

(a) Informing and periodically reminding employees of their IA responsibilities and current IA policies. A critical point is that employees need to be taught the significance of IA policies to the organization and why they need to comply with such policies. The benefits of IA need to be communicated to employees, as do the costs associated with not complying with established policies. Examples of how the organization both benefited and suffered a loss would prove very useful to communicating these points.

(b) Maintaining an awareness of the IA program within the organization.

(c) Providing basic, intermediate, and advanced IA training for employees.

(d) Providing opportunities for select IA professionals to enroll in IA educational courses and advanced degree programs at colleges and universities.

Third, the various types of employees should be identified, along with the variety of privileges and responsibilities that should be provided to them. For example, employees who are responsible for administering the organization's information systems (i.e., system administrators) are provided with greater privileges than a general user of those systems. Also, certain "general users" of information systems may have greater responsibilities and greater privileges than other "general users." For example, supervisors and managers within organizations may be assigned authority to approve the access of employees to organizational information and IA baseline resources.

Fourth, in order for an organization to utilize its IA education, training, and awareness dollars sufficiently, the location, scope, and magnitude of employee training needs must be determined. The primary purpose is to provide a competent workforce by satisfying job-specific IA needs. There is a need to recognize the difference between IA training needs and IA training wants. Determine what is required or expected for the various types of employees and the extent to which these requirements are being met. This difference, or performance deficiency, identifies the organization's IA training needs.

There are several questions that should be considered to help determine this difference:

- What does the organization want concerning the IA proficiency of its employees?
- What do the various types of employees want concerning IA proficiency?
- What do the various types of employees know concerning IA?
- What are the various types of employees doing now concerning IA?
- What are the levels of experience for the various types of employees concerning IA?
- What are current IA problems that confront the organization?
- What is the job performance of the various types of employees?

Fifth, having determined a level of need, there are two other factors affecting the development of the IA education, training, and awareness program that should be considered. These factors involve the content of the program and the resources required for its implementation. From a content perspective, the subjects of the IA education, training, and awareness program need to be determined as well as the availability of subject matter experts to implement the program. There are a variety of subjects that can be included within the program. The following provides a listing of the more significant subjects:

- Threats to the successful operation of employees and the organization
- Types of vulnerabilities
- The concept of risk, how employees can identify and manage it, and the impact that it can have on employee performance and organizational operations
- The concept of the confidentiality, integrity, and availability of information
- The statutory and organizational requirement to protect information
- Distinguishing between IA technical (hardware and software); policy, procedures, and practices; and, education, training, and awareness countermeasures
- The concept of trust and the establishment of trust relationships
- Distinguishing between the security disciplines such as information security, operations security, transmission security, emanations security,

personnel security, administrative security, and information systems security (INFOSEC)

- Employee accountability for organizational information
- Distinguishing between identification and authentication (I&A), access controls, auditing, and object reuse
- Employee protection of passwords
- Organizational policies concerning the remote access to organizational information; the use of magnetic and optical media; and the use of laptop and handheld computing devices
- The organizational security incident handling process
- The organizational configuration management process
- The role of IA in the systems development process
- Automated IA tools
- Contingency planning
- The organizational IA structure and points of contact

The extent and availability of resources also affect the implementation. There are several issues that need to be addressed. Examples include the establishment of a budget; the definition of requirements for staff and locations to implement the program; the determination as to whether organizational personnel are sufficient to implement the program or whether contracting will be required; and the development of an annual and five-year implementation schedule.

Sixth, there needs to be a distinction between some different approaches for providing IA education, training, and awareness. Basically, IA education is a formal process that is provided by external entities such as colleges and universities. IA training can be provided internally or by specialized external entities such as training institutes and training centers. Generally, IA awareness results from internal formal and informal activities. New employees should receive an initial IA orientation and annual refresher orientations that describe their responsibilities; specific precautions that employees must always take in order to protect both themselves and the IA baseline from possible compromise; how and where to report suspected and actual IA incidents; and some prohibitions such as attempting to access data or perform a function for which employees do not have authorization and leaving a live terminal unattended. Informally, employees receive IA awareness and training as a result of their daily interactions with fellow employees, their experiences as a user of the IA baseline, and their efforts to learn more about IA and their IA responsibilities.

Finally, an organization's IA education, training, and awareness program will consist of several major components. Examples of these components are as follows:

- *Introductory film.* This film will feature a high official in the organization to provide an indication of management support for IA and the IA education, training, and awareness program. It would be very beneficial if the organization's top executive were in the film as well as the Chief Information Officer (CIO).
- *Briefings and seminars.* These will address significant IA topics for the various types of employees within the organization.

- *Employee IA handbook.* This handbook should explain in nontechnical terms the purpose and procedures involved in the organization's IA program including its structures and points of contact.
- *Ongoing IA awareness.* The intent of providing ongoing IA awareness is to maintain employee awareness of potential threats, vulnerabilities, IA policies, IA procedures, and IA standards. A variety of means can be used to maintain this awareness, including Web sites, electronic mail, handouts, videotapes, and help desks. Help desks can be an especially valuable means of providing information and support to employees with IA questions or problems. For example, help desks can improve password management by not only helping employees change passwords, but also providing guidance on strengthening and protecting them. Also, help desks can be valuable on-call repositories of IA policies, procedures, practices, and standards. A trained help-desk operator can answer employees' IA policy questions, often directly from the manuals. Only the more serious questions need be directed to the IA staff. Another important factor to consider is that help-desk operators can also collect information on and respond to actual IA events or alerts. Those operators can serve as backup destinations for alerts, both from employees and from the automated systems within the IA baseline. Many of those alerts would still escalate directly to automated system technicians, IA personnel, or other managers. However, help-desk personnel could apply their existing tracking mechanisms to ensure that reported security incidents are addressed in a timely manner.

SUMMARY

An organization needs to establish an IA education, training, and awareness program to help ensure the confidentiality, integrity, and availability of its information. This program must be comprehensive enough to consider the needs of the various types of employees who access the organizational information as well as those employees who are responsible for managing and maintaining the IA baseline that generates this information. Employees must be fully aware both of their basic IA responsibilities and of the availability of opportunities to improve their awareness and enhance their IA knowledge and skills.

REFERENCES

ARCA, *INFOSEC Handbook—An Information Systems Security Reference*, 2nd ed. San Jose, CA: ARCA, 1993.

Burge, T., "Making a Day of It—With the Right Preparation, a Security-Awareness Day Can Spread the Word with a Smile." *Infosecurity News* (January–February 1997).

Russell, D., and G. T. Gangemi, Jr. *Computer Security Basics.* Sebastopol, CA: O'Reilly & Associates, Inc., 1991.

14. Layer 9: IA Policy Compliance Oversight

CHAPTER OBJECTIVE

- Provide an understanding of how the organization can monitor and assess its compliance with its established IA policy. There are a variety of automated and nonautomated techniques and approaches that are available to an organization. A proper combination of these techniques and approaches needs to be developed and operated to sufficiently manage an organization's IA posture and maintain an acceptable level of risk.

THE NECESSITY OF IA POLICY COMPLIANCE OVERSIGHT

As discussed in Chapter 6 ("Layer 1: IA Policies"), IA policies are the first layer of any organization's Defense in Depth strategy. IA policies essentially define the bounds of acceptable behavior and actions that are needed to achieve the IA needs of the organization. These policies are intended to control and influence the behavior and actions of people, automated systems, people's interactions with automated systems, and the interactions between automated systems. Therefore, there must be means of monitoring and assessing the extent to which the IA policies are being achieved. The intent of an organization's IA policy compliance oversight function is to provide a means of detecting, reporting, and correcting noncompliance with the IA policies.

THE IMPLEMENTERS OF IA POLICY COMPLIANCE OVERSIGHT

The implementation of the compliance oversight can be performed both internally within the organization and by external parties.

First, the implementation of the oversight can be performed by the IA staff within the organization or by employees who have been designated to support the IA staff.

Second, an organization's internal audit staff can perform compliance oversight as a result of their implementation of audits, inspections, investigations, and studies.

Third, compliance oversight can be performed by "third parties." These "third parties" generally are external contractors or public accounting firms. Many organizations undergo annual audits of their financial statements. A significant part of this audit process involves an independent assessment of the internal controls of the organization. Also, organizations may decide to use independent organizations to perform periodic assessments and studies to determine the extent of compliance with IA policies. These assessments and studies could be rather broad or concentrated on a particular aspect of the compliance. For example, a vulnerability assessment could be performed of the organization's wide-area network (WAN) or its firewalls.

MECHANISMS OF IA POLICY COMPLIANCE OVERSIGHT

There are five basic mechanisms of IA policy compliance oversight. These mechanisms involve intrusion detection systems (IDS), scanners, the automated auditing and review of predefined events, virus detectors, and periodic assessments of IA management and vulnerabilities. Each of these methods will be discussed.

Intrusion Detection Systems (IDS)

Firewalls and authentication mechanisms are methods used to prevent unauthorized users from accessing the organization's information. However, these methods cannot detect all the potential attacks that could be happening in the organization's network. The history of IA incidents has proven that it is possible to successfully attack through a firewall or to bypass its controls entirely by gaining access by means of a dial-in connection through the use of modems. Therefore, there is a need for a mechanism to be capable of monitoring the network behind the firewall and authentication mechanisms.

IDS mechanisms constantly scan network traffic or host audit logs to determine what kind of activity is occurring on the organization's network and whether any activity is not in compliance with the organization's IA policy. These mechanisms can identify attacks based on predefined signatures of known methods of intrusion as well as identifying statistical anomalies that veer from normal operation. For example, an IDS may monitor CPU use and the number and types of network packets moving through the network.

An IDS mechanism generally operates as a system with four distinct phases:

- *Detection phase.* The detection phase begins as soon as a detector or sensor reacts to stimuli it is designed to detect. The sensor alarm condition is then transmitted over cabling located within the protected area to the premise control unit (PCU). The PCU may service many sensors. The PCU and the sensors it serves comprise a "zone" at the monitor station. This is used as the definition of an alarmed zone.
- *Reporting phase.* The PCU receives signals from all sensors in a protected area and incorporates these signals into a communications scheme. Another signal is added to the communication for supervisors to prevent compro-

mise of the communications scheme. This supervised signal is intended to disguise the information and protect the ISD against tampering or injection of false information by an intruder. The supervised signal is sent by the PCU via the transmission link to the monitor station. Inside the monitor station, either a dedicated panel or central processor monitors information from the PCU signals. When alarms occur, an annunciator generates an audible and visible alert to IA personnel. Alarms result normally from intrusion, tampering, component failure, or system power failure.

- *Assessment phase.* The assessment period is the first phase that requires human interaction. When alarm conditions occur, the operator assesses the situation and dispatches the response force.
- *Response phase.* The response phase begins as soon as the operator assesses an alarm condition. A response report must immediately respond to all alarms. The response phase must also determine the precise nature of the alarm and take all measures necessary to protect confidentiality, integrity, and availability of organizational information.

Generally, IDS mechanisms are either host-based or network-based. Host-based mechanisms reside on hosts and monitor operating system and application audit and event log files, providing policy enforcement by detecting unauthorized activity. If they notice a change during their file scanning, they will look for attack signatures based on a knowledge database. If evidence of tampering is found, the IDS mechanism can then notify the system administrator. These mechanisms can provide a fine granularity of information. Examples of such information include who is accessing specific files and when users log in and out of servers. Also, the host-based IDS mechanism can detect changes in system files through the use of trigger alarms, and knows if anyone tries to install potentially malicious software such as backdoors.

Network-based mechanisms perform real-time monitoring of network traffic. This leads to faster administration notification and faster response to any attacks in progress. These mechanisms actually read packet headers, unlike host-based IDS mechanisms. Therefore, they can detect attacks such as denial of service, which can only be detected through packet examination. There are two basic approaches to network-based IDS mechanisms.

First, the IDS would monitor network traffic, searching for data that suggests known types of computer attacks. This "signature-based" monitoring requires the IDS to capture data packets traveling the network and to compare them to predefined attack signatures stored in the IDS's search engine. Also, they can read the contents of a packet, not just the packet header, which could reveal backdoor attacks. Of great significance is the fact that they can terminate attacks as they happen since they are looking for intrusions in real time.

There are some issues associated with signature-based IDS. The security provided by the system will only be as good as the signatures in the search engine. Poorly defined signatures can result in false positives, in which good packets are labeled as bad packets and the transmission is interrupted. Therefore, the utility of the IDS partially depends on keeping the signatures up-to-date. This can be done either by the vendor or by internal staff. Also, there is an emerging breed of computer attack known as the distributed attack. This involves the attack packets being sent over a long period of time, thereby eluding some commercially available IDS products. However, vendors have recognized this as a problem and initiated improvements to their products.

The second approach to network-based IDS mechanisms involves capturing and analyzing packets to define patterns of usage on the network. Once the IDS has developed statistics on what is considered normal network activity, it will audit network traffic by capturing packets and analyzing them for any deviations from the normal statistics. This heuristic approach to IDS methodology is also known as behavior-based IDS.

Scanners

Scanner mechanisms are distinct from IDS mechanisms. Generically speaking, IDS mechanisms try to detect attacks in progress while scanners are probing for vulnerabilities in the network to prevent an attack from happening in the first place. These mechanisms contain large databases of known attacks that they try against the network. Therefore, the database needs to be continuously updated as new attacking methods are discovered or determined to be possible.

After the scanner software is loaded, administrators can specify a range of Internet Protocol (IP) addresses to check. The scanner then checks operating systems, servers, routers, firewalls, Web servers, applications, and any other network product that uses IP. Scanners can detect a wide range of security vulnerabilities, including areas that are not password-protected, misconfigured software, server buffer overflows, and other areas that could cause problems. These mechanisms should be able to prioritize potential risks, recommend corrections, and provide recommendations on controls to counter the vulnerabilities.

Automated Auditing

Fundamentally, to *audit* something is to inspect or examine it to evaluate its safety, efficiency, profitability, and so forth. The intent is to examine a history of information processing, which includes generation, distribution, exchange, modification, and destruction of data, to evaluate the security of the processing in a broad sense. The basic goals are to collect sufficient data to reconstruct system events after a security violation has occurred and to provide a means of surveying users' actions before violations occur.

Auditing has a derived, technical meaning, in the context of an automated information system. That is, it often refers to the creation of a log of transactions made by the system. Generally, to support auditing, the automated information system generates logs that indicate:

- What happened
- Who did it
- What went wrong
- How far some information spread
- Who had access to some information

Therefore, logging by an automated information system provides data for auditing by creating an audit trail of events that makes it possible to assess damage and take corrective action.

The National Computer Security Center's "A Guide to Understanding Audit in Trusted Systems" (NCSC-TG-001, Version 2) defines an "audit trail" as a set of records that collectively provide documentary evidence of processing used to aid in tracing from original transactions forward to related records and reports, and/or backward from records and reports to their component source transactions. Audit trails are used to detect and deter penetration of an automated information system and to disclose usage that identifies misuse. At the discretion of the organization, audit trails may be limited to specific events or may encompass all the activities on an automated information system.

As defined by NCSC-TG-001, the audit mechanism of an automated information system has five important security goals.

1. "The audit mechanism must allow the review of patterns of access to individual objects, access histories of specific processes and individuals, and the use of the various protection mechanisms supported by the system and their effectiveness."
2. "The audit mechanism must allow discovery of both users' and outsiders' repeated attempts to bypass the protection mechanisms."
3. "The audit mechanism must allow discovery of any use of privileges that may occur when a user assumes a functionality with privileges greater than his or her own, i.e., programmer to administrator. In this case there may be no bypass of security controls, but nevertheless a violation is made possible."
4. "The audit mechanism must act as a deterrent against perpetrators' habitual attempts to bypass the system protection mechanisms. However, for this to act as a deterrent, the perpetrator must be aware of the audit mechanism's existence and its active use to detect any attempts to bypass system protection mechanisms."
5. "The audit mechanism should supply an additional form of user assurance. Attempts to bypass the protection mechanisms should be recorded and discovered."

Even if the attempt to bypass the protection mechanism is successful, the audit trail will still provide assurance by its ability to aid in assessing the damage done by the violation, thus improving the system's ability to control the damage.

The organization needs to adequately administer automated auditing. There are four basic factors associated with the administration of automated auditing. First, there needs to be a definition of the content of the audit trail. This involves defining a minimal set of auditable events. Generally, there is a definition of these auditable events at the workstation platform and network levels. Examples of auditable events at the workstation level are as follows:

- Login
- Logoff
- Operating system changes

- User-invoked operating system commands
- User-invoked applications
- All security maintenance events

Events will be audited by audit class. These audit classes include kernel-level and user-level events. Some examples are listed below:

- Read of data
- Write of data
- Access of object attributes
- Change of object attributes
- Creation of object
- Deletion of object
- Close object
- Turn off event preselection
- Process operations
- Network events
- Interprocess communications (IPC) operations
- Nonattributable events
- Administrative actions
- Login and logout
- Application auditing
- Set file/process security attributes
- Information label floating
- Use of privilege
- Events that may exercise covert storage channels
- The setting of all flags

The second aspect of administering automated auditing involves the process of collecting and analyzing the recording of the logged events. This information can be centrally or decentrally collected. The decentral collection would involve the storage of the logged events within each of the platforms (workstations, routers, servers, and so forth). Also, the logged events could be captured at the individual platform level but transferred to a central audit server platform. The size of the logged events may vary depending upon the amount of activity on an automated information system and the number of events selected for logging. The audit trail could grow to sizes that would necessitate some form of audit data reduction software. The intent of this software tool is to allow the selective retrieval of audit data based on a number of factors such as the following:

- The identity of individuals
- The identity of objects
- The security level of objects accessed
- The types of events
- Time and data

The audit data reduction tool would generally be a batch program that would interface to the system security administrator. This batch run could be a combination of database query language and a report generator with the input being a standardized audit file. The reduction of the collected audit data would permit more effective real-time or periodic analysis of the data to determine discrepancies and trends.

Third, the collection and analysis of the audit data should result in the generation of daily audit reports. These reports would provide IA management with the ability to detect violations to the organization's IA policy and to have the historical data associated with these violations. Fourth, the audit data needs to be stored and archived. The exact time period required for retaining the audit trail data is dependent on the organization and statutes and should be documented as one of the organization's IA policies.

Virus Detectors

Virus detection software mechanisms, also known as antiviral software, looks for, identifies, and in most cases, one hopes, eradicates viruses. The virus detection software must be installed on all clients and servers to be monitored. Electronic mail (e-mail) servers should continuously scan for viruses in both e-mail and file attachments to the e-mail. The key to an effective antiviral defense is to ensure that the virus detection software is updated with the latest virus profiles. Virus detection shortfalls occur when these profiles are not kept current; when unprecedented viruses are used; and during the gap in time between the discovery of a new virus and the release and implementation of an effective antiviral inoculation.

Periodic Assessments of IA Management and Vulnerabilities Assessments

The organization can require that periodic assessments are performed of the organization's IA management and vulnerabilities. These can be performed by the internal IA staff, by the organization's internal audit staff, or by external businesses that specialize in such assessments. The assessments would be performed using predefined testing and evaluation procedures and vulnerability assessment tools. Any resulting findings would need to be formally documented and reported. The confidentiality of these findings is critical. Also, the findings would have to be corrected within specified periods of time based on the risks to the organization associated with the findings. The findings may indicate that one or more of the IA policies may need to change to reflect a more realistic assurance of their adherence.

SUMMARY

An organization requires a means of ensuring that its prescribed IA policies are in full compliance. A variety of automated and nonautomated approaches were discussed in this chapter. The responsibility of the organization's IA management is to consistently use these approaches in varying degrees of intensity over time to ensure the compliance with its IA policies and to adjust those policies as circumstances require.

REFERENCES

Klander, L. *Hacker Proof—The Ultimate Guide to Network Security.* Las Vegas, NV: James Press, 1997.

National Computer Security Center (NCSC). *A Guide to Understanding Audit in Trusted Systems.* NCSC-TG-001, Version 2 (June 1, 1988).

15. Layer 10: IA Incident Response

CHAPTER OBJECTIVES

- Understand what constitutes an IA incident
- Discuss what members comprise the incident handling team
- Determine a measured approach and appropriate procedures for incident handling

REACTING AND RESPONDING TO IA INCIDENTS

Introduction

The best-laid defenses will eventually fail. When that happens, the security team needs to turn to preexisting battle plans. . . . The incident response plan needs to be in place before it is needed. The critical steps that should be included in the incident response plan are: regain control of the situation, analyze the intrusion, recover from the incident, improve your security to prevent the same type of attack, reconnect to the Internet, and update the security policy to reflect changes (Miller, 2001, p. 5).

What Is an Incident?

It is critical that all users understand what constitutes an IA incident, not only to avoid committing incidents, but to know how to recognize and report IA incidents when they occur. An *IA incident* could be any event that has an actual or potentially adverse affect on information or information systems. Think of the incident as the symptom; the cause of the incident is a threat. An IA incident may also involve a violation of law. The following are examples of realized threats that result in IA incidents:

- A virus-infected e-mail attachment executes upon opening, deleting critical system files
- A disgruntled employee maliciously modifies or destroys critical information
- An unscheduled power interruption causes a denial of service
- A system administrator abuses his privileged access by gaining unauthorized access to a protected directory
- A hacker engages in unauthorized probing of an organization's IP address range

- Unauthorized changes to a system's software security configuration result in a loss of audits
- A manager disregards the organization's classification marking procedures, resulting in an unauthorized disclosure of information

Incident Severity

The way we respond to incidents will depend on the severity of the threat. The more severe the damage, the bigger the impact to operations; or the faster an incident spreads, the more quickly we must react to the incident. This reaction must be a measured and appropriate response, proportional to the threat. A password compromise is a security violation, but all compromises are not alike: the compromise of a privileged password is more serious than the compromise of a password for a regular user account. Detection of malicious code constitutes a reportable incident, but not all viruses are created equal: a fast-spreading virus affecting an entire LAN is more serious than a macro-virus affecting a single e-mail attachment. The organization's incident handling procedures must account for these varied measures.

Because IA incidents may involve criminal activity, the IA manager must know either what specific circumstances need to be reported to law enforcement agencies or whom to contact when in doubt. Responsibility for a security violation or for possible compromise of classified information should be established through investigation. The causes of IA incidents are often complex. When individual responsibility cannot be established, responsibility typically falls to the supervisor or manager involved.

Incident Reporting Policy

All suspected or actual security incidents, security policy violations, or practices dangerous to security should be immediately reported to the responsible security manager (i.e., ISSO/ISSM, IA manager). The organization should have written policy stating this requirement for all employees. The policy should also spell out procedures for reporting incidents during duty hours and after-duty hours. Security training and awareness should emphasize this individual responsibility. Security point-of-contact telephone numbers should be prominently posted throughout the workplace.

Examples of Reportable Incidents

The following relevant IA incidents must be reported:

- Unauthorized access attempt from locations external to the facility
- Unauthorized access attempt internal to the facility
- Unauthorized monitoring
- Malicious code
- Virus attack
- Virus detection

- Failure of a network or system security feature
- Breeches of policy or procedure resulting in practices dangerous to security
- Compromise or possible compromise of classified information
- Other incident deemed important but not covered in any of the above

Causes of IA Incidents

Incidents can occur for a variety of reasons and rarely result from a simple or single cause. Most are the result of a complex combination of factors:

- Failure to apply patches and updates to mitigate software vulnerabilities
- Lack of training or awareness
- Failure to follow established policy
- Poorly written or outdated policies
- Holes in existing procedures
- Overdependency on automated processes
- Negligence
- Deliberate or malicious acts

Incident Reporting Assumptions

- Not all incidents get reported. It is not known what percentage of actual incidents goes unreported; therefore, it is uncertain what percentage reported incidents actually represent of the organization's total incidents.
- Users must be trained to recognize an incident; understand how to report an incident; and know to whom to report the incident.
- Security officials must be available/accessible, approachable, and competent to handle incidents.
- Incidents vary in degree of severity and scope. Tracking the number of incidents is important, but reporting numbers alone does not reflect the extent of damage caused by each incident.
- There must be appropriate deterrents for discouraging willful, deliberate, or negligent breaches of IA policy and procedure that result in security incidents.

Incident Response Team Composition

The organization should have an incident response policy that defines the roles and responsibilities of the individuals performing incident handling. Examples of team member roles include the following:

- *Dispatchers* take incident hotline calls, initiate the incident report, and dispatch the response handler to the scene.
- The *response handler* is the individual who initially reacts to the incident. This individual must be capable of securing the incident/crime scene and proficient in gathering evidence for all types of incidents.
- The *director* directly represents and communicates with the senior manager (e.g., President, CEO) and acts as public spokesperson.

- The *lead investigator* oversees the response activities; prepares the incident report; and reports directly to the director.
- *Technicians* are skilled in computer forensics and systems operations.
- The *evidence handler* ensures that evidence is properly controlled and protected so that legal chain-of-custody requirements are satisfied.
- *Legal counsel* advises the organization on legal matters (incident response fundamentals briefing).

Incident Reporting Benefits

- Incidents are indicators of systemic problems. By understanding the underlying causes of these incidents, the organization can make adjustments to business processes and, thereby, reduce incidents.
- A history of incidents can be used as a tool for measuring the effectiveness of the business process improvement initiatives.
- We have a community responsibility to report incidents so that others can benefit from our experiences.

Incident Response Capability

According to NIST, a Computer Security Incident Response Capability (CSIRC) "provides computer security efforts with the capability to respond [reactively] to computer security-related incidents such as computer viruses, unauthorized user activity, and serious software vulnerabilities, in an efficient and timely manner. A CSIRC further [proactively] promotes increased security awareness of computer security-related risks so that [the organization is] better prepared and protected." A Computer Emergency Response Team (CERT) and Computer Incident Response Team (CIRT) are examples of a CSIRC.

The organization either needs to develop an internal CSIRC or make arrangements to use an existing CSIRC. Consideration should be taken if the organization's CSIRC is dependent on external sources or outsourcing. There should also be checks and balances built into the CSIRC; for example, incident reports should be screened by security personnel to determine legitimacy before raising the alarm and to ensure that all reportable incidents get reported.

The IA manager or staff must ensure that security vulnerability reports, alerts, and advisories are received on a timely basis. The IA manager or staff must then ensure that all applicable alerts and advisories are acted upon quickly (e.g., patches applied, system vulnerabilities eliminated or reduced). There is usually a reporting responsibility back to the CSIRC to notify them of action taken.

Incident Handling Considerations

- Policy must define what constitutes an incident and the roles and responsibilities of the incident handling team.
- Management must ensure that adequate resources and processes exist for detecting, responding to, and recovering from IA incidents.

- Incident handling often requires concurrent actions to ensure timely response. Incident handling itself is not a one-person job, but there should only be one incident handling coordinator to oversee clean operations, reporting, and investigation.
- Public release of information about any incident must be conducted by the director (or equivalent); ensure that all employees understand and honor this rule.
- After-hours notification lists must be kept up-to-date and provide both primary and alternate contact information.
- Simply deleting the offending file from a local server does not necessarily undo the damage and may actually hinder the investigation. Ensure that everyone knows to phone security first, before destroying evidence.
- Backup copies, shadow files, search engine copies, caching proxies, etc., all need to be checked in the event of data spill to ensure they do not contain copies of the offending file/data.
- Everyone has a responsibility to report incidents.

General Incident Handling Procedures

In addition to defining roles and responsibilities, the incident response policy needs to identify the procedures to follow when an incident is detected. These procedures must be clear and complete enough to leave no doubt in anyone's mind as to what to do next. When an incident occurs there is no time to deliberate about what needs to be done, in what order, and by whom — a quick and proper response is critical to minimizing damage and ensuring that legal requirements are not jeopardized by mishandling evidence. The response needs to be based on established procedures and should be tested/exercised prior to responding to a real-world event (i.e., pre-incident preparation).

Basic incident response and handling procedures should include the following steps:

1. **Determine appropriate response.** Please refer to Appendix K for a sample threat response matrix. Malicious code is the example threat analyzed to assess its severity, urgency, and gradual response options.

   - Identify the problem
   - Initially, assess the situation to determine current status (e.g., Did an incident occur? Is it over? Is it still spreading?)
   - Determine if criminal in nature; if so, contact law enforcement; else dispatch the response handler to the scene to preserve evidence
   - Determine if keystroke monitoring is required

2. **Collect and safeguard the information**

   - Ensure that audits are turned on (they should be already on) and that they cover the entire period during which the file was accessible
   - Obtain the most volatile evidence, including human testimony (Mandia and Prosise, 2001, p. 17)

- Record everything: annotate date/times, actions taken, interviews/contacts, extent of problem, etc.
- Log the information in a medium that maintains the integrity of the investigation (i.e., a bound legal notebook that would reveal missing pages using ink rather than pencil)

3. **Contain the situation.** At this point, the threat (e.g., malicious code) has occurred.

- Determine if the system/network must be shut down or taken offline
- Estimate the impact to operations if the system/network is taken offline
- Determine best course of action to minimize downtime
- Follow procedures for appropriate measured response for isolation

4. **Assemble the incident management team**

- Ensure that everyone recognizes only one team leader/coordinator
- Estimate the level of effort involved
- Determine if additional expertise outside of the team's skills is required
- Agree on a best course of action
- Ensure management approval and support

5. **Create evidence disk(s) and printouts**

- Find the evidence; employ active and passive techniques to determine full extent of problem; if e-mail is involved, ensure that all envelope/header information is included
- Determine what evidence is relevant to the case at hand
- Collect evidence in order of volatility, working from the most volatile to the least volatile (i.e., registers, cache, operating system tables, kernel statistics and modules, main memory, temporary files, router configuration) (Braid, 2001, p. 3)
- Copy the evidence to two compact disks: one to be safeguarded as part of the legal chain-of-custody and the second to be used in the investigation (use CD-R versus CD-RW media to prevent the possibility of modification to copies)
- Manage the evidence chain-of-custody
- Assess the damage

6. **Eradicate/clean up/recover**

- Ensure that the latest virus signature files are installed and the system is inoculated
- Search for all instances; check backup/archived files, shadow/mirrored files, search engines, caching proxies, and meta-data for instances of the offending file/information; don't forget to check wastebaskets
- Notify users prior to fully restoring system/network operations
- Restore system/network to a secure operational state (Mandia and Prosise, p. 17)

7. **Prepare preliminary status report for management and other authorities**

- Analyze the forensic evidence to reconstruct the events and determine cause, time, place, etc.

- Estimate damage and costs
- Obtain information damage assessment from the data owner(s)

8. **Document and report all activity**
   - Create memos recording daily status to keep interested parties "in the loop"
   - Report the incident to cognizant authorities (e.g., management, data owners, accreditation authorities, law enforcement, Computer Emergency Response Team)

9. **Lessons learned: make appropriate process improvements to prevent similar incidents**
   - Analyze causes of the incident (remember that it is usually a combination of factors)
   - Determine whether policies and procedures need to be modified to prevent reoccurrence
   - Determine whether additional training is required
   - Determine whether administrative actions are warranted
   - Follow-up to ensure corrective actions are implemented

Incident Report Content

When reporting incidents, the following information should be included:

- Type of incident
- Name and contact number of person reporting incident
- Date and time of report
- Date and time (GMT) the incident occurred
- Name, location, and classification of the victimized system
- How and when the incident was detected
- Description of the incident
- Actions taken so far
- Impact of the incident on organization operations
- Point of contact (POC) for the system

SUMMARY

Despite all your efforts to protect and defend your information and assets, it is inevitable that an IA incident will occur. A user may disregard an IA policy, endangering the security of information. Another user may cause a security violation by causing the compromise of sensitive or classified information. Yet another may engage in criminal activity that requires intervention by law enforcement authorities.

The IA manager must know how to appropriately respond to each and every kind of IA incident that arises. Detecting and responding to an incident is only the beginning. Incident handling procedures must be followed to ensure that necessary steps are not omitted and that response is appropriate to the threat.

Established and proven procedures for responding to incidents will allow the organization to react quickly and decisively when incidents occur.

REFERENCES

Braid, Matthew. "Collecting Electronic Evidence after a System Compromise." *SANS Institute* (April 17, 2001).

Farrow, Rik, and Richard Power, "Can You Survive a Computer Attack?" Online Network Defense article for Networkmagazine.com (August 1998).

Incident Response Fundamentals Class Briefing Slides, Presented at the National Information Systems Security Conference, Baltimore, MD (October 16, 2000).

Mandia, Kevin, and Chris Prosise. *Incident Response: Investigating Computer Crime.* New York: Osborne/McGraw-Hill, 2001.

Miller, Matthew K., "Sun Tzu and the Art of (Cyber) War: Ancient Advice for Developing an Information Security Program," *SANS Institute* (April 2, 2001).

NIST Special Publication 800-3, "Establishing a Computer Security Incident Response Capability (CSIRC)" (November 1991).

NIST ITL Bulletin, "Computer Attacks: What Are They and How to Defend Against Them" (May 1999).

Ross, Steven, and Vikram Bhat, "Incident Management." *IS Audit & Control Journal* (1999; Vol. I).

SANS Step-by-Step Consensus Guide, "Computer Security Incident Handling: Step-by-Step." SANS Institute Publications, 1999.

16. Layer 11: IA Reporting

CHAPTER OBJECTIVES

- Describe the significance of establishing a formal IA reporting structure and process within an organization
- Describe the significant factors to consider in developing an IA reporting structure and process

THE DEFINITION OF FORMAL IA REPORTING

A formal reporting structure and process is one that has been defined, documented, approved, and accepted by an organization as official. Formal reporting structures and processes generally exist throughout any organization. For example, organizations have formal structures and processes for reporting the statuses of their assets and their financial performance (e.g., balance sheets, income statements, and cash flow statements), as well as their operational performance (e.g., production, sales, market shares, customer satisfaction, and so forth). The organization needs to establish a comparable reporting structure and process for its IA program. This is critical because the organization's financial, operational, and IA performances are so inextricably interrelated and interdependent.

IA reporting provides a means of integrating the IA program within an organization from two perspectives. First, a formal IA reporting structure and process serves to integrate each of the underlying layers of the organization's IA program into a cohesive functional component. Second, formal IA reporting provides a means of integrating the IA program within the organization's overall management structure and process. Therefore, formal IA reporting benefits both those responsible for specifically managing the IA program and those responsible for managing the organization as a whole entity.

THE DEVELOPMENT OF AN IA REPORTING STRUCTURE AND PROCESS

There are seven significant factors that an organization needs to consider in developing a formal IA reporting structure and process. First, the objective of IA reporting must be defined. Basically, the objective of IA reporting is to collect and assess predefined information related to the performance of the IA program and the historical, current, and projected IA posture of the organization. The intent of the reporting is to determine the effectiveness and efficiency of the IA program relative to established managerial goals.

Second, the organization must determine the information that must be collected and assessed in order to reach conclusions on the performance of the IA program and the status of the organization's IA posture. For example, IA management should receive current and accurate information related to the following:

- Existing and newly defined organizational Critical Objects
- Existing and projected physical and virtual boundaries
- The organization's capabilities to properly prevent, detect, and correct IA incidents and contingencies
- The extent to which employees are properly aware, trained, and educated relative to their IA responsibilities
- The existing and projected network infrastructure, enclave boundaries, and computing environments, and the extent to which changes to these components are properly controlled via documentation, approval, and oversight to determine that they are implemented correctly
- The extent to which organizational units are in compliance with established IA policies
- The extent of IA incidents and the statuses of these incidents

Third, the organization should determine who will be held responsible for collecting and disseminating the predefined information. As emphasized several times throughout this book, security is everyone's responsibility within an organization. The IA management staff is not capable of performing all that is necessary to adequately protect the organization's IT Critical Objects to ensure its survival, coexistence, and growth. Therefore, select personnel throughout the organization have to assume additional responsibilities. The emphasis must be on building a cross-organizational team. Everyone within the organization is a part of that team, and certain individuals will have higher levels of responsibility as members of that team. Everyone should be held accountable for accomplishing these responsibilities. The following are examples of team members:

- Suppliers of information
- Consumers of information
- Owners of information
- System administrators
- Network administrators
- System access control officers
- Network security officers
- Information system security officers (ISSO)
- Database administrators

The managers of the subdivisions of the organization (e.g., operating divisions, departments, and branches) may be responsible for assigning certain IA responsibilities to the employees under their authority. For example, systems administrators, network security officers, database administrators, and ISSO might not fall directly under the authority of the organization's IA manager. However, reporting relationships should be established with these individuals based on specified conditions. The IA management staff will need to interact and work with a wide variety of individuals throughout the organization in order to collect the information it needs to assess the performance of the IA program.

Fourth, the reporting structure must be clearly defined throughout the entire organization. Each individual in the reporting structure must clearly understand to whom he or she is to report and under what circumstances. A critical aspect of the reporting process is the free and timely flow of accurate information to the organization's IA manager, and from the IA manager to senior-level organizational management. The IA manager needs direct and immediate access to senior management based on specified circumstances. For example, senior management must be informed and updated as to the status and financial/operational impact of IA incidents that result in the corruption, improper exposure, or unavailability of the organization's information and IT capabilities. Also, senior management must be aware of any weaknesses in the organization's IA capabilities that could potentially result in adverse financial/operational impacts to the organization's survival, coexistence, and growth. IA management must be prepared to provide senior management with recommendations to avoid such problems and the budgetary issues associated with these recommendations. The intent is to minimize surprises as much as possible.

Fifth, the IA reporting process must clearly define when predefined information is to be reported, the method that should be used to report the information, and possible responses to reported information. Information could be reported on a consistent, exceptional, or unusual basis. From a consistency perspective, predefined information could be reported on a daily, weekly, monthly, quarterly, or annual basis. This reporting would occur regardless of whether the information is considered acceptable or unacceptable based on goals or whether the information has changed from the previous reporting time period. For example, at the very least, "no change" or "no problems" could be reported. Information could also be reported on an exceptional basis based on predefined circumstances such as the occurrence of IA incidents or when specific IA goals are not being accomplished. From this perspective, information could be reported on unusual circumstances that have not been previously predefined as requiring reporting. Also, the information could be reported by a variety of methods, including telephone calls, e-mail, formal written reports, video teleconferencing (VTC), and verbal briefings. Over time, the organization should develop possible responses based on the information that is reported. For example, the varying impact and scope of IA incidents would require a variety of actions to correct the incidents and to prevent their reoccurrences.

Sixth, the IA reporting requirements, structure, and process should be officially formalized within the organization. An IA reporting policy document should be developed and signed by the highest level of senior management. At the very least, the Chief Information Officer (CIO) should sign the document.

Seventh, to ensure success, there must be recognition and acceptance within the organization of the approved IA reporting policy document that defines the structure and process of IA reporting. IA management could use formal IA reporting as a means to control, recognize, and reward performance. There may be occasions when IA management has to notify senior management when individuals are not complying with IA reporting requirements as specified in the policy document, which might be detrimental to organization-wide acceptance of the policy. On the other hand, the recognition and rewarding of performance would significantly contribute to the acceptance of IA as an integral function of the organization and would encourage compliance with its requirements.

SUMMARY

IA management should have a formally documented and recognized structure and process for reporting organizational IA performance and the IA posture. Everyone within an organization can be considered to be part of a team that is responsible and accountable for timely and accurate IA reporting. Such reporting is critical for both IA management and senior-level organizational management to understand the extent to which the organization's IA performance and its IA posture have reached objective and acceptable levels.

REFERENCES

Fink, S. L., R. S. Jenks, and R. D. Willits, *Designing and Managing Organizations.* Homewood, IL: Richard D. Irwin, Inc., 1983.

Hitt, M. A., R. D. Middlemist, and R. L. Mathis, *Management — Concepts and Effective Practice.* 2nd ed. St. Paul, MN: West Publishing Company, 1986.

Kreitner, R., *Management — A Problem-Solving Process.* Boston: Houghton Mifflin Company, 1980.

APPENDICES

Appendix A: Listing of IA Threats

Significant IA threats can be divided into the following categories.

THREAT CATEGORY

Unauthorized Access Threats

- Unauthorized use by an authorized user of system resources for which he or she lacks formal approval
- Unauthorized access by former users whose accounts were not deleted on departure
- Unauthorized use of system resources by individuals who have physical access to the resources but who are not authorized users of the resources
- Hacker penetrations of system resources
- Undetected or uncorrected vulnerabilities that, when exploited, allow unauthorized access
- Masquerading, which involves posing as an authorized user or program to gain access to system resources — for example, a program such as a Trojan horse may act like another program to gain information (e.g., logon passwords or information files), or an unauthorized user may impersonate a network control center user to request router passwords and filter definitions
- Replay, which involves recording a stream of previously transmitted encrypted text, such as an encrypted logon sequence, and retransmitting the stream at a later time in place of the wiretapper's own logon sequence
- Unauthorized use of access or technology, including privileged access, for the purpose of subverting, modifying, or bypassing security mechanisms
- Criminal or terrorist acts, including emanation interception for military or economic espionage and state-sponsored terrorism, as well as "physical destruction or vandalism, organized insider theft, armed robbery, or physical harm to personnel" (Krutz and Vines, 2001, p. 20)

Information Compromise Threats

These threats can only be implemented by someone (or a process acting for someone) with access to the system, whether that access is authorized or unauthorized. They include:

203

- Inappropriate access controls that allow unwanted browsing
- Wrong file or directory permissions that allow unwanted access to owner or group files

Active Intercepts

These interceptions involve the deliberate modification of a message stream to gain access to information.

Passive Intercepts

This is the observation (but not modification) of information transmissions by someone not authorized to view those transmissions. Such attacks involve passive monitoring of communications transmitted over public media (e.g., radio, satellite, microwave, and public switched networks). Examples of passive intercepts are as follows:

- Monitoring plaintext — an attacker who monitors the network could capture user or domain data that is not protected from disclosure.
- Decrypting weakly encrypted traffic.
- Password sniffing/network eavesdropping — involves the use of protocol analyzers to capture user identifiers and passwords.
- Traffic analysis — an attacker can gain valuable information by observing external traffic patterns, even without decryption of the underlying information. Information about changes in traffic patterns could permit the attacker to reach conclusions about organizational intentions.
- Browsing — involves searching through storage to locate or acquire information without necessarily knowing of the existence or the format of the information being sought.
- Denial of receipt/denial of shipment — involves falsely denying that a message was received or disavowing responsibility for a message that has been sent.
- Inserting malicious software. There are a variety of different types of malicious software. An adversary could use trapdoors to set up entry mechanisms, Trojan horses, viruses, worms, and time bombs. The impact could involve a modification or misrouting of information, a modification of system operations, and a bypassing of security mechanisms.
- Spoofing — involves inducing a user or a system resource to take an incorrect action. For example, there could be masquerading as the sending (provider) device to deceive a receiver (consumer) in believing the message was legitimately sent can be accomplished by spoofing the address, or by means of a *playback*. A playback involves capturing a session between a provider and consumer of information, and then retransmitting that message (either with header only, with new message contents, or the whole message).
- System spillage/misrouting — generally, unintended delivery of information to a communications channel, network device, or workstation; attributable to system failures or operator errors.
- Theft of documentation — documentation that contains detailed descriptions of the operations, components, and security features of systems needs

to be protected. Possession of such documents could provide very useful information for an individual who has malicious intent.

- Theft of equipment or storage media, digital information, and printed output — such items need to be protected since they may contain program files and information.
- Unauthorized reading of critical and sensitive information — a consumer of information may gain access, intentionally or inadvertently, to information for which he or she does not have access privileges.

Information Corruption Threats

Information corruption threats may involve information, software, or message transmissions.

- Unauthorized destruction or modification of existing information and software — results from unauthorized changes (additions, deletions, or modifications) to files or software programs.
- Unauthorized destruction or modifications of information transmissions — occurs when unauthorized changes are made to any part of the message including the contents and addressing information, usually by means of active intercepts.
- Inserting malicious software
- Inserting misinformation
- Tampering by disgruntled employees
- Ineffective software applications or scripts that cause denials of service or data errors
- "Data aggregation or classification that results in data inference, covert channel manipulation, a malicious code/virus/Trojan horse/worm/logic bomb" (Krutz and Vines, 2001, p. 20)

Denial of Service (Availability) Threats

- Disrupting/disabling or destroying a system — this threat involves degradation of system performance, physical sabotage, or destruction of files. For example, an internetworking device could be disabled by an unauthorized user, which could result in the loss of the availability of network traffic. Another example involves the unauthorized alteration of a user's access privileges to deny him or her access.
- "Hardware equipment failure, program errors, operating system flaws, or a communications system failure" (Krutz and Vines, 2001, p. 20).
- Flooding — involves placing such an excessive quantity of traffic on a network that delay becomes intolerable and services are denied.
- Delays or reductions in productivity or transmissions resulting in a loss of income, increased expenses, or penalties.
- Environmental hazards, utility failures, power outages, and natural disasters.

Software Corruption Threats

- Inserting malicious software
- Subverting or modifying software — system or application software executing within organizational systems can be surreptitiously reprogrammed so that it produces results that appear correct but are in fact incorrect

Hardware Corruption Threats

- Inserting hardware to disrupt operations — involves the insertion by an intruder of malicious implants within hardware located within organizational facilities. These malicious implants would be intended to set up entry mechanisms, to bypass security procedures, to modify system operations, to alter or misroute information, or to record or transmit information.

Hardware/Software Distribution Threats

These threats focus on modification of hardware or software at the factory, or modification or substitution during distribution. Malicious code could be easily imported into protected organizational facilities through shrink-wrapped software, users swapping media with machines outside the facilities, or other paths that are implemented to import information from outside a protected network. The hardware/software distribution threat refers to the potential for malicious modification of hardware or software between the time it is produced by a developer and the time it is installed and used. If a user has a remote access capability, such attacks could occur while the remote user's computer is being configured, if it is left unattended (i.e., without proper physical security), or while software is communicated to it either over the network or via physical means (e.g., floppy disks).

- Modification of software during development and prior to production — an unauthorized individual can modify the source code after it has been reviewed and approved if it is not kept under rigid physical control
- Malicious software modification during production and/or after distribution — can be performed by affecting the configuration of software during its production or distribution

Network-Based Threats

These threats relate to the network backbone, the exploitation of information in transit, electronic penetrations into a local-area network (LAN), or attacks on an authorized remote user when he or she attempts to connect to the network. Network-based threats could be placed within three groups as follows:

- *Denial of service (availability).* There are a variety of threats in this group including Internet Control Message Protocol (ICMP) bombs to disable a router, flooding the network with bad packets, and flooding mail hubs with junk mail.

- *Malicious code insertion and exploitation.* A network attacker could get an authorized user to execute malicious code by including the code in seemingly innocent software/e-mail that is downloaded. The malicious code could possibly be used to destroy or modify files, especially files that contain privilege parameters or values. Examples of such attacks involve PostScript, Active-X, and MS Word macro viruses.
- *Penetration attempts.* There are a variety of methods that attackers have used to penetrate systems to gain unauthorized access to information. Three examples will be provided. First, an attacker could exploit vulnerabilities in protocols to spoof users or reroute network traffic. Domain Name Servers (DNS) have been spoofed to gain unauthorized remote login. Second, *social engineering* is a method attackers use to trick users to gain unauthorized access to organizational systems and information. An attacker can obtain system or user information through phone calls or e-mails that fool the victim into disclosing passwords or other information that the attacker uses to gain access or privileges. Third, an attacker could masquerade as an authorized user/server. The attacker identifies himself or herself as someone else and therefore improperly uses and accesses resources and information. Sniffers could be used to obtain user/administrator information and then use that information to log in as an authorized user. Also, rogue servers can be used to obtain critical and sensitive information after establishing what is believed to be a trusted service relationship with the unsuspecting user.

DEFINITIONS

See Table A-1.

Table A-1   Threat Descriptions (continued on following page)

Threat	Description
Virus	Malicious software that attaches itself to other software
Worm	Malicious software that is a standalone application
Trojan horse	A worm that pretends to be a useful program, or a virus that is purposely attached to a useful program prior to distribution
Time bomb	A virus or worm designed to activate at a certain date/time
Logic bomb	A virus or worm designed to activate under certain conditions
Rabbit	A worm designed to replicate to the point of exhausting system resources
Bacterium	A virus designed to attach itself to the operating system in particular (rather than any application in general) and exhaust system resources, especially central processing unit (CPU) cycles
Spoofing	Getting one computer on a network to pretend to have the identity of another computer, usually one with special access privileges, so as to obtain access to the other computers on the network

Table A-1   Threat Descriptions (continued)

Threat	Description
Masquerade	Accessing a computer by pretending to have an authorized user identity
Sequential scanning	Sequentially testing passwords/authentication codes until one is successful
Dictionary scanning	Scanning through a dictionary of commonly used passwords/authentication codes until one is successful
Digital snooping	Electronic monitoring of digital networks to uncover passwords or other data
Shoulder surfing	Direct visual observation of monitor displays to obtain access.
Dumpster diving	Accessing discarded trash to obtain passwords and other data.
Browsing	Usually automated scanning of large quantities of unprotected data (discarded media, or online "finger"-type commands) to obtain clues as to how to achieve access
Spamming	Overloading a system with incoming message or other traffic to cause system crashes
Tunneling	Any digital attack that attempts to "go under" a security system, by accessing very low-level system functions (e.g., device drivers or operating system kernels)
Hardware malfunction	Hardware operates in abnormal, unintended mode
Software malfunction	Software behavior is in conflict with intended behavior
Trapdoor (backdoor)	System access for developers, inadvertently left available after software delivery
User/operator error	Inadvertent alteration, manipulation or destruction of programs, data files, or hardware
Fire damage	Physical destruction of equipment and programs due to fire or smoke damage
Water damage	Physical destruction of equipment and programs due to water (including sprinkler) damage
Power loss	Computers or vital supporting equipment fail due to lack of power
Civil disorder/ vandalism	Physical destruction due to criminal activities

REFERENCE

Krutz, Ronald L., and Russell Dean Vines, *The CISSP Prep Guide: Mastering the Ten Domains of Computer Security.* New York: Wiley, 2001.

Appendix B: Listing of Threat Statuses

This table provides a means of representing the status of specific types of threats relative to the past, present, and future. As indicated in Appendix A, specific threats are listed under each of the seven threat categories.

Threat Category	Threat Occurrence	Threat Detection	Threat Prevention	Threat Correction	Threat Impact
Unauthorized Access Threats	Past Present Projected	Past Present Projected	Past Present Projected	Past Present Projected	Past Present Projected
Information Compromise Threats	Past Present Projected	Past Present Projected	Past Present Projected	Past Present Projected	Past Present Projected
Information Corruption Threats	Past Present Projected	Past Present Projected	Past Present Projected	Past Present Projected	Past Present Projected
Denial of Service (Availability) Threats	Past Present Projected	Past Present Projected	Past Present Projected	Past Present Projected	Past Present Projected
Software Corruption Threats	Past Present Projected	Past Present Projected	Past Present Projected	Past Present Projected	Past Present Projected
Hardware/ Software Distribution Threats	Past Present Projected	Past Present Projected	Past Present Projected	Past Present Projected	Past Present Projected
Network-Based Threats	Past Present Projected	Past Present Projected	Past Present Projected	Past Present Projected	Past Present Projected

Appendix C: Listing of Major Sources of Vulnerability Information

GENERAL SOURCES OF VULNERABILITY INFORMATION

- http://cve.mitre.org
- http://xforce.issnet
- http://seclab.cs.ucdavis.edu/projects/vulnerabilities/#databases/
- http://www.cs.purdue.edu/coast/projects/vdb.html
- http://www.rootshell.com/

VENDOR-SPECIFIC SECURITY INFORMATION

Berkeley Software Design, Inc.
http://www.bsdi.com/services/support
E-mail: info@bsdi.com

Cisco Systems, Inc.
http://www.cisco.com/warp/public/707/sec_incident_response.shtml
E-mail: security-alert@cisco.com

Compaq Corporation
http://www.compaq.com/
E-mail: rich.boren@compaq.com

The FreeBSD Project
http://www.freebsd.org/security/
E-mail: security-officer@freebsd.org

Hewlett Packard
http://us-support.external.hp.com/
E-mail: security-alert@hp.com

IBM
http://www-1.ibm.com/services/continuity/recover1.nsf/ers/Home
E-mail: era@ers.ibm.com

Linux (Caldera)
http://www.calderasystems.com/support/security
E-mail: linux@caldera.com

Linux (Debian)
http://www.debian.org/security/
E-mail: security@debian.org

Linux (Red Hat)
http://www.redhat. .com/cgi-bin/support/
E-mail: support@redhat.com

Microsoft Corporation
http://www.microsoft.com/security/
E-mail: secure.microsoft.com

Novell
http://www.support.novell.com
E-mail: secure@novell.com

The Open BSD Project
http://www.openbsd.org/security.html

Santa Cruz Operation
http://www.sco.com/support/ftplists/index.html
E-mail: cse-security-alert@sgi.com

Silicon Graphics, Inc.
http://www.sgi.com/support/patch_intro.html
E-mail: cse-security-alert@sgi.com

Sun Microsystems, Inc.
http://www.sunsolve.sun.com/pub-cgi/secBulletin.pl
E-mail: security-alert@sun.com

VENDOR-SPECIFIC SECURITY PATCHES

BSDI	ftp://ftp.bsdi.com/bsdi/patches
Caldera OpenLinux	ftp://ftp.caldera.com/pub/OpenLinux/security/
Debian Linux	ftp://ftp.usdebian.org/debian
Compaq	http://www3.compaq.com/support/files
FreeBSD	ftp://ftp.FreeBSD.org/pub/FreeBSD/
Hewlett Packard	http://us-support.external.hp.com/
IBM	http://service.software.ibm.com/support/rs6000
NT	http://www.microsoft.com/security/
OpenBSD	http://openbsd.com/security.html
RedHat Linux	http://www.redhat.com/corp/support/
SCO	ftp://ftp.sco.com/SSE
SGI	ftp://ftp.sgi.com/patches/
Sun	http://sunsolve.sun.com/

Source: SANS Institute, *Network Security Roadmap 2001.*

Appendix D: IA Policy Web Sites

- Electronic Frontier Foundation (EFF): http://www.eff.org/pub/CAF/policies
- Georgia Institute of Technology Computer and Network Usage Policy: http://www.gatech.edu/itis/policy/usage/contents.html
- General Services Agency (GSA) Policies: http://www.itpolicy.gsa.gov
- SANS Institute Information Security Reading Room: http://www.sans.org/infosecFAQ
- Information Systems Security (Infosyssec) Portal: http://www.infosyssec.com
- IA Support Environment (IASE) Policy & Guidelines: http://www.iase.disa.mil/policy.html
- National Institute of Standards & Technology (NIST) Computer Security Resource Center (CSRC): http://www.csrc.nist.gov
- Information Systems Audit and Control Association (ISACA) Standards: http://www.isaca.org/down.htm

Appendix E: IA Policy Basic Structure and Major Policy Subjects

BASIC STRUCTURE

- *Purpose.* Explains why the document exists, its intended usage, and its relationship to other organizational documentation.
- *Scope.* Explains the scope or limits of the document. Factors to consider discussing include whether the document includes all or subsets of information within the organization; whether the document applies to the confidentiality, integrity, and availability of information; whether the document applies to organizational employees as well as to suppliers, contractors, business associates, customers, and so forth; and, whether the document applies to information in a logical or physical state or both.
- *Roles.* Defines the roles or players that are relevant to the document. Such roles could include information owners, application owners, information custodians, application developers, and users. The responsibilities and authorities for each role should be defined.
- *Enforcement.* Explains the basis for enforcing the policies stated in the document and the organizational elements responsible for such enforcement.
- *Administrative Considerations.* Explains the frequency with which the policies should be reviewed with each individual and organization that is accountable to adhere to the policies; points of contact to enable the addressing of questions or issues; and the date of the last revision of the document.
- *Definitions.* Significant words may require definition to avoid confusion and ensure consistency of implementation. This could include definitions of the various types of organizational information such as critical information, sensitive information, and proprietary information, as well as IA terms such as confidentiality, integrity, and availability.

MAJOR POLICY SUBJECTS

Acceptable Use of IT Resources

- Defines appropriate use of IT resources by the various roles
- Individuals should be required to read and sign Acceptable Use Policy as part of the account request process

- Defines responsibility of roles in terms of protecting information stored on their accounts
- Defines whether roles can read and copy files that are not their own but are accessible to them
- Defines whether roles can modify files that are not their own but for which they have write access
- Defines whether roles are allowed to make copies of systems configuration files (e.g., /etc/passwd) for their personal use, or to provide to other people
- Defines whether roles are allowed to use .rhosts files and what types of entries are acceptable
- Defines whether roles can share accounts
- Defines whether roles can make copies of copyrighted software
- Defines level of acceptable usage for electronic mail, Internet news, and Web access

Account Management

- Defines the requirements for requesting and maintaining an account on the organizational systems
- Roles could be required to read and sign an Account Policy as part of the account request process
- Defines who has the authority to approve account requests
- Defines who is permitted to use IT resources
- Defines any citizenship/residency requirements
- Defines whether roles are permitted to share accounts or whether the various roles are allowed to have multiple accounts on a single host
- Defines the rights and responsibilities of the roles
- Defines when the account should be disabled and archived
- Defines how long the account can remain inactive before it is disabled
- Defines password construction and aging rules

Remote Access

- Defines acceptable methods of remotely connecting to the organizational internal network
- Covers all available methods to remotely access internal resources. These include dial-in (SLIP, PPP), ISDN/Frame Relay, telnet access from the Internet, and the cable modem
- Defines who is permitted to have remote access capabilities
- Defines what methods are permitted for remote access
- Defines whether dial-out modems are allowed
- Defines who is permitted to have high-speed remote access such as ISDN, Frame Relay, or cable modem and any extra requirements that need to be imposed
- Defines any restrictions on information that can be accessed remotely
- Defines requirements and methods for connections by organizational partners

Information Protection

- Defines guidelines to roles on the processing, storage, and transmission of sensitive information to ensure that information is appropriately protected from modification or disclosure
- New individuals assuming the roles could be required to sign a policy statement as part of their initial orientation
- Defines the sensitivity levels of information
- Defines who can access sensitive information, under what circumstances, and the requirement for the signing of nondisclosure agreements
- Defines how sensitive information is to be stored and transmitted (encrypted, archive files, uuencoded, etc.)
- Defines on what systems sensitive information can be stored
- Defines what levels of sensitive information can be printed on physically insecure printers
- Defines how sensitive information is removed from systems and storage devices (i.e., degaussing of storage media, scrubbing of hard drives, shredding of hardcopy output)
- Defines any default file and directory permissions contained within system-wide configuration files
- Defines information storage media marking and control

Firewall Management

- Defines how firewall hardware and software is managed and how changes are requested and approved
- Defines who can obtain privileged access to firewall systems
- Defines the procedure to request a firewall configuration change and how the request is approved
- Defines who is allowed to obtain information regarding the firewall configuration and access lists
- Defines review cycles for firewall system configurations

Special Access Account Management

- Defines requirements for requesting and using special system accounts (root, bkup)
- Defines how the roles can obtain special access
- Defines how special access accounts are audited
- Defines how passwords for special access accounts are set and how often they are changed
- Defines reasons why special access is revoked

Network Connection

- Defines requirements for adding new devices to the organizational network
- Defines who can install new resources on network

- Defines what approval and notification must be done
- Defines how changes are documented
- Defines the security requirements
- Defines how unsecured devices are treated

Wireless Networks

- Defines the process for requesting and using wireless communications

Router Configuration

- Defines the process and parameters for configuring organizational router devices

System Development

- Defines the process for designing, developing, installing, and testing new systems to ensure their compliance with established security requirements

Configuration Management

- Defines how new hardware/software is tested and installed
- Defines how hardware/software changes are documented
- Defines who must be informed when hardware and software changes occur
- Defines who has authority to make hardware and software configuration changes

Contingency Management

- Defines which file systems are backed up
- Defines how often backups are performed
- Defines how often storage media are rotated
- Defines how often backups are stored off-site
- Defines how storage media are labeled and documented

Disaster Planning and Response

- Defines tasks to keep critical IT resources operating and to minimize impact of disaster
- Defines a plan to ensure that critical information needed for disaster response is kept off-site and easily accessible after the onset of a disaster
- Defines several operating modes based on the level of damage to resources
- Defines the need for "hot" or "cold" sites
- Defines plans to perform disaster preparedness drills several times a year

Security Incidents Handling

- Defines who to contact and when
- Defines initial steps to take
- Defines initial information to record
- Defines how to handle intruder attacks
- Defines areas of responsibilities for members of the response team
- Defines what information to record and track
- Defines who can release information and the procedure for releasing the information
- Defines how a follow-up analysis should be performed and who will participate

Monitoring and Auditing Management

- Defines the process and conditions for performing the monitoring and auditing functions within an organization

Education, Training, and Awareness

- Defines the process and requirements for IA education, training, and awareness within an organization

Laptop Computer Management

- Defines the process for controlling the use of laptop computers within the organization

Appendix F: Sample IA Manager Appointment Letter

(Letter should be done on official business letterhead.)

SUBJECT: Appointment of Information Assurance (IA) Manager for the XYZ Organization

1. Effective [INSERT DATE], the following individual is appointed as the XYZ Organization IA Manager:

    [NAME GOES HERE]

2. Authority: [Reference applicable policy or regulation(s)]

3. Purpose: To perform the duties and responsibilities assigned to the IA Manager for each XYZ Organization information system as prescribed by [References]

4. Period: Until officially relieved or released from appointment or assignment.

5. Special Instructions: The IA Manager is authorized to cause operations to be suspended, partially or completely, upon detection of actions that may affect the security of any information system for which the IA Manager is responsible.

6. This letter supersedes all previously issued IA Manager appointment letters.

SIGNATURE BLOCK of Appointing Official

Appendix G: Sample Outline for IA Master Plan

I. Current IA Posture [What does your organization look like today?]
   A. Scope of Responsibilities
   B. Governing Policy
   C. IA Personnel and Staffing
   D. IA Training and Awareness
   E. Current Threat Assessment
   F. Current Security Architecture
   G. Residual Risk
   H. Mission Needs

II. IA Strategic Plan [Where do you want to be?]
   A. IA Goals and Objectives for IA Resourcing, Training, and Operations
   B. Objectives for Defending the Network Infrastructure
   C. Objectives for Defending the Enclave Boundary
   D. Objectives for Defending the Computing Environment
   E. Objectives for Defending Supporting Infrastructures

III. IA Implementation Plan [How are you going to get there?]
   A. Strategy for Resourcing IA
   B. Strategy for Improving IA Training and Awareness
   C. Strategy for IA Operations
   D. Strategy to Achieve Objectives for Defending the Network Infrastructure
   E. Strategy to Achieve Objectives for Defending the Enclave Boundary
   F. Strategy to Achieve Objectives for Defending the Computing Environment
   G. Strategy to Achieve Objectives for Defending Supporting Infrastructures

Appendices
   A. References
   B. Glossary
   C. IA Master Training Plan
      1. New Employee Security Indoctrination
      2. Employee Refresher Training
      3. Security Training for Management
      4. Security Training for System Administrators
      5. Security Awareness Program
      6. IA Course Descriptions and Outlines
      7. IA Training Calendar

Appendix H: Things to Do to Improve Organizational IA Posture

LIFE-CYCLE MANAGEMENT

- Determine what needs protecting and identify the threats; focus on real needs and real, foreseeable threats.
- Decide on what priorities will be and what trade-offs can be made (e.g., constraints on operations).
- Know the value of your critical information; identify critical processes and systems, and know why (and how much) protection is required.
- Ensure that security is planned and developed into any prospective new system.
- Certify that security features are performing properly and tightened down before allowing the system to operate.
- Approve and track configuration changes to the baseline, verifying the changes do not affect the terms of the system's accreditation.
- Assess the status of security features and system vulnerabilities through manual and automated reviews (i.e., simple scans and self-inspection audits).
- Destroy and dispose of hardcopy printouts and nonvolatile storage media in a way that eliminates possible compromise of sensitive or classified data.

PASSWORD AND ACCESS CONTROLS

- Use strong authentication (e.g., one-time passwords), if possible.
- If static passwords must be used, follow best practices for password characteristics, selection, protection, and expiration.
- Control and verify physical access to servers and workstations; escorting those not fully authorized for unescorted access.
- Turn monitor displays away from open doorways and windows.
- Provide outside verification that the enclave boundary (e.g., routers and firewalls) is properly configured and that IP access control lists are complete and up-to-date.
- Routinely check for and purge inactive or closed accounts.
- Employ the least privilege principle; limit privileged access to the absolute minimum privileges and number of individuals necessary to accomplish the job.

- Verify that file permissions enforce strict need-to-know.
- Implement automated and manual procedures for screen saving the monitor during periods of nonuse when still logged on.
- Control use of modems.
- Place publicly accessible Web servers outside of the operation's wide- or local-area network.

SYSTEM AUDITING AND MONITORING

- Ensure that audits are operational and collecting required events.
- Install intrusion detection systems (IDS) on all network paths.
- Disallow anonymous, guest, and shared accounts and multiple logons.
- Review system logs and audit trails for anomalies; logs of privileged access should be reviewed daily.
- Prohibit unauthorized monitoring and use of sniffers.
- Check periodically for unauthorized modem connectivity.

SECURITY OPERATIONS/MANAGEMENT

- Promulgate realistic, written policies and procedures to ensure that all employees understand roles and responsibilities and expected security practices; review regularly for relevance.
- Follow best practices identified by successful businesses.
- Where possible standardize procedures, forms, and training.
- Assign and train a security point of contact for each system or set of systems.
- Provide security training and awareness for general and privileged users to include security incident reporting and emergency response.
- Configure the system to implement security features, tighten security controls, and turn off vendor default settings/accounts (i.e., guest accounts).
- Keep antiviral software definitions and vendor patches up-to-date.
- Stay abreast of known system and networking vulnerabilities, keeping current with service packs, vendor patches, and version upgrades.
- Control, label, and protect removable media; where possible, limit the use and proliferation of access to removable media drives (e.g., floppy drives, CD-ROM drives).
- Electronically display a legally approved warning banner stating the terms for system access and the potential ramifications of misuse.
- Eliminate all unnecessary network protocols and connections; disable unneeded services (e.g., Web, mail, print, file sharing).
- Make security an enabler; sell management on the return on investment that security can provide by protecting the organization's information, reputation, and continued operations.

CONFIGURATION MANAGEMENT

- Keep system and network configuration documentation current, reflecting patches, version upgrades, and other baseline changes.
- Track hardware and software changes through a process that ensures changes are approved and tested before installation and operation; ensure that the IA manager or representative is part of that approval process.
- Control privileges and authority for modifying software.

CONTINGENCY PLANNING

- Implement virus protection for all files introduced into the system and keep virus definition software current.
- Centralize storage of data and prohibit storage of critical information on the workstation.
- Perform frequent backups of data and system files and store off-site.
- Develop and exercise a disaster recovery plan.

INCIDENT RESPONSE AND HANDLING

- Develop policy to define what constitutes an incident and the roles and responsibilities of the incident handling team.
- Ensure adequate resources and processes exist for detecting, responding to, and recovering from security incidents.
- Develop flexible procedures for responding to various threats, allowing for graduated measures to be implemented, as required (e.g., IP blocking, turning off selected network services, isolation subnets, etc.).

Appendix I: Information Assurance Self-Inspection Checklist

Information Systems Security Plan	YES	NO	N/A
Does your organization have a written security policy? If so:			
Are security roles and responsibilities clearly delineated in the policy?			
Are all those individuals aware of their responsibilities?			
Does the policy cover expectations of behavior, enforcement procedures, and penalties for policy breeches?			
Does a security plan exist based on the security policy?			
Is security documentation available that includes:			
Security concept of operations?			
Security architecture?			
Security certification test & evaluation report?			
Security accreditation?			
Does the organization have an accurate mission or vision statement?			
Does the organization have a long-term strategic Information Assurance plan to meet in keeping with the mission or vision statement? If so:			
Have goals and objectives been developed to meet the strategic plan?			
Have short-term tactical plans been developed to meet these objectives?			

Physical Security	YES	NO	N/A
Are the following physical security documents available:			
Facility security plans?			
Facility security certification/accreditation?			
Physical security policies and procedures?			
Facility access control lists?			
Facility modernization plans?			
Emergency action plan?			

	YES	NO	N/A
Continuity of operations plan addressing alternate facilities?			
Disaster recovery plan?			
Are procedures in place to address the following:			
Physical access to facilities?			
Fire safety?			
Loss of supporting utilities (e.g., electricity, air conditioning/heating)?			
Structural collapse?			
Portable computing devices entering/exiting facilities?			
Are site baseline components and associated information protected by physical barriers to prevent access by unauthorized individuals?			
Are physical access controls used for employee entrance/exit of facilities?			
Do procedures address securing office doors after hours? If so:			
Are these procedures enforced?			

Visitor Control	YES	NO	N/A
Does the organization have a policy and procedures for visitor control? If so, do procedures address:			
Badging or other identification to easily distinguish the classification/access level of a visit?			
Visitors with authorized access?			
Visitors without authorized access?			
Official visits by family members (retirements, award presentations, etc.)?			
Unofficial visits by family members (emergency situations when childcare is unavailable)?			
Unofficial visits by others (e.g., flower or pizza deliveries)?			
Non-disclosure agreements for authorized vendors, contractors, and visitors?			
Escort policy for visitors, cleaning staff, and maintenance personnel?			
Portable computing devices and associated media carried in/out of the facilities by visitors?			
Procedures for sanitizing work spaces prior to visits from personnel without proper clearances or need-to-know?			

Personnel Security	YES	NO	N/A
Is the following personnel security information available:			
Clearance process?			
Contact listing of key personnel?			
Organizational structure?			
Continuity of Operations to address augmentation and cross-training?			

	YES	NO	N/A
Access authorization list?			
Training and awareness program?			
Proof of user training for minimum security requirements?			
Proof of privileged user certification?			
Do procedures exist for employee in-processing and out-processing?			
Is a background check required for new employees to determine eligibility for handling sensitive or classified information?			
Are all employees required to sign a non-disclosure agreement as a condition of employment?			
Does a process exist for immediate termination of employee access to facilities and systems upon voluntary or involuntary separation?			

System Deployment	YES	NO	N/A
Does the organization have a written plan for system deployment that adequately addresses all IA requirements for hardware, operating system, network services and connectivity, software, user access, auditing and accounting, backup and recovery, administration, maintenance, and disposal?			

Account Management	YES	NO	N/A
Are written procedures in place detailing the process for establishing, activating, modifying, and terminating a user account?			
Are procedures in place for issuing a user account only after confirming that the account owner has met minimum security training prerequisites?			
Are procedures in place for disabling an account when an employee is fired?			
Are procedures implemented to force review of user accounts for disabling or possible purging after ___ days of inactivity?			
Are anonymous, guest, generic, shared, or group accounts prohibited?			
Have all guest, vendor, or other accounts and passwords been removed?			
Are procedures in place for monitoring inactive accounts?			
Do all personnel with access to site baseline components and associated information have their clearances verified before being granted access?			
Are system administrator and security administrator (ISSM) functions separate, providing checks and balances in the account management process?			

Identification & Authentication (I&A)	YES	NO	N/A
Are userids (and UIDs) unique for each valid user able to be correlated to specific actions in order to enforce individual accountability?			
Is logging on as ROOT prohibited in writing?			
Is an I&A mechanism in place that ensures a unique identifier (e.g., user identification) for each user and that attributes all accountable actions of the user with that unique account?			
Does the protection level of the information stored, processed, or transmitted within the IS warrant strong authentication (i.e., an authentication method that is resistant to replay attacks)?			
Are tokens, certificates, or digital/electronic signatures used for authentication or access control?			
If static passwords are used, is a password history maintained to prevent recycling of passwords?			
Is a system-generated password feature available on this system?			
If users must choose static passwords, are written guidelines available to the user to assist in choosing a password that is not easily breakable?			
Are passwords securely disseminated, controlled, and protected at the highest classification level of the IS/network?			
Are passwords stored in the password file encrypted?			
Are scripts with embedded passwords prohibited?			
Are passwords issued to users in a secure manner? (Passwords should never be recorded online or sent to users via e-mail. Procedures should be in place to ensure passwords are passed via trusted channels.)			
Are procedures in place for handling forgotten passwords?			
Are passwords required to be a minimum of ___ characters in length?			
Does the system force password aging?			
Are static passwords changed a minimum of every ___ days (e.g., 30, 60, 90, 120, 180)? (If automatic password aging is not available, are procedures implemented to manually force a password change at least every 90 days?) NOTE: If any password is compromised or suspected to be compromised, it must be changed immediately.			
Are passwords required to contain at least one number or special character for protection against standard dictionary attacks?			
Are passwords suppressed (not echoed to screen) upon keyboard entry?			
Is vulnerability assessment software (e.g., password cracking program) run against the password file to identify and correct weak static passwords?			

	YES	NO	N/A
Does the system lock the user's account after three consecutive unsuccessful login attempts from a single access port or against a single userid (i.e., break-in detection) and immediately notify the IA manager or ISSO?			
Are authentication data, password files, etc., protected from normal user access?			
Can the /etc/password file be read anonymously over the network via UUCP or TFTP?			
Are all password files encrypted?			
If applicable, have any lines beginning with a "+" in the password or group files on any NIS server been eliminated?			
If applicable, has an * been placed in the password field of any line beginning with a + symbol in both the password and group files of any NIS client?			
Does the system positively identify all user terminals and other user-employable devices before allowing them to access system resources?			

Mandatory & Discretionary Access Controls	YES	NO	N/A
Does written policy state the access control requirements for the protection of files, devices, and objects within the organization's information systems?			
Are data access controls automatically set to limit access when any new file or data set is created?			
Is need-to-know determination made before access to classified information is granted?			
Are access privileges limited to only the most restrictive set of privileges necessary to perform assigned tasks (i.e., least privilege)?			
Is access to command line (shell) processes restricted to only those individuals who require access to such process in the performance of their official duties?			
Does the ISSM or ISSO oversee the assignment of special accounts (e.g., sys admin, oper, ROOT, floppy tool, tape tool) and other such privileges that would permit an individual user to exceed the authorizations of a "normal" system user and thereby override or negate the automated and/or technical safeguards provided by the system?			
Is root access limited to a manageable number of individuals? Note: "Manageable" is a relative term and will be limited by the ability of the IA manager or IA staff to effectively oversee the total number of privileged users.			
Does the ISSM or ISSO have a current list of all root access holders?			
Does the ISSM or ISSO own and control the root password?			

Does the system control access of named users to named objects such as files and programs?			
Does the enforcement mechanism (e.g., self, group, public controls and access control lists) allow users to specify and control the sharing of named objects with individuals who are identified either by name, by membership in defined groups of individuals, or both?			
Does the DAC mechanism, either by explicit user action or by default, protect objects from unauthorized access?			
Are controls capable of including or excluding access to the granularity of a single user?			
Are there controls to limit the propagation of access rights to additional users?			
Can the list of those permitted access to DAC-controlled information be changed only by persons who are themselves authorized users of the information?			
Is a mandatory access control (MAC) policy required for this IS to force access control labels that reflect the sensitivity (i.e., classification level, classification category, and handling caveats) of the information?			
If applicable, does the IS provide a means to ensure that labels a user associates with information provided to the system are consistent with the sensitivity levels that the user is allowed to access?			
Has the ISSM or ISSM agent reviewed the umask and permission settings for system files and directories?			
Are users briefed on the implications of changing permissions on their data files to allow world read/write capability?			
Have file permissions and ownership on critical data files been verified to ensure proper configuration?			

Session Control	**YES**	**NO**	**N/A**
Are users notified about the last successful or unsuccessful logon attempt?			
Is a screen locking feature with forced password re-entry installed on all terminals/workstations to prevent unauthorized personnel from gaining access to information?			
Is the screen locking feature activation period by explicit user action or by keyboard/mouse inactivity for a specified period of time (e.g., 15 minutes or less)?			
Can the screen blanking mechanism be invoked manually?			
Does the screensaver require authentication before re-entry into the session?			
Are users aware that activation of the screen lock is not a substitute for logging off the IS?			

	YES	NO	N/A
Are procedures in place requiring session logoff at the end of the day?			
Does a "dead man timeout" feature force automatic logout of any active sessions after an additional system-defined increment of time has passed with no user activity?			
Do session controls include an electronically displayed notification to all users prior to gaining access to the IS that explains that use of the IS may be monitored, recorded, and subject to audit?			
Do the session controls include electronic notification to all users that use of the IS constitutes consent to monitoring and recording; that unauthorized use is prohibited and subject to criminal and civil penalties?			

Data Flow Control	YES	NO	N/A
Does the network transmit information at a specified maximum classification level and at one specified accredited security enclave and each IS and/or other attached network pass information to, or receive information from, the network at the same security level?			
Does the network constrain the transfer of information between network components in accordance with the network security policy?			
Are separately accredited ISs attached to the network accredited to operate in one of the authorized modes to process and store information at the security level for which the network is accredited?			
Are procedures for data exchange (e.g., automated guards, "sneaker nets") between ISs of differing security levels established, approved, and implemented?			

Interconnection Controls	YES	NO	N/A
Has the IA manager identified all remote and network connections to the appropriate Certifying Organization/Agent to ensure connections meet site security requirements?			
Has the controlled interface been certified, accredited, and approved to operate in the current configuration?			
When connecting two separately accredited networks, has the Designated Approving Authorities (DAA) given written approval for the controlled interface in the form of a Memorandum of Agreement for the interconnection?			
Are mechanisms or procedures in place to prohibit general users from modifying the functional capabilities of the controlled interface?			
Are safeguards in place to ensure that these mechanisms or procedures cannot be circumvented?			

	YES	NO	N/A
Are mechanisms in place to ensure the controlled interface is monitored for failure? Are these mechanisms themselves protected against failure or compromise?			
Is the controlled interface physically protected?			
Can routing information that controls the release of outgoing traffic or delivery of incoming traffic be changed only through the security mechanism of the controlled interface?			
Is the controlled interface configured to prohibit all incoming and outgoing communications protocols, services, and communications not explicitly permitted?			
Are all direct user access to and actions on the controlled interface audited?			
Is remote access to the controlled interface prohibited? If not, is strong authentication used on physically or logically separated communications paths?			
Is strong authentication required for direct user access to the controlled interface?			
Have tests been conducted to confirm that upon failure, the controlled interface does not allow the unauthorized release of information outside the enclave boundary?			
Does the controlled interface provide a capability to screen for inappropriate or malicious content?			
Is an audit capability implemented for the controlled interface to include the following events:			
Identity of sender?			
Identity of recipient?			
Device (port) ID?			
Date and time of event?			
Have network cabling diagrams been provided to the IA manager?			
Have the following been configured to prevent unauthorized access to site ISs/networks:			
Guard filters?			
Firewall filters?			
Gateways?			
Filtering routers?			
Replication servers?			
Authentication servers?			
Strong authentication?			
IP Security/Virtual Private Networks?			
Has approved network vulnerabilities assessment software (e.g., SPI, COPS) been run on this system to detect vulnerabilities in the IS or network configuration?			

	YES	NO	N/A
Has the ISSO ensured the + sign has been removed from the /etc/hosts.equiv file?			
Are ISs connected to a telephone data port or modem?			
If an IS is connected to a telephone data port or modem, has permission been received from the proper authority and in accordance with all IA requirements?			
Is the Red/Black criterion separation being strictly enforced?			
Do patch panel breakouts prevent cross patching of different classification levels?			

Marking Human-Readable Output	YES	NO	N/A
Are documents required to be conspicuously marked to show the highest classification of information they contain?			
Does the system automatically mark the top and bottom of each individual page with the classification, controls, and handling restrictions that pertain to the data printed on that page (or does it mark each page to reflect the overall sensitivity of the printed output)?			
Can system marking be suppressed as a default option?			
Is overriding automatic page bannering or individual page marking an audited event?			
Has the IA manager or ISSO verified the default classification for output?			
Does the system, by default and in an appropriate manner, mark other forms of human-readable output (e.g., maps, graphics, imagery) with human-readable classification, controls, and handling restrictions that properly represent the sensitivity of the output?			

Media Requirements	YES	NO	N/A
Are mechanisms in place to scan media introduced into the IS to detect and eradicate viruses or other malicious code?			
Are standard operating procedures in place for conspicuously labeling or marking the exterior of removable and non-removable storage media indicating the highest classification ever stored on the media?			
Are standard operating procedures in place for conspicuously labeling or marking the exterior of hardware components indicating the highest classification ever stored on the device?			
Are procedures implemented to provide appropriate controls and accountability for removable media (i.e., comparable to those requirements for equivalent hardcopy documentation)?			
Is the location for storing media (e.g., vault, library) protected against physical and environmental threats?			

Are procedures implemented for the transporting of removable media outside of the installation?			
Are procedures in place for preventing unauthorized use of public domain or shareware software?			
Is a policy implemented prohibiting personally owned software?			

Reliable Human Review Requirements	**YES**	**NO**	**N/A**
Is written policy in place to delineate organizational requirements for a reliable human review process?			
Is a reliable human review conducted prior to releasing sanitized or downgraded information?			
Is a quality control process in place to verify policy compliance for human review requirements?			

Integrity	**YES**	**NO**	**N/A**
Are system programs and data protected against unauthorized (or accidental) alteration or deletion?			
Does the IS/network employ safeguards (e.g., checksum) to detect and minimize inadvertent or malicious modification or destruction of data?			
Does the network ensure the integrity of the information it transmits?			

Network Security	**YES**	**NO**	**N/A**
Does the organization have an Internet access policy?			
Is the organization's internal network architecture hidden from untrusted external users?			
Are procedures and/or technical measures in place to control access to network services?			
Does the ISSM/ISSO or Network Security Officer routinely run network vulnerability assessment tools to test system and network defenses?			
Does the ISSM have regular access to advisories and support services (e.g., CERT Advisories) to stay abreast of network developments, threats, and vulnerabilities?			
Does the network identify and authenticate the devices from which users attempt to access the network and the devices that originate data exchanges?			
Does the network enforce individual accountability by providing the capability to uniquely identify each individual user and associate this identity with all auditable actions taken by that individual?			

	YES	NO	N/A
When systems are interconnected, is there an exchange of security information ("security handshake") between the ISs or between the ISs and the network to ensure that security aspects of a data exchange will occur in a legitimate and secure fashion?			
Are procedures in place for approving the use of network sniffers in advance of installation and use?			
Are mechanisms (e.g., wrappers) in place to log requests for service and provide an access control mechanism for network services?			
Does the ISSM/ISSO routinely review and inspect host tables, IP addresses, firewalls, and access control lists (ACLs) or filters?			
Is exporting file systems using root access prohibited?			
Is exporting mounted partitions with world or group-writable directories prohibited?			
Are NFS directories prevented from being mounted across domain boundaries?			
Is anonymous ftp or tftp prohibited?			
Are procedures in place for secure dial-in connections?			

Modem Security	YES	NO	N/A
Does the organization have a written policy for modem use?			
Are modems prohibited from being connected to networked workstations?			
Are modems prohibited from being connected to network servers, except to provide authorized dial-in access?			
Is modem use controlled and tracked?			
Is immediate termination of modem access part of the organization's procedures for termination of employment?			
Are modems automatically disconnected after a specific period of inactivity?			

Firmware	YES	NO	N/A
Is the BIOS or EEPROM password feature enabled?			

Operating System	YES	NO	N/A
Are applicable patches and version updates promptly applied?			
Have all generic, anonymous, and vendor-supplied user accounts been removed or disabled?			
Has the OS kernel been configured to perform only the most restrictive set of essential functions?			

Has the OS been configured to disallow all unnecessary network services?			
Have unneeded TCP/IP ports been disabled?			
Has remote privileged administration been prohibited?			

Server Security	YES	NO	N/A
Where possible, are network servers dedicated to a single service or purpose (e.g., e-mail server, Web server, audit server)?			
Is information stored on Public access servers limited only to general information authorized for release to anyone with access to the public access network?			
Are all Web servers with public access isolated from the organization's internal network(s) through the use of firewalls, proxy servers, or filtering routers?			
Are proxy servers used to prohibit direct public access to operational databases?			
Are certificates required for HTTP access?			
Are certificates only issued by an approved Certificate Authority?			
Are all certificates protected by an approved authentication mechanism?			
Are secure Web technologies (e.g., Secure Socket Layer, Secure HTTP) used where possible?			
Do Web pages alert users to the highest classification or level of sensitivity of the Web site, as well as the classification/ sensitivity level of each Web page?			

Mobile Code Security	YES	NO	N/A
Is mobile code or executable content authorized for use on critical information systems? If so, is a code review for mobile code and executable content conducted prior to operational use?			
Are systems or controlled interfaces configured to prohibit the downloading of mobile code or executable content?			

Electronic Mail	YES	NO	N/A
Are mechanisms in place to scan incoming and outgoing electronic mail to detect and eradicate viruses contained in e-mail and attachments?			
Is a policy in place to require classification marking of electronic mail?			

Collaborative Computing	YES	NO	N/A
Is collaborative computing software configured to prevent remote activation?			
Does activation and deactivation of collaborative computing peripherals (e.g., desktop camera and microphone/headset) require explicit action by the user (i.e., user must deliberately activate an on/off switch on the camera and microphone)?			
Do collaborative computing peripherals provide conspicuous indication that the devices are operating (i.e., manual on/off or mute switch; indicator lights on the device)?			
Does the server portion of client–server collaborative computing mechanisms require use authentication?			
Are operations and environmental security procedures in place for reducing the risk of inadvertent disclosure of sensitive information from the use of cameras and microphones?			

Portable Computing Devices	YES	NO	N/A
Do written policy and procedures exist for authorizing and controlling portable computing devices and associated media within organizational facilities?			
Are organizational laptops stored in a secure location when not in use?			
Have policy and procedures been implemented establishing criteria for allowing modem connectivity?			
Is encryption used to protect hard drives and removable media in portable computing devices (e.g., laptops) used by traveling employees?			

Encryption	YES	NO	N/A
Do procedures exist for accessing files encrypted by a user key, after the user has terminated employment with the organization?			

Configuration and Change Management	YES	NO	N/A
Does the organization have a configuration control plan?			
Does a formal change management process exist to control and approve changes to the approved baseline? If so:			
Does the process allow for emergency modifications or repairs?			
Are only authorized individuals allowed to move and install information systems equipment?			
Do network and system diagrams exist?			
Does an inventory list of all information systems resources exist?			

	YES	NO	N/A
Is the ISSM a participant and voting member of the organization's Configuration Control Board?			
Are proposed changes to the baseline configuration of operating system, applications, utilities, and security features tested and approved by the IA manager prior to operational use?			
Have mechanisms been implemented to allow an enterprise view of the network to include identifying hardware devices?			
Does the CM plan include procedures for identifying and documenting system connectivity, including any software, hardware, and firmware used for all communications (including, but not limited to, wireless and IR)?			
Does the CM plan include procedures for identifying and documenting the type, model, and brand of system or component; security relevant software, hardware, and firmware product names and version or release numbers; and physical locations?			
Are procedures implemented to ensure no software will be loaded into any IS unless approved by the ISSM and the change control/configuration management process?			
Are procedures implemented to ensure any external data files, whether from a network download or a removable magnetic medium, are checked for active virus infection prior to being introduced into any site IS/network?			
Are system startup files and configuration files regularly reviewed for additions and changes?			
Does policy exist requiring data integrity while in storage?			
Are procedures implemented for the physical and technical protection of the backup during storage?			
Are mechanisms in place to record the time and date of the last modification to data?			
Are mechanisms or procedures implemented to ensure that data modification is accomplished only by authorized personnel?			

Security Testing and Evaluation	YES	NO	N/A
Has an ISSO been appointed in writing for this IS/network and been briefed on his/her responsibilities?			
Has the ISSM verified that the Certifying Authority as accreditable has certified this IS/network?			
Is the IS/network under configuration management?			
Are the following documents available, if applicable:			
Information systems security plan?			
Security concept of operations (SECONOPS)?			
Security requirements?			
Certification test plan?			

	YES	NO	N/A
Certification test procedures?			
Threat assessment/risk analysis?			
Security test and evaluation report?			
Security certification and accreditation?			
Verification of approval to operate/approval to connect?			
Standard operating procedures?			
Emergency action plan?			
Contingency operations plan?			
Disaster recovery plan?			
Backup procedures?			
Destruction procedures?			
Operator manuals for applications?			
Rules of behavior?			
Has the physical security manager granted approval to bring the hardware into the facility?			
Has the ISSM granted approval for installation and testing of the IS/network?			
Is the security certification testing for this system being conducted in a development (non-production) environment?			
If so, does the development environment mirror the production environment and configuration in which the system will be used operationally?			
If certification testing is being conducted in the production environment, was development and integration testing of this system conducted in a non-production environment?			
Are formally approved policies and procedures implemented to cover the following security-related topics:			
Security responsibilities of the users?			
Security marking of hardcopy output?			
Procedures for downgrading and/or releasing output/media?			
Media degaussing, destruction, and/or downgrading?			
Generating and reviewing the audit data?			
Adding or removing user accounts?			
Control and issuance of passwords?			
Setting access control privileges for users?			
Maintenance policy and procedures?			
Secure system startup and shutdown?			
Generating and storing system backups?			
Software and hardware media labeling?			
Use of dial-up, STU-III, FAX, and modems connections?			
Security incident reporting?			
Disaster recovery plan?			
Configuration management plan?			

Are standards used to verify the operating system is secure (e.g., security checklist, system technical implementation guides)?			
Is a vulnerability scanning tool run against the system to identify known weaknesses?			

Development and Acquisition Phase	YES	NO	N/A
Were security requirements identified and clearly delineated? If so:			
Were these requirements included in the acquisition specifications?			
Were security benchmarks agreed upon to provide a measurement for success or failure during the security testing and evaluation?			
Have periodic design reviews been conducted through the development phase to ensure security control design meets security requirements?			

Implementation Phase	YES	NO	N/A
Was the system tested using established and/or ad hoc test procedures to ensure security control meets or exceeds benchmark standards? If so:			
Does a written security test and evaluation report exist that identifies security findings and recommendations?			
Has the completed system undergone a technical security evaluation to meet or exceed federal laws, directives, regulations, policies, standards, and guidelines?			
Has the cognizant Certification Authority certified the system?			
Is this certification in writing?			
Has the Designated Approving/Accreditation Authority (DAA) rendered an accreditation decision in writing?			
Has the system been granted an approval to operate by the Certification Authority and/or the DAA? If so:			
If the approval is an interim approval due to outstanding security findings, does a get-well plan exist for correcting and closing these findings?			

Operational and Maintenance Phase	YES	NO	N/A
Does the organization have a policy and procedures addressing maintenance of IT equipment?			
Do the procedures address emergency repair and maintenance situations?			
Are all maintenance personnel cleared to the same security level in which the IS/network is operating?			
Are only trusted personnel permitted to perform IT maintenance?			

	YES	NO	N/A
Are diagnostic test program media used on classified systems permitted to leave secure facilities?			
Are IS parts being removed from the facility purged of all sensitive or classified information; verified by security; and actions appropriately documented before removing the equipment?			
Do procedures exist for escorting of uncleared individuals?			
Are procedures for conducting remote diagnostics from a cleared site documented in the site CONOPS and approved for use?			

Disposal Phase	YES	NO	N/A
Do procedures exist for the secure destruction of:			
Hard drives?			
Removable magnetic media?			
CD-ROMs?			
Printed hardcopy?			

Purging & Sanitization	YES	NO	N/A
Does the organization have a policy and procedures for the sanitizing and disposal of sensitive information on removable media (e.g., floppy disks, tapes, CDs)?			
Does the organization have a policy and procedures for the sanitizing, removal, and disposal of sensitive information on non-removable media (i.e., internal hard drives)?			
Is memory remanence being controlled and safeguarded in the manner prescribed for the most stringently protected data ever processed on the IS until the data is purged or the media is destroyed?			
Does policy address who is responsible for ensuring that sanitization has occurred before disposal?			
Are all personnel familiar with applicable sanitization procedures for this IS/network hardware, software, and firmware?			
Are approved destruction facilities available?			

Backup Procedures	YES	NO	N/A
Does the organization have a backup policy and applicable recovery procedures for critical systems? If so:			
Are backup frequencies delineated for system and user files for all systems?			
Does the policy clarify who is responsible for performing backups?			
Does the policy address archived data?			
Do procedures exist to promptly restore the system in the event of a natural disaster or intentional/unintentional denial of service?			

Are adequate backups of all information on the system made on a frequent basis in accordance with written procedures?			
Is a process implemented for the regular and frequent backup of data (complete or incremental)?			
Are backups conducted prior to any major hardware, software, or firmware change?			
Are backups retained for a minimum of ____ months/years?			
Are backups stored at an off-site location?			
Is restoration of backups exercised every ____ months?			

Continuity of Operations	YES	NO	N/A
Is an emergency action plan (EAP) established for reacting to natural and man-made disasters? If so:			
Does the plan identify who is responsible to implement the EAP?			
Are employees trained regarding their responsibilities in reacting to an EAP implementation?			
Is the EAP posted or kept in a place that lends itself to being used under emergency conditions?			
Are alternate means of communications available when the primary communications capabilities are unavailable?			
Is a disaster recovery plan established?			
Is a site continuity of operations (COOP) plan current and implemented?			
Does the COOP explicitly state the priority order in which critical systems must be restored to full operational capability?			
Do adequate alternative hardware, firmware, software, power, and cooling exist in the event that primary equipment is unavailable?			
Are the EAP, COOP, and disaster recovery plan exercised to ensure procedures work and users understand responsibilities?			
Is the system/network supported by an uninterruptable power source (UPS) system?			
Do procedures allow for the timely transfer of the system's power supply to an alternate power source?			
Does a secure audit trail exist for the re-creation of data changes?			
Are procedures or mechanisms available to prevent and detect known denial-of-service attacks?			

Malicious Code Prevention	YES	NO	N/A
Is a virus prevention policy in place?			
Is antiviral software installed and operational on all information systems to detect and eradicate malicious code?			

Are processes in place for obtaining the latest antiviral software profiles and distributing the profiles to all systems?			
Is antiviral software configured to scan all software introduced into the information system?			
Are employees trained to recognize and report viruses and other malicious software upon detection?			

Intrusion Detection	YES	NO	N/A
Is a host-based intrusion detection system (IDS) implemented? If so:			
Are sufficient numbers of IDS agents placed for optimal coverage?			
Is IDS software configured to provide real-time notification of critical events?			
Is 24 × 7 monitoring of IDS conducted?			
Are incident handling and reporting procedures in place?			
Are these procedures exercised to ensure all personnel understand their roles and responsibilities?			
Are network-based IDS monitoring tools implemented to identify attacks and suspicious network activity?			
Are all IDS tools properly configured based on reliable assessments?			
Is an IDS analysis capability available (e.g., audit review, routine internal audit capability, computer forensics capability)?			

Penetration Testing	YES	NO	N/A
Is penetration testing routinely conducted in order to determine software vulnerabilities? If so:			
Is this testing conducted internally?			
Is this testing conducted externally?			

Auditing and Monitoring	YES	NO	N/A
Does a process exist for ensuring that audit mechanism features are operating and collecting the audit information?			
Does the system create and maintain an audit trail of accesses to the files and programs it protects?			
Is the system configured to crash upon audit failure (i.e., the system is not allowed to continue operations without recording required audit events)?			
Does the system protect the data in the audit trail from unauthorized access, modification, or destruction?			
Does the system limit access to online audit data only to those authorized to read it?			

Does the audit process record the successful and unsuccessful use of: I&A mechanisms, the introduction of files into a user's address space, the deletion of files, actions taken by privileged users, and other security-relevant events?			
Does an automated or manual audit trail document the following:			
Identity of each person or device that has access to the system?			
Time of the access?			
User activities, sufficient to ensure user actions are controlled?			
Activities that might bypass, modify, or negate safeguards?			
Security-relevant actions associated with the changing of security levels or categories of information?			
For each recorded event, does the audit record identify the date and time of the event, the user identification, the type of event, and the success or failure of the event?			
When the event involves I&A, does the audit record include the origin of request (e.g., the identity of the terminal/workstation used by the requester)?			
For events that delete files/programs or introduce files/ programs into a user's address space, does the audit record include the name of the file/program?			
Can the ISSO focus the audit process on the actions of selected individual users and/or groups?			
Are audits and reviews conducted to verify compliance with applicable license and copyright agreements?			
Are effective tools available for analyzing the audit trail of security-related events, either on the system itself or as part of a central support facility?			
Do network audit records create and maintain an audit trail of information about connections between systems, to include identification of each connection and its principal parameters, the start/stop time of each connection, and any other security-related events?			
Are appropriate network software/tools provided to assist in collecting, reducing, analyzing, and reporting audit trail information?			
Is audit trail data being reviewed in accordance with established site policy, to include at minimum:			
Manual or automated verification that audit daemons are operational?			
Daily review and analysis of privileged account audit records?			
Random or complete review of all audit records weekly?			
Is audit information archived and maintained for a minimum of ___ year(s)?			

Security Incident Reporting	YES	NO	N/A
Has the organization developed a computer security incident response capability? If so:			
Is the capability internal to the organization?			
Is the capability dependent on outsourcing or other external sources?			
Is the handling or reporting of incidents dependent on privileged users without security checks and balances?			
Does the IA manager or IA staff receive alerts and advisories on a timely basis?			
Does the IA manager/staff ensure applicable alerts and advisories are quickly acted upon (e.g., patches applied, vulnerabilities tightened down)?			
Do procedures establish a formal incident reporting mechanism to report compromise, or possible compromise, of classified information; internal and external unauthorized access attempts; malicious code; virus attacks; failure of a network or IS security feature; and any other security-relevant event?			
Are all employees aware of the security incident reporting procedures and the importance of timely reporting?			
Is an incident database maintained for statistical reporting and lessons learned?			

Security Awareness & Training	YES	NO	N/A
Are all users and IS personnel actively participating in a security awareness program?			
Have all users and IS personnel been indoctrinated in the proper operation and their responsibility for protecting the information being processed and/or stored within the IS/network?			
Have all users read and signed a responsibility briefing and statement of understanding prior to receiving their user account and password?			
Have all system superusers read and signed for the ROOT password and understand the additional responsibilities that come with added privilege?			
Have users been provided with names and contact numbers for account/password management POC, ISSO, and ISSM?			
Have the following personnel been given adequate system/application training to ensure proper operation of the IS/network and to reduce risk of denial of service:			
Users?			
Operators?			
System administrators?			
Security administrators/ISSOs?			

	YES	NO	N/A
Have manuals for users, operators, system administrators, and security administrators been provided?			
Has the ISSM agent received training in the following areas and is confident in performing his/her automated information system (IS) security duties:			
Audit collection?			
Audit review?			
Incident reporting?			
Virus detection and eradication?			
Purging and sanitation of storage?			
Media labeling?			

Appendix J: Sample Outline for a Disaster Recovery Plan (DRP)

I. Purpose Statement (e.g., to provide established procedures for surviving/recovering from a disastrous event in order to reestablish normal business operations)
II. Scope of Procedures (To whom and what do the procedures apply?)
III. DRP Planning Assumptions
IV. Organizational Process for Developing, Approving, and Updating of the DRP
V. DRP Procedures:
   A. Normal Operating Procedures
      1. Standard Operating Procedures/Operational Instructions
      2. Backup Procedures
      3. Disaster Prevention Measures
   B. Procedures Used during a Disaster
      1. Emergency Notification Procedures
      2. Safety Procedures for On-Site Personnel during a Disastrous Event
      3. Continued Operations Procedures for Critical Functions
      4. Procedures for Maximizing Protecting/Minimizing Disruption to Critical Assets
   C. Post-Disaster/Recovery Procedures
      1. Procedures for Damage Assessment
      2. Procedures for Short-Term, Medium-Term, and Long-Term Outages
      3. Recovery of Organizational Assets
         a. Facilities
         b. Communications
         c. Hardware
         d. Software
         e. Databases/Data Files
         f. Operational Functions
         g. Customer Services
         h. Other
      4. Critical Systems and Prioritized Order of Recovery
      5. Alternative Plans for Continuity of Operations
      6. Alternate Operational Sites/Hot Sites
         a. Remote Management Services
         b. Vendor Consignments
         c. Other

Appendix A: References

Appendix B: Organizational Process for DRP Testing

Appendix C: Risk/Business Impact Assessment of the Organization

Appendix D: Memorandums of Agreement

Appendix E: Inventories

- Telephone Contact List/Employee Recall Roster
- Customer Lists/Distribution Lists
- Documentation (Critical Information, Forms, Policies/Procedures/ Checklists)
- Equipment (Hardware, Software, Communications/Telephone, Photocopiers/Facsimile machines, etc.)
- Property Book Inventories/Office Supplies
- Off-Site and Temporary Storage Site lists

Appendix F: Associated Service and Maintenance Costs

- Recovery and Backup Services and Equipment Fees

Appendix G: DRP Training and Awareness Program

REFERENCES

Computing & Networking Services, "Disaster Recovery Planning." Toronto: University of Toronto, 2000.

Wold, Geoffrey H., "Disaster Recovery Planning Process." *Disaster Recovery Journal* (Vol. 5, No. 3; 1997).

Appendix K: Sample Threat Response Matrix

Table K-1   Assess Threat

	Characteristics	High Threat	Medium Threat	Low Threat
WILD	Measures the extent to which a virus is already spreading among computer users	1000 machines OR 10 infected sites OR 5 countries	50–999 machines OR 2 infected sites/ countries	Anything else
DAMAGE	Measures the amount of damage that a given infection could inflict	File destruction or modification OR very high server traffic OR large-scale nonrepairable damage OR large security breaches OR destructive triggers	Noncritical settings altered, buggy routines, easily repairable damage, nondestructive triggers	No intentionally destructive behavior
DISTRI-BUTION	Measures how quickly a program propagates	Worms OR network-aware executables OR uncontainable threats (due to high virus complexity or low AV ability to combat)	Most viruses	Most Trojan horses

Derived from Symantec Antiviral Research Center (SARC) Model.

Table K-2   Determine Threat Category

	WILD			DAMAGE			DISTRIBUTION			Category
	L	M	H	L	M	H	L	M	H	
IF	X		AND	X		OR	X		THEN	1
IF	X	X	OR		X	X	OR		X	X	THEN	2
IF		X	X	OR		X	X	AND			X	THEN	3
IF		X		AND		X		OR		X	THEN	4
IF		X		AND		X		AND		X	THEN	5

Derived from Symantec Antiviral Research Center (SARC) Model.

Table K-3   Detremine Appropriate Response

Action	CAT 1	CAT 2	CAT 3	CAT 4	CAT 5	OPR	Comment
Verify existence and threat status of virus	X	X	X	X	X		
Coordinate incident response	X	X	X	X	X		
Ensure latest definitions are installed on all workstations and servers	X	X	X	X	X		
Check calendar of virus trigger dates	X	X	X	X	X		
Check online site for antiviral updates		X	X	X	X		
Notify organization's network operations center		X	X	X	X		Upon detection of virus on systems
Notify all users			X	X	X		Upon detection of virus on systems
Enable content filtering and/ or IDS software to filter for user characteristics		X	X	X	X		If no signature definitions updates are available yet
Disable e-mail and ftp services; discontinue floppy disk use				X	X		Upon confirmation of cases of virus on LAN; enact logon pop-up notice for new logons
Disconnect high assurance guard connectivity			X	X	X		Upon detection of virus on systems
Coordinate incident reporting		X	X	X	X		
Brief status to senior management		X	X	X	X		Any incident that threatens the organization's systems/networks
Report incident to DIA CERT		X	X	X	X		Upon detection on local systems/networks
Notify other ISSOs/ISSMs			X	X	X		Upon detection on local systems/networks
Coordinate and oversee cleanup operations		X	X	X	X		
Verify that all virus instances are eradicated from systems		X	X	X	X		
Check backup copies for instances of viruses	X	X	X	X	X		
Determine source of virus on system or network	X	X	X	X	X		
Notify external sources of viruses	X	X	X	X	X		
Notify external sites that may have received virus from source within the organization	X	X	X	X	X		

About the Authors

Joseph G. Boyce, CISA, is a Senior Information Assurance (IA) Analyst within the Department of Defense (DoD). He has over 25 years of experience as an IA INFOSEC professional, with particular expertise in developing and managing large-scale organizational IA programs to ensure the protection of highly critical and sensitive information. Mr. Boyce attended the Advanced Management Program of the U.S. National Defense University's Information Resources Management College and holds an M.S. degree in Information Systems from the U.S. Naval Postgraduate School and an M.P.A. degree from Harvard University.

Dan W. Jennings has over 20 years of IT experience within the U.S. Department of Defense and has held security management positions within the U.S. European Command (USEUCOM) for the past 10 years. He is well known and respected as the USEUCOM theater's Department of Defense Intelligence Information System (DoDIIS) security representative at the national level. He holds a bachelor's degree in Information Systems Management from the University of Maryland.

Index